The Illustrated History of

LMS

STANDARD
COACHING STOCK

I : General Introduction and
Non-Passenger Vehicles

The Illustrated History of

LMS

STANDARD
COACHING STOCK

I : General Introduction and Non-Passenger Vehicles

David Jenkinson and Bob Essery

Oxford Publishing Co.

A FOULIS-OPC Railway Book

British Library Cataloguing in Publication Data
Jenkinson, David
   An illustrated history of LMS coaches.
   1. Rolling stock
   I. Title   II. Essery, R. J. (Robert John)
   625.24

   ISBN 0-86093-450-0

Library of Congress catalog card number
91-71119

Published by:
Haynes Publishing Group
Sparkford, Near Yeovil, Somerset. BA22 7JJ

Haynes Publications Inc.
861 Lawrence Drive, Newbury Park, California 91320, USA.

Printed by: J. H. Haynes & Co. Ltd

Publisher's note: Although there are several references to
Volumes II and III of *The Illustrated History of LMS Standard
Coaching Stock* in this first volume, these are not yet available
and are to be published at a later date.

Contents

List of Drawings

List of Tables of Vehicles Built etc

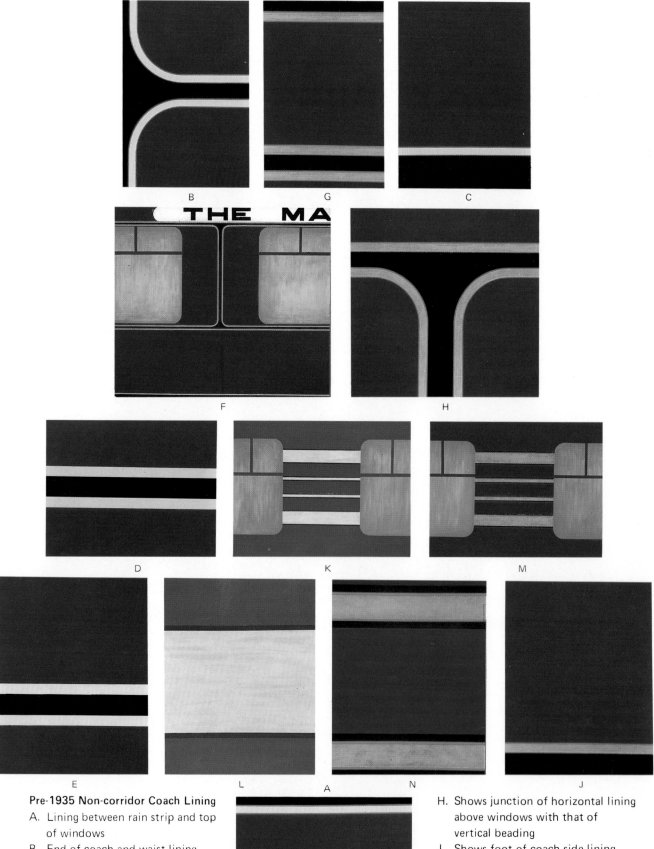

Pre-1935 Non-corridor Coach Lining

A. Lining between rain strip and top of windows

B. End of coach and waist lining

C. Foot of coach side lining

1935–1946 Coach Lining

D. At waist of coach corridor and non-corridor

1946 Coach Lining

E. At waist of coach

Pre-1935 corridor Coach Lining

F. Section of corridor coach side

G. Shows lining from rainstrip to top of window lining

H. Shows junction of horizontal lining above windows with that of vertical beading

J. Shows foot of coach side lining

Coronation Coach Stock

K. Blue coach side showing lining details

L. Shows upper and lower band of K illustration, silver edged with darker blue line

M. Red coach side showing lining details

N. Shows two central bands of the four main lining bands

O.

P

Q

O. Simplified coach livery (1934 onwards) showing waist lining and seriffed pattern 'LMS' in chrome yellow and fully shaded. The style of LMS lettering from 1923 onwards was of this type but before the adoption of the simple livery, the base colour was gold (gilt).

P. LMS 'Coat of Arms' as used on carriage stock. The version illustrated is the post-war variety with 'straw' coloured letters/ surrounds. Before the war, the same design had been provided with gold lettering &c (full livery) followed by chrome yellow lettering, &c (simple livery).

Q. Simplified livery showing fully shaded sans serif numerals in chrome yellow. This style of running number was used during the 1934–40 period.

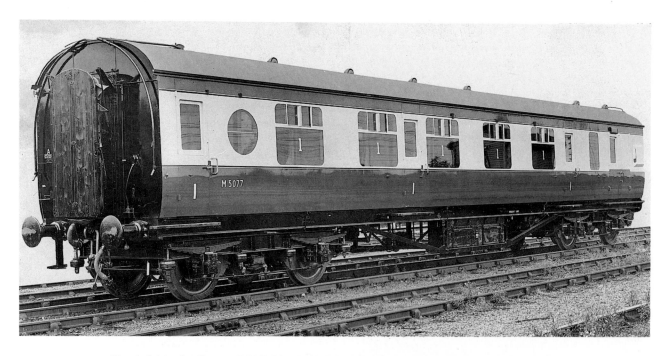

'Porthole' brake first to D2168 No. M5077 in BR crimson/cream livery as built. These were 60ft coaches and the only LMS pattern BFKs to be built to this length. Note the extra corridor door, the window opposite the toilet and five main windows. They were five-compartment coaches

Authors' Introduction to the Third Revised Edition

Something like a generation or so ago, the two of us embarked on what turned out to be the most comprehensive single research project we have ever jointly undertaken: the discovery and recording of as much as we could of the still remaining information about the locomotives and rolling stock of Britain's largest privately owned railway company. The publication of this volume marks the start of what we hope will be the final detailed phase of that endeavour.

We first told the LMS standard carriage story in outline as early as 1970 and in 1977, OPC kindly re-issued this initial survey with some augmentation in terms of pictures and drawings. Since then, we have completed our expanded review of locomotives and one of us has dealt with the LMS wagon fleet in some detail, also for OPC. At that, we thought it might have ended but since then the revised version of *LMS Coaches* has long since gone out of print and it was suggested to us by OPC that rather than re-issue it, we might like to expand it to the same sort of comprehensive levels as the other surveys had now reached.

This we have now done and this book marks the first of a fully revised three-part survey in which, as well as including all the detail previously published, we have also included full details of every item of passenger coaching stock built to LMS standard design. There will thus now be found within these pages a great number of drawings not previously present, along with those which were. We have similarly incorporated a large number of official pictures which space did not allow to be published before, even though we already had them in our possession. Lastly, the extra space now available enables us also to give the full pre-1933 LMS carriage number series (where applicable) which, hitherto, had only appeared in 'sample' form.

The data we have used mostly stemmed originally from the PR&PO's office of the London Midland Region and most of the official pictures should be assumed to have come from this source unless otherwise stated. But it must be pointed out that since we obtained our copies back in the 1960s, the bulk of this picture collection has now been rehoused at the National Railway Museum to which any interested readers should refer for any copies they might require. The pre-1933 numbers come from one of very few known full copies of the official LMS list which has survived. Happily, it is now safely in our possession, having been rescued from a waste stack destined for the incinerator (along with the LMS engine history cards) well over twenty years ago!

The revised work is still structured broadly as before – that is a general introductory section followed by a detailed analysis of each generic vehicle type rather than chronologically by age. However, when deciding which groups to put in each book after the introductory section (Chapters 1-4 of this volume), we thought it might be appreciated if, before we expanded the passenger-carrying sections, we were first to feature the full details of the vehicles which were covered most briefly in the previous survey: ie those which were classified 'non-passenger coaching stock'. As it has turned out, by giving this fascinating group full measure, we have just nicely filled the rest of the first volume! The passenger carrying vehicles do not, therefore, appear in detail until Volumes 2 and 3.

Readers of the previous surveys will naturally find much that is familiar in this new work; this is rather inevitable if we are to be fully comprehensive. For one thing, there were very few changes found necessary in the original text and the original four introductory chapters are repeated without major amendment in this volume; but we reckon that at least two thirds of the subsequent material is genuinely new in terms of having not been published before. In effect, we are now offering a fully illustrated version of the complete LMS carriage diagram book with as much supplementary narrative as we can manage to incorporate. For this reason, and also to save much time and cost in preparation, we have quite deliberately chosen to make exclusive use of the official diagrams themselves rather than have them re-drawn. This, in itself a fortunate accident of their total survival, also offers a rather interesting reflection of LMS policy; for as the years went by, the gradual but very noticeable deterioration in the quality of draughtsmanship was no more than symptomatic of the Company's wish to cut out all unnecessary frills!

After the introduction, each detailed chapter will follow broadly similar lines; basically a general introduction to the type in question (broadly speaking the narrative information formerly contained in the earlier survey), followed by a detailed review of each specific design of that type, accompanied by the diagram itself, photograph(s) and full running number and other details.

Finally, though we are getting quite accustomed to having to revise our views in the light of our increasing knowledge, we do honestly think that there can be little of substance left to say about this particular subject once Volume 3 is published. If there is, then we think we shall leave it to others to tackle! In the meantime, it only remains, as always, for us to thank our many friends, too numerous to record in detail, for their constant help over many years and in particular in this case, to OPC for having suggested this very comprehensive enlargement in the first place. We very much doubt if either of us ever thought that a comprehensively illustrated version of the full LMS Carriage Diagram Book without a single significant omission was even the remotest of possibilities way back in the 1960s. That it can now be offered with little compromise, is a very fascinating reflection of the change which has taken place both in the readers' expectation and perception of railway books since we started out on the trail. So, in thanking our publishers, we sincerely hope that their faith is justified.

DJ
Knaresborough
1991

RJE
Solihull
1991

Explanation of Terms

DIAGRAMS AND LOTS

LMS coaches were built to various *Diagrams*. Basically the Diagram was a drawing which defined the precise type of coach which was to be built although not, in itself, a working drawing. The various Diagrams have identifying numbers, not necessarily in consecutive sequence through the years, and in this book will be referred to throughout as Dxxxx. Several Diagrams were current for a number of years and each separate batch of coaches built to a particular diagram was given an identifying *Lot Number*. In general, Lot numbers, while not always consecutively numbered on a particular Diagram, were in ascending order as the years went by. Thus Lot 954 of D1915 would represent later coaches than Lot 843 of the same Diagram.

Whenever a design was changed—even to a minor extent— a fresh Diagram was almost always issued. As far as can be ascertained there were very few exceptions to this policy and these have been noted in Vol II. Several Diagrams have been used as illustrative material in this book.

PLATING

This term will be used to refer to the LMS practice of putting works plates on the coach. These were carried on the solebar and on the coach end. The solebar plate generally gave details of the works where built and the date of building, including Lot numbers from 1934/5, while the plate on the coach end was a dimension plate giving length, width and tare weight, to the nearest ton. Sometimes the plates were slightly at variance with the official Diagram version. The policy in this book will be to give the Diagram version drawing attention where necessary to any discrepancies in the coach plating details as observed in traffic.

DIMENSIONS

Unless otherwise stated, basic coach dimensions will be given as follows:

Height: Rail level to top of roof, not counting roof ventilators.
Length: Over Headstocks—with LMS coaches, which almost always had flat ends, this dimension was some 1in to 1½ins less than the body length of the coach.
Width: Over projections—i.e. a coach with a 9ft 0in wide body but with projecting handles would be quoted as 9ft 3in if this dimension was the width over the handles.

STRUCTURAL TERMS

The following definitions have been adopted as a standard for this work.

Beading: Raised wooden strips covering the panel joints on wood panelled stock.

Cantrail: The point at which the coach side meets the roof.

Cornice: The moulding, often of slightly ornamental nature, which was frequently found along the line of the cantrail.

Chassis: The complete underframe together with bogies, buffing and draw gear &c.

Gutter: The rainwater channel along the top of the cornice.

Headstock: The end section of the underframe which carried the buffing and draw gear.

Light: A generic term for a carriage window, sub-classified as follows:

Droplight:	An opening window which moves in the vertical plane—usually wood framed but there were aluminium frame and frameless variants.
Fixed Light:	A window which will not open.
Quarterlight:	The small fixed light flanking the doors of all compartments which had outside doors.
Toplight:	A small window situated between the cantrail and the top of the main carriage window.

Panelling: A generic term relating to the method of covering the exterior of the coach—e.g. wooden panelling, steel panelling, flush panelling &c. The following principal sub-classifications should be noted:

Eaves Panel:	The section of the body panelling located between the window top and the cantrail.
Flush panelling:	Used to refer to any coach which did not have any form of raised body projections in the form of wooden beading.
Matchboarding:	The name used in reference to the type of coach end panelling which consisted of a series of tongue and groove boarding running vertically from roof level to headstocks. This was a technique generally confined to coaches with an 'all wood' exterior finish.
Tumblehome:	The incurving portion of the bodyside panelling as it approaches the solebar.
Waist Panel:	The portion of the body panelling situated immediately below the windows and on LMS coaches, having a depth of some 8in. Waist panelling was generally confined to high waisted fully beaded coaches of wood panelled style.

Plates 1-2 LMS period I corridor third to D1695 No. 14318 (later 1485)—*above* and LMS (ex-MR) 56ft 6in corridor third No. 58 (later 3214)—*below*. Comparison of these two pictures reveals the almost total adoption of MR styling features in most early LMS standard stock. The MR coach was originally built as a World War 1 ambulance, converted to corridor in 1922. Note that it is carried on an older type of underframe, has beaded end panels and is fitted with recessed door handles.

Roof Types: The LMS, for the most part, adopted two types of roof as follows:

Rainstrip roof: This was of wood and canvas construction with a continuous rainstrip from end to end and on each side of the roof.

Ribbed roof: This was the Stanier pattern metal clad roof with a series of strengthening ribs from one side of the coach to the other, rainstrips if present at all, being generally confined to the section of the roof immediately above the doors. Some coaches had flush welded roof panels without external transverse ribs.

Semi-elliptical: This is a term used to refer to the roof profile above the cantrail when in the form of a semi-ellipse.

Solebar: The heavy section forming the main side members of the coach underframe. On LMS design coaches this was a steel channel section, generally with the channel facing outwards.

Truss-rods: The angle section fixed underneath the underframe between the bogies, giving additional strength to the underframe itself and acting as a support for some ancillary fittings.

Underframe: The supporting frame of the coach on which the body was mounted, but not counting the bogies, buffers, ancillary fittings &c.

Ventilators: The following principal sub-classifications should be noted:

Door ventilators: These were the ventilators situated on outside doors above the droplight, either hooded or louvred.

Hooded ventilators: External ventilators (generally on doors or above windows) which were covered by a plain metal 'hood'.

Louvre ventilators: External ventilators (usually mounted over door drop-lights) which consisted outwardly of a series of horizontal wooden louvres, usually three.

Shell and Torpedo ventilators: The two types of roof ventilator generally used by the LMS. Torpedo ventilators were of several styles and the differences are best appreciated by comparing pictures of the various types.

Sliding ventilators: The type of ventilator used in the upper part of the big side windows of Stanier pattern gangwayed coaches.

Stones ventilators: These were ventilators generally placed above the main windows of coaches in the eaves panel. They had swivelling glass vanes (six or nine elements) which could be adjusted by the passenger to 'face' or 'trail' the airstream past the coach.

Dewel ventilators: Similar to Stones ventilators but even shorter (five moving vanes).

TYPES OF COACH

The following definitions will be adopted throughout:

Corridor coach: A coach with a side corridor for all or part of its length and with gangway connections to adjacent vehicles.

Dining Car: A vestibule coach containing a kitchen as well as passenger seating accommodation.

Vestibule coach: An open coach with gangway connections to adjacent vehicles. Note that a vestibule coach used exclusively for dining purposes but *not* having a kitchen was referred to as a 'vestibule dining coach' and was *not* called a dining car.

Non-corridor coach: Any coach without gangway connections.

Lavatory coach: A non-gangwayed coach with toilets serving individual compartments either directly or from a short side corridor.

The nomenclature of other types of coaches is self explanatory.

COACH CODING

Where it seems appropriate, the standard British Railways coach codes have been adopted for ease of reference. These are, in fact, based on the old LNER system but the familiarity of present day usage will, it is felt, make them easier to understand for most readers than the official LMS codes. Full details are given at Appendix I, together with the old LMS code letters.

COACH NUMBERING

Until 1932, new standard LMS coaches were numbered somewhat haphazardly in the gaps available between the various batches of pre-group coaches which themselves, apart from the ex-MR vehicles, had been numbered in blocks in 1923. The ex-MR coaches retained their pre-group numbers except for the M&GSW and M&NB Joint Stock vehicles which were given vacant numbers in the ex-MR allocation, generally at the end of this series.

From 1933, the whole coaching stock (pre-group and standard) was renumbered systematically by generic vehicle types and these 1933 numbers are the ones which are used throughout this book. Details of the renumbering principles are given at Appendix II. At Nationalisation, LMS coaches generally retained their numbers and newly built coaches to LMS/LMR diagrams were given numbers in the appropriate LMS series. From 1948 until 1951, the LMS number was prefixed by a letter 'M' to denote the company/region of origin of the design. At about the time of the introduction of BR standard coaching stock, the prefix/suffix system was introduced. The prefix letter now denoted the region of allocation and the suffix letter was introduced as the identification of the vehicle's origin. Thus, for example, LMS coach No. 1234 would first have become M1234 in 1948 and then, if allocated to, say, Scotland, would have finally become Sc1234M. For the sake of consistency, it will be the policy in this book to omit the prefix/suffix letters in all references to LMS/LMR coaches—even those which entered service carrying such prefix or suffix letters.

Part One

A General Survey of LMS Coaching Stock

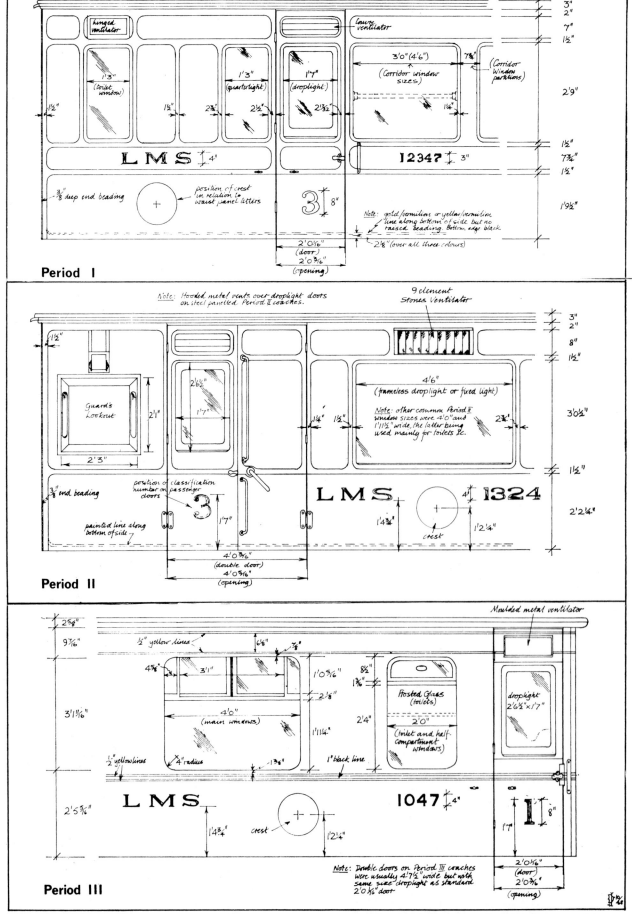

Figure 1 LMS standard Coaches—typical external details

These drawings reproduced approximately to $\frac{3}{8}$ in—1ft scale, which are of no particular vehicles, are designed to illustrate typical external details of the three main periods of LMS standard coach design. They also show the location and size of insignia in relation to windows etc, but should only be taken as giving an approximate representation of the shape of LMS insignia. Period II steel panelled stock was the same as drawn but without the beading strips.

(Drawn by D. Jenkinson)

Plates 3-4 The ancestry of the early LMS open stock is apparent by comparison of these two pictures. LMS standard open third No. 4649 (later 7784) was built to D1353 and still retained the MR type recessed door handles, dimension plate on the solebar and hooded vents over the door lights. M & GSW open third class dining coach No. 394 (1st LMS 4028, later 9617), designed by Reid c. 1917, exhibits the final version of the characteristic 'twin-window per bay' feature adopted as standard by the LMS. The underframe and bogie design also anticipated LMS practice but the reduced body width at the entrances was not perpetuated in LMS designs.

Chapter 1 - The Design and Evolution of the LMS Coach

Introduction; Period I—1923 to 1928/9; Period II—1929 to 1932; Period III—1933 onwards; Post-nationalisation: Conclusions

FROM almost the very inception of the LMS Railway, the design and building of coaches followed a very standardised pattern. There were very many types of coaches built to suit the various services and needs but, in general, the progression of design features was a logical one and is not unduly difficult to analyse. Three quite distinct periods of design can be recognised, the last of which continued until after nationalisation. For a variety of reasons it has been felt desirable to build the study of LMS coaches round these three periods, drawing attention to any departure from the normal practice at the time concerned.

PERIOD I—1923 TO 1928/9

The characteristic Period I LMS coach was a wooden framed and panelled, high waisted vehicle. It was fully beaded on the outside with a wood and canvas roof, matchboard ends and mounted on a steel underframe derived from the final MR design. Corridor coaches had a full complement of external compartment doors and the door ventilators of all vehicles were generally of the louvre pattern. Roof ventilators were generally of the torpedo type. The coaches were fitted with non-automatic screw couplers and gangwayed stock made use of the British standard pattern corridor connection of scissors type (as used also on the GWR), rather than the Pullman type gangway. For inter-company working to the LNER and SR, gangway adaptors were fitted. Most coaches ran on two four-wheel bogies which were of a 9ft 0in wheelbase single bolster design which hardly changed for the whole of the company's life. Some special vehicles ran on twelve wheel chassis and the six-wheel bogie on these vehicles was of 12ft 6in wheel-base, based on the LNWR design. All coaches except kitchen cars were electrically lit and normally fitted with vacuum brake as standard. In this connection one might add that the general design of the LMS coach chassis scarcely changed at all once it was settled in the early post-grouping years.

In terms of general styling, early LMS coaches followed much the same ideas as were prevalent elsewhere in Britain. The wooden framed and panelled, fully beaded body with a semi-elliptical roof, doors to all compartments of corridor coaches, window ventilation mainly by droplight and mounted on a steel underframe was fairly typical British design. However, certain characteristic Midland Railway features were incorporated in the design of early LMS coaches which distinguished them from those of other lines. Most noticeable of these was the twin-window arrangement in each seating bay of the vestibule coaches. This took the form of two rectangular windows side by side (one fixed and one drop-light), rather than a single window or centre drop-light with two flanking quarterlight arrangement. There was generally a Stones pattern ventilator in the eaves panel above the fixed light of these window pairs.

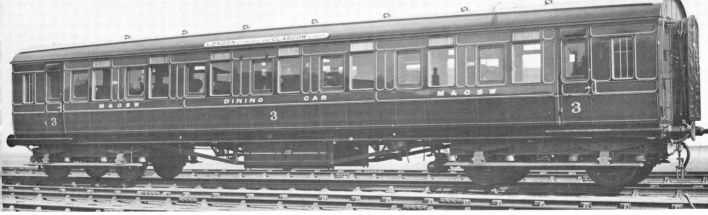

Plates 5-6 These two pictures show the corridor side elevations of LMS standard corridor brake composite No. 16435 (later 6653) to D1755 and Midland Railway corridor composite No. 2811 (LMS 4904 after 1933). The similarities are too obvious to need additional comment. These pictures are not of the highest quality but, on the originals, lining can just be distinguished on the narrow pillars between the windows on the MR coach—a feature which was not perpetuated by the LMS which painted the whole of the pillar in black.

Other ex-MR features were also perpetuated to a limited extent for the first year or so in the form of countersunk locks and door handles. This gave an overall width of 9ft 1½in rather than 9ft 3in which latter dimension, however, rapidly became universal on all new construction. A 57ft underframe was also rapidly standardised for most general service stock although for certain areas (e.g. the LT&S Section), a 54ft length was preferred for non-corridor stock. Other lengths employed during this first design phase included a 68ft 12-wheel chassis for sleeping and dining cars and a 50ft chassis for full brakes and kitchen cars.

During this period, the new company introduced a considerable quantity of conventional coaches which were comfortable and well built but it cannot be denied that, although their comfort left little to be desired by comparison with other lines, the designs were not particularly revolutionary. Externally, of course, these early LMS coaches were extremely attractive in the fully panelled and beaded style and with the fully lined Crimson Lake livery; but in terms of interior styling and amenity, the time was, perhaps, getting a little overdue for a change.

The first indication of changing ideas were some very handsome corridor vehicles in 1927. For the first time, the LMS abandoned outside compartment doors in corridor coaches and introduced larger windows in their stead. At first there were two such windows in each compartment (one fixed and one frameless droplight) in the manner of the characteristic Midland pattern vestibule coaches already considered, but only the first class passenger could, initially, enjoy the privilege of having no draughty door. Furthermore, not many were built (25 BFKs to D1654 and ten FKs to D1748). They differed from the normal twin-window style in having frameless droplights and Stones ventilators over both windows and the style soon became adopted for other vehicles. By 1930 it had made its appearance in some composites (CKs to D1716 and BCKs to D1704), this time with but one Stones ventilator centrally over the window pair and with large 4ft 6in wide corridor side windows.

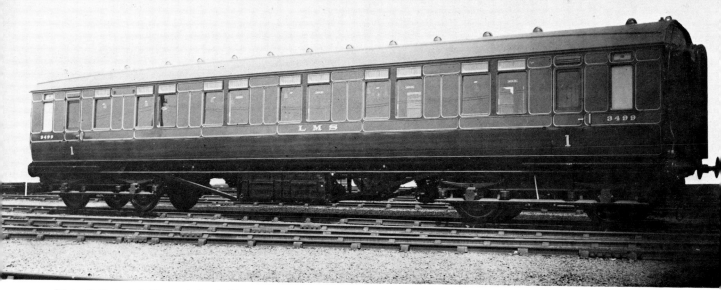

Plate 7 Period I 'Two-window' 5½ compartment corridor first to D1748 No. 3499 (later 1013). Note the Stones ventilators over both compartment windows and the frameless droplights in the left hand windows of each pair.

All the same, except for these few composites and, of course, the vestibule carriages, the third class passenger, although enjoying a comfortably cushioned ride in the best Midland tradition, was still being provided with a full complement of compartment doors in the third class corridor coaches.

The next development in the somewhat tentative progression towards more up to date amenity was the development of a single window per bay design which was introduced in 1928 with the building of ten very palatial carriages for inclusion in the 'Royal Scot' and other prestige trains. Five of these coaches were semi-open firsts to D1707 and these had three compartments all finished in a different style with only four seats in each; each passenger thus had a corner seat. The open end was rather more conventional, seating 18 in two-and-one arrangement. These coaches were classed as dining vehicles and generally ran next to a kitchen car. The other five coaches were equally luxurious lounge brakes with accommodation for 10 first class passengers in eight individual armchairs and a settee (D1741). They again had large single windows instead of the two-window arrangement.

These 10 vehicles, beautiful examples of the coach builder's art, were closely followed in 1929 by a similarly styled batch of 25 neutral vestibule coaches for either first or third class passengers to D1706. These were 42 seaters with seven bays arranged two and one and again designated as dining vehicles. With these, the single window style could finally be said to have 'arrived' in LMS gangwayed coaches.

There were, however, snags. Although these 1928/9 coaches had single windows, they were still of the 'high waisted' design with full exterior beading—as indeed were most LMS coaches to this time—and there is some evidence that although the single window was more appreciated than the earlier arrangement, it was not always easy to see out of it because of the high waist. This was, apparently, particularly irksome in the lounge brakes which with their very low seated chairs were, seemingly, never very popular. Thus it was that the single window design was not perpetuated in the high waisted style.

At this point, mention ought also to be made of the introduction in 1925/6 of some all-steel coaches. These were open thirds and brake thirds, together with a large number of full brakes, which were built by outside contractors, probably to assist the steel industry at that time (TOs to D1745, BTOs to D1746 and BGs to D1715). Construction apart, however, their 'two window' style and interior layout showed no advance on the other coaches of the time while externally they were finished in pseudo fully beaded style.

Plate 8 Period I 'All Steel' full brake to D1715 built by Birmingham C & W Co. in 1926/7 (No. 6996, later 30546).

Plates 9-10 *(above)* Early LMS 12-wheel stock owed much more to the LNWR than the MR, except for the angle-trussed underframe adopted by the LMS. These two pictures clearly illustrate the LNWR influence on sleeping car design. LMS standard car No. 10371 (later 323) is to D1705; West Coast Joint Stock No. 445 (1st LMS 10323, later 485) represents the final pre-group style adopted by Wolverton. The slightly recessed doors were not adopted by the LMS and the waist panel was slightly shallower than on the LMS version.

Plate 11 *(below)* The single window Period I styling appeared on a variety of coaches. This view shows the corridor side of the pioneer third class sleeping cars to D1709. This coach (No. 14247) became No. 522 in 1933.

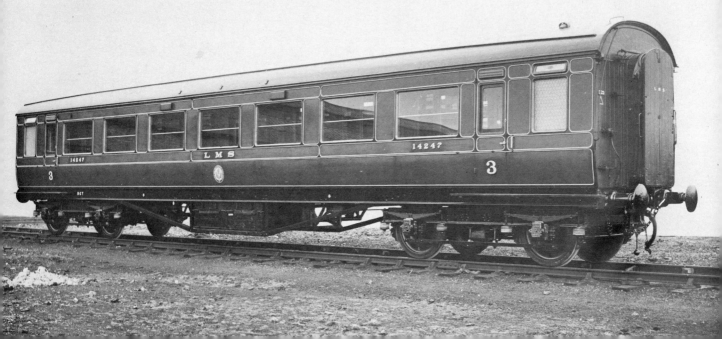

Meanwhile, the more specialised branches of coaching stock seemed of lesser importance. The LMS had inherited a considerable number of dining cars from its constituents, particularly the LNWR and MR, and few new ones were built for some seven years after grouping. Those that were (a batch of six RCs to D1743), largely followed LNWR practice in exterior styling. However, considerable numbers of kitchen only cars were built to run with the new vestibule dining vehicles so it is possible that the need at this time was for rather more dining accommodation than could be provided by a completely self-contained coach.

Sleeping cars were, however, needed and it is interesting to note that as with the first few dining cars, no real attempt was made to depart from pre-group policy—at least externally. The LNWR tradition was perpetuated in the first class cars to the tune of over 50 new 12 wheel sleepers between 1924 and 1929 (D1739 and D1705). The third class passenger, on the other hand had no sleepers until 1928 when the first of an eventual 85 convertible coaches was put into service to D1709. Externally these were pure LMS Period I standard coaches except for the absence of compartment doors. They were, however, mounted on 60ft underframes which introduced this length to LMS standard vehicles. The corridor side had the large 4ft 6in windows which were soon to become more familiar on the 'single window' stock of 1928/9 (see remarks above).

However, kitchen cars and sleepers were relatively few in number compared with the vast quantity of general service vehicles built in this first phase of LMS coach building. By the time of the first basic change in style, over 2000 new gangwayed carriages had been built of which no fewer than 851 were vestibule thirds, followed by 571 corridor composites and thirds—about equal numbers of each style.

This emphasis on the open carriage was very characteristic of the LMS and may possibly have been influenced by the long Midland Railway tradition of allowing passengers to travel all the way in the dining cars which probably led to a greater number of open carriages being needed. In fact, of the 1902 general service gangwayed coaches of all classes built during this first period, over 1000 were open vehicles and this proportion was to be exceeded even more noticeably during the next phase of coach design.

Meanwhile, a considerable quantity of non-corridor coaches had been put into service during this period. Most were on 57ft underframes for short distance stopping services and suburban use but a number were built on 54ft chassis (mostly for the LT&S Section). A number of 57ft non-corridor coaches were also built with lavatories for cross-country inter district services but all the coaches shared the characteristic Period I styling features. There were, however, some small batches of non-corridor coaches built with outside steel panelling but otherwise Period I characteristics. These were built by outside contractors and were of somewhat spartan nature—the composites being only 51ft long and with five a side seating in the first class section! They were built for use on the Cathcart Circle services in Glasgow and are interesting as representing the forerunners of the Period II non-corridor stock.

During the first design phase, the LMS also built new compartment type stock for the Euston—Watford and Liverpool—Southport electrified lines. These were 'all steel' in construction and, when new, were given full livery with imitation waist panelling.

Plate 12 Third class trailer coach for the London-Watford electric suburban services built in 1929 to D1684. This vehicle, although steel panelled, was given the fully lined livery, including the waist panel.

PERIOD II—1929 TO 1932

The start of the second phase in LMS carriage design was almost contemporary with the introduction of the previously mentioned high waisted single window designs and the new trend of thought was first exemplified by the appearance in 1929 of six luxury brake firsts with two-a-side compartment seating and somewhat palatial toilet accommodation. All the compartments were differently finished and the coaches seem to have been introduced in preference to repeating the earlier lounge brakes. These six were closely followed by 10 more of the luxury semi-open firsts of the kind already mentioned in connection with the single window designs at the end of Period I. These 16 new carriages all had single windows but the waist of the coach was much lower than hitherto. The principal external difference was the elimination of the waist panel consequent upon the deepening of the windows. The new coaches were, however, still wood panelled and fully beaded and with the full lining represented very handsome designs. As with their Period I predecessors, these coaches went to the more important trains like the 'Royal Scot' and 'Merseyside Express'. One more of each type was built with steel panelling and no raised beading as replacement for the similar coaches destroyed in the Leighton Buzzard crash of 1931.

This low waisted trend in design only partially set the pattern for new construction because corridor composites continued to come out in the fully beaded 'two window' style and the corridor thirds/brake thirds continued to have full compartments doors until 1930. Thus there was a certain amount of overlapping styles during the first part of the second period of LMS coach building.

It was again the vestibule coach which received the bulk of attention during this second phase. First were a series of spacious 60ft long 42 seaters. Some of these were built as firsts but downgraded a few years later on the advent of the Stanier 65ft firsts. These 42 seat coaches, of which 50 were initially built to D1721 and D1722, were classed as dining vehicles and were followed by a 56 seater for general service. More 42 seat coaches followed which, although identical to the original 42 seaters, were not classed as diners. All these 60ft coaches had the new low waist and were wood panelled with full outside beading. However, a much larger group of low waisted vestibule coaches was the 57ft, 56 seat version of which 300 were built to D1807. These were built in 1931/2 and differed from the 60ft version in that they were steel clad with simulated external beading in paint. They did, however, follow the Period II style in all other respects and retained the raised window edge mouldings.

Eventually in 1930/31, the new low waisted style was adopted for all corridor stock too. Although mainly confined to composites and brake composites, it was a batch of corridor thirds in 1930 that really set new standards (D1782). These coaches were but 10 in number but had only seven compartments on a 60ft underframe. Although the traditional four on each side seating was retained, the compartments were no less than 6ft 6in between partitions. They were again wood panelled and fully beaded and were, reputedly, extremely comfortable to ride in—presumably no more were built because they were a little extravagant of space and large numbers of the earlier designs had, in any case, been built between 1924 and 1928.

On the specialised coaching side, this second phase of design was represented mainly by dining cars of which 36 were built (24 RFs and 12 RCs). Mention has already been made of the relative lack of new dining cars during the first six years of the LMS but these new 68ft, 12 wheel coaches amply made amends. Like the above mentioned 57ft vestibule thirds, these diners were steel panelled with painted 'beading'.

There were also two batches of 12 wheel composite sleeping cars built at this time to D1781 which were rather in the nature of 'odd men out'. They retained a high waist and certain LNWR styling features but were flush clad with frameless droplights. They are fully described in Volume II but must be regarded as distinctly outside the main trend of LMS coach design.

Plate 13 *(below)* Period II BFK to D1717 from the corridor side. This coach, No. 5006, is shown running on experimental twin bolster long wheelbase bogies which give every appearance of having been derived from the standard six wheel type but without the centre pair of wheels. On this coach, the solebar appears to be red.

Plate 14 *(opposite top)* Period II open third to D1807 No. 2744 (later 8737).

Plate 15 *(opposite centre)* Period II corridor composite to D1791 No. 14993 (later 3810) taken from the corridor side.

Plate 16 *(opposite below)* Period II composite sleeping car No. 10637 (later 709). This design (D1781) still showed some residual LNWR influence.

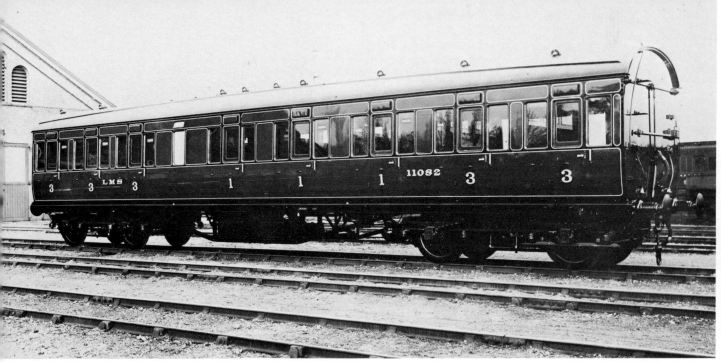

Plate 17 A typical period II non-corridor coach. This is a lavatory composite to D1736 No. 11082 (later 19190).

From the point of view of other changes, the most noticeable detail alteration from the Period I coach during this 1929–32 period was the change in window ventilation. Over the tops of the main windows almost exclusive use was made of the Stones or Dewel pattern glass vane ventilator. These features had always supplemented the droplight in the 'two window' and high waisted single window designs but did not become universal for all gangwayed coaches until the complete adoption of single window designs. There were some partial exceptions. Some of the 1932 built 57ft vestibule thirds had hooded ventilators over many of the windows while it was by no means unusual to find hooded ventilators or even no ventilators at all over the windows on the corridor side of non-vestibule coaches. Outside doors, of course, still retained droplights and top ventilators but, on steel clad stock, the latter were exclusively of the plain hooded pattern rather than the more usual louvre type on the wooden coaches.

With the Period II vestibule coach, most of the windows were of fixed light design with raised mahogany mouldings round the edges. There were, however, generally two or three frameless droplights incorporated in each side of the vehicle. The whole window could be partially lowered in its surround (usually made of aluminium) and from the outside could be identified by the lack of raised wood mouldings and the two hand grips which were fixed to the glass near the upper edge. Needless to say, compartment windows of Period II corridor stock were all of this type while corridor windows were mostly fixed lights.

Non-corridor Period II stock continued to have the high waist and was little different from its Period I predecessor except in the steel panelling and absence of beading. It retained the raised window mouldings and full livery but, unlike the Cathcart Circle and early electric stock mentioned did not have a pseudo waist panel in paint. There were no innovations at all in the design of Period II non-corridor coaches but it should be mentioned that the LMS did build a considerable quantity of electric stock of Period II style as well as the locomotive hauled variety.

Summing up the second phase of LMS coach design, it should be emphasised that, although steel panelling had occasionally been used before 1929, it was this second period of design which saw the genuine transition from wood to steel panelling and the abandonment of raised external beading. The design period itself was somewhat short lived, spanning less than four years. During this time, however, some very good coaches of more than normally handsome aspect had been built and, with the gradual introduction of outside steel panelling, the precedent had been well and truly established for the final change to completely flush exteriors which was to characterise LMS coaches for the rest of the company's lifetime.

PERIOD III—1933 ONWARDS

In 1932, Mr. William Stanier took up his appointment as Chief Mechanical Engineer to the LMS and the first of the completely flush sided LMS coaches emerged soon enough after his assumption of office to lead to the coaches ever afterwards being referred to as Stanier stock. Just what real influence the CME had on external coach styling is rather conjectural but most sources refer to the flush sided designs as Stanier coaches and it seems less likely to confuse matters if this term is adopted.

The LMS flush sided coach, of which many examples still remained as late as 1967–8, differed in appearance from its predecessor mainly in the shape of its windows which now exhibited well rounded corners. All the earlier coaches had, of course, been built with slightly rounded window corner mouldings but by comparison with Stanier vehicles the Period I and II coach window was almost 'square' cornered. The second major visible difference was also in the window area. During Period I, the favoured method of admitting fresh air was the droplight which was frequently supplemented by and finally (in Period II) in large measure superseded by the Stones and Dewel pattern glass vane ventilator. With the Stanier stock was introduced the now familiar sliding ventilator incorporated in the upper part of the window. Initially this was quite shallow with only one section moveable but in 1934 this was replaced by the deeper ventilator with two wide sliding sections which remained almost until the end. From about 1947/8, the sliding portions were somewhat shortened and in this form were retained as a feature of the BR standard coach.

Plate 18 *(above)* The first ever Stanier gangwayed coach design for the LMS was this corridor brake composite to D1850 No. 9318 (later 6784). The picture here was probably taken when the coach was given luxury style seating to D1939 in 1933. Note the shallow window ventilators, pre-1933 series running number and fully lined livery.

Plate 19 *(below)* Period III BTK No. 5518 to D1905. This was one of the batch which had the projecting lookouts removed for working on the 'Sunny South Express'. It was also one of the only batch of Period III BTK with the standard deep window ventilators to receive full livery.

There were, however, other points of difference in the Period III coach. Firstly, the roof now became of the 'ribbed' pattern rather than the wood/canvas/rainstrip variety while almost from the start of construction, torpedo roof ventilation gave way to shell ventilators and side lamps were omitted above the guard's lookout on brake coaches. The torpedo ventilators returned after the second World War but in modified form as perpetuated on a great number of BR standard coaches. The Stanier coach also marks the general introduction of the 'suspended' type of British Standard corridor connection to the LMS. As this feature first seems to have made its appearance on some of the 1932 Period II 57ft vestibule thirds, one wonders if Stanier imported the idea from Swindon where it had been in use from about 1925. Since shell ventilators were also used at Swindon before Stanier came to the LMS, it seems quite possible that these detail changes were at the behest of the CME himself. Some Stanier ideas—e.g. the removal of the lamps above the guard's lookout—were applied retrospectively to older coaches.

The Stanier coach was still a wood framed vehicle; the total employment of flush steel outer panels and the ribbed roof being the main differences from the Period I/II coach as far as construction was concerned. The underframe changed but little except to develop a few more length variations. In general the 57ft length remained the standard where possible but the 60ft length, first introduced in 1928 with the convertible third class sleepers, was the common standard for open firsts, corridor composites and corridor brake composites. The extra 3ft of length was useful in giving the first class passenger a little more leg room while it was invaluable in the composites in helping to do away with the half, or coupé compartment which, as will be seen in Volume II, caused a certain amount of trouble to the design staff. Certain other coaches by virtue of their more specialised purpose were even longer and these mainly came in the following categories.

69ft long	12 wheel sleeping cars
68ft long	12 wheel dining cars
65ft long	Eight wheel third class sleeping cars and eight wheel vestibule first class dining vehicles
62ft long	Later designs of corridor brake composites

Plate 20 Period III high capacity open third No. 9174 to D1915. This design, with 7½ seating bays, had the highest seating capacity of any LMS standard design of gangwayed open coach.
Plate 21 LMS third class dining car No. 142 to D1923, typifies most features exhibited by the Stanier period coaching stock.

The final distinguishing feature of the Stanier coach was probably its livery. While the first year or so of new construction saw the perpetuation of a fully lined quasi-beaded style (in paint), the characteristic simplified livery was much more common with horizontal lining only, this variation being introduced only a short time after the introduction of the deeper window ventilators. As time went on, all coaches were, of course, finished in this simplified style but during the middle thirties, the difference of livery was also, more often than not, indicative of a difference in coach style too.

To many people, flush sided coaches are much of a muchness with little visible difference between those of Stanier, Thompson, Bulleid, Hawksworth or even the BR standard designs. While it is undoubtedly true that the flush sided style introduced a greater monotony into the external appearance of the coach, the differences were still there. It is, however, to the interior layout of the coach that one must look for changes and in this respect the full progression of interior design and layout and of detail changes in the Stanier coach is best appreciated by considering the detailed analysis of each type of coach in the later chapters. However, in this preliminary survey it *is* worth mentioning that the Stanier coach, amongst other things, introduced a general policy of three a side seating in the third class compartments of LMS corridor coaches for the first time.

In passing, it is interesting to note that in this respect the first BR standard coaches followed their regional predecessors. The LMS from 1933 was wedded to the three a side third class corridor coach whereas the GWR and SR tended to favour the more frugal four a side seating. This may have been to keep down dead coach weight per passenger but it was a source of some surprise to the writers to find the BR standard coaches built for the Western and Southern Regions long after 1950 still perpetuated this somewhat uncomfortable feature when otherwise identical vehicles built for the Northern main lines were given armrests. Possibly the heavier holiday traffic carried by the Southern and Western region was the main reason for the four a side policy.

As well as general service vehicles, the Stanier era introduced further examples of specialised coaches, all bearing the common house style. Possibly the most noteworthy *new* designs (at least as far as LMS standard coaches were concerned) were the first LMS fixed berth third class sleeping cars, the massive third class dining cars and the rather neat Engineers' saloons of the 1940s. Mention ought also to be made of the building of various articulated coaches mainly for general service and/or excursion use in the Central and Northern Divisions (see Volume III), but not forgetting the magnificent special vehicles built for the second Coronation Scot train–regrettably never to run as such in this country. During the Stanier period too, experiments were also conducted in lightweight design, welded bogie construction and so forth. From these experiments there stemmed a partial adoption of welded underframes and bogies from about 1935/6 onwards although the basic design of these features remained substantially unchanged and the riveted style continued to be used alongside the welded chassis.

Although the third period of LMS coaches introduced many desirable features into the gangwayed stock, sufficient indeed to make it compare more than favourably with almost anything built by BR until recent years, the same cannot be said about the non-corridor stock which remained of pretty nondescript character right to the very end. It is true, of course, that there is little scope in the non-corridor vehicle for large scale innovation but at the same time it seems a little

Plate 22 Corridor side elevation of the pioneer Stanier first class sleeping car. Note the wider body profile.

surprising that a company which in its heyday produced some of the best riding and most comfortable corridor and vestibule stock in the country, did not do more for the stopping passenger services. One wonders, perhaps, why nothing was attempted along the lines of the ex-LNER semi-corridor cross-country coaches. On the other hand, it might be argued that as the LMS seemed more prone to use older corridor coaches on its cross-country services than did the other companies, there was less need for specialised cross-country sets.

Be that as it may, during the Stanier period, non-corridor coaches varied but little from the pattern laid down in the 1920s except for the flush clad exterior. The design was still high waisted and the seating arrangements never changed from the earlier years. No inter district lavatory sets were built during the Stanier régime and apart from a few lavatory composites for the LT&S Section, all the Stanier non-corridor stock was of the 'suburban' type. There was an interesting batch of articulated triplets made in 1938 but these do not seem to have been very popular. They were, perhaps, less flexible in the traffic sense than they were mechanically.

The Stanier period is also interesting as witnessing the bulk of newly built LMS standard motor fitted (push-pull) stock. Again it is somewhat surprising that in view of the many GWR imports which Stanier brought to the LMS, there seems to have been no attempt to build an LMS equivalent of the GWR auto-trailer. Yet the LMS had need of a considerable stock of motor fitted vehicles and one can only conclude that reasons of standardisation at Wolverton and Derby were the main factors behind the appearance of LMS motor fitted trains which looked scarcely any different from their suburban contemporaries. For this reason, motor fitted coaches do not suggest themselves as topics for separate discussion in the LMS coach story and have been included with their associated non-corridor vehicles in Volume III.

Plate 23 Period III non-corridor third brake to D1735 No. 20609. This is a very typical Stanier period non-corridor type but has a few features which were not retained for long (torpedo roof ventilators, side-lights over the guard's lookout and full livery). This coach was actually built to a Period II diagram.

Plate 24 A train of Liverpool-Southport open stock seen in service c.1946. Note the post-war type of insignia.

Apart from locomotive hauled stock, the third period did witness some changes in the type of vehicle provided for some of the electrified lines. In the Wirral and between Liverpool and Southport there were introduced some new open coach multiple unit sets rather reminiscent of the London Transport style. They had sliding doors and other characteristic type features. Livery apart, they would have looked reasonably at home on the Circle Line! They do not, therefore, fit into the mainstream of LMS coach design and have been considered separately in Volume III.

POST NATIONALISATION

LMS design coaches continued to be built for several years after 1947 until the introduction of the BR standard designs. This short-lived period was, in fact, little more than a continuation of the Stanier era and was not really a new phase in the same sense that the flush sided stock itself was. Later corridor coaches have, however, been distinguished by the name Porthole stock by virtue of the circular toilet window feature which they introduced. This stock actually commenced building a year or two after 1947 and was, therefore, not strictly LMS stock as such but it was in the direct tradition of LMS coachbuilding practice and has, therefore, been included in this survey. It differed from the last versions of the Stanier stock proper (which themselves were built well into BR days) principally in the circular toilet windows which replaced the earlier rectangular ones, but also in having post-war torpedo ventilators and the final style of sliding window ventilators.

Plate 25 Period III CK No. M4878M from the corridor side. This picture shows the first post-war D2117 version with two extra corridor doors. Note also the shorter sliding portions of the window ventilators. The picture was taken in 1962 to illustrate the newly introduced yellow band above the first class section of the coach.

Plate 26 'Porthole' BTK No. M26668 to D2161 built new in 1950 with BR crimson and cream livery. This is a compartment side view; note the longer pattern of sliding window ventilators used on this example.

One batch of 'Portholes' was however, of particular significance. These were 'all steel' corridor composites to D2159 and although retaining many LMS features they saw the first real change from their predecessors in that the coach profile was changed. In these particular coaches, the profile was more clipper-sided with a slightly more accentuated tumblehome. Moreover the junction between sides and roof at the cantrail was sharper and the roof lost its pure semi-elliptical shape. As a final point of difference, the sides met the ends in a small radius curve rather than a sharp angle. One can presume that but for Nationalisation, these coaches, of which large numbers were still in use as late as 1967/68 would have probably set the pattern for subsequent design development at Derby. The drawings date from 1947 and they bequeathed their roof profile and rounded off side/end junction to their BR standard successors.

Another post-1947 innovation entirely in the LMS tradition was a batch of twin berth third class sleeping cars to D2169. These did not appear until 1951 and they perpetuated the more traditional LMS sleeping car profile in spite of being built after the above mentioned composites. Because of their twin berth arrangement, they looked more like the standard Stanier first class sleeper than their first class predecessors. However, they ran on LMS standard 65ft chassis.

On the non-corridor side, amongst the more interesting points to note is the fact that considerable numbers of LMS pattern motor fitted coaches were built after 1947, presumably to replace the outmoded conversions of pre-group coaches which were hitherto frequently used for motor train working. Another interesting batch was a group of fifteen non-corridor firsts built in 1951 to a Diagram issued in 1938 (D1997). These were amongst the last vehicles to be built to any LMS design and their late building may have been a contributory reason for the non-appearance of a BR standard non-corridor first. However, the oddest feature of all is undoubtedly the fact that the last general service coaches of all to be given LMS series numbers were actually built at Swindon to a pre-war GWR design. These were 59ft composites to D2189 and it is understood that they were built at Swindon because the need for them was urgent and the ex-LMS works were all fully occupied at the time building BR standard stock. Details have been included in Volume III for the sake of completeness but the coaches were not, of course, LMS designs. In addition to these, LMS type TPO vehicles appeared until 1956/7 and a batch of LMS design Mersey/Wirral electric stock emerged in 1956/7.

Finally, after 1948, several ex-LMS coaches were converted for other uses. These included conversion to buffet cars, heating vans &c. and where it has been possible to trace these conversions, details have been included.

Plate 27 Period III CK No. M24623 as built new in late 1949 with BR crimson and cream livery. This coach clearly illustrates the slightly altered end profile of the final LMS design corridor coaches.

Plates 28-29 The above two views show how little the end profile of LMS coaches changed during almost the whole of its lifetime. On the left is a Period I gangway end exhibiting matchboard panelling. Period II was similar but from 1930 had steel sheeting. Coach 5403 was an ambulance conversion—hence the safety chains on the headstock. The right hand view shows a Period III gangwayed brake end. The coach was BTK No. 26321 of D1968, built in 1945.

CONCLUSIONS

The high degree of standardisation of LMS coaching stock has been mentioned and this may well be one of the reasons why the company never seemed particularly anxious to build special vehicles for its glamour trains. Apart from the 1939 Coronation Scot stock, the nearest it came were probably such coaches as the already mentioned lounge brakes and semi-open firsts. Even the 1933 'Royal Scot' tour train to the USA was composed of standard stock and in this matter of special vehicles, the LMS came rather a poor third to the LNER and GWR whose streamlined and centenary stock respectively set new standards on their own lines.

All the same, when the LMS so wished, it *could* build extremely fine coaches and its supporters could argue with some justification that the general high standard of LMS coaches, together with the high replacement rate of sub-standard pre-group stock was sufficient not to warrant the provision of specially designed luxury vehicles. In any case, these would probably interfere with the mass production techniques of the works at Derby and Wolverton and, moreover, cost far more than the standard designs for which the works were laid out. This seems the only logical explanation for the lack of new coaches for the Coronation Scot train of 1937 which has often been unfavourably compared with its LNER rival. What seems generally to have been overlooked is that the 1937 train was itself a very fine set of coaches and it speaks volumes for the quality of the Stanier coach that a cheap refurbishment of three sets of standard vehicles could compare favourably, if not totally with a specially built prestige train. When the LMS did wish to build some special vehicles for the exhibition of the Coronation Scot in America in 1939, it showed itself more than capable of matching anything that the rest of British railways could produce. It seems a thousand pities that the three sets which were finally completed after the war were never reformed into full trains.

The first type of BR standard coach did not, superficially, owe much to its LMS predecessor as the length, gangways and couplers were all of a different standard and nearer to that of Bulleid than Stanier. Yet in some ways the coach owed as much to the LMS as any company for it should be viewed in relation to the last batch of 'Portholes' which, as suggested above, really represent the final expression of LMS design ideas. Experience of the early BR standard coach tempts the thought that in some respects it would have been better to perpetuate more LMS features. In particular, in preferring a narrow single sliding door to the compartment to the LMS arrangement of wider double doors, the BR coach seems to have taken a major step backwards.

Throughout the rest of this survey, the above sub-division into Periods I, II and III will be adopted for convenience* since the design periods are also reflected in the non-corridor and other passenger stock built by the LMS, remembering, of course, that the low waist, first introduced in the Period II gangwayed stock was never adopted in non-corridor vehicles.

---

*In the above chapter, no mention has been made of certain non-standard coaching type vehicles which the LMS owned. Included among these were such vehicles as the Sentinel steam railcars and the experimental diesel articulated streamline train. These vehicles do not really form part of the mainstream of LMS standard coach development and have therefore, been confined to Volume III where all are considered together. The same is also true of much of the non-passenger carrying stock (except full brakes and TPO coaches) which exhibited a considerable variety of exterior styling features which do not lend themselves to the Period I/II/III generalisations.

Chapter 2 - Constructional Methods and Coach Interiors

Introduction; Underframes; Body construction; All-steel coaches; Coach interiors (open stock, compartment and corridor stock, sleeping cars)

INTRODUCTION

THE technique of construction of LMS coaches varied but little throughout the company's existence and seems to have directly evolved from methods adopted by the Midland Railway. During early years, LNWR techniques were employed at Wolverton on a few specialised vehicles and an odd batch of non-corridor coaches was built at Newton Heath with slightly different compartment dimension (See Volume III, D1767). As well as constructional methods, body dimensions too became remarkably standardised within a very short space of time and although there were many superficial external differences between coach types, all exhibited standard panel, door, gangway, seat and other dimensions.

The LMS at grouping took over control of a considerable number of locomotive, carriage and wagon works but only three (Derby, Wolverton and Newton Heath) were ever involved in the building of LMS standard coaches. Of these, Newton Heath was only involved for a short period and to a limited extent and the vast bulk of LMS coaches were built at Wolverton and Derby. There were also batches of coaches built by outside contractors but the coaches thus supplied were of standard LMS type except, in some cases, for the all-steel constructional methods adopted.

UNDERFRAMES

With very few exceptions, generally all-steel coaches built without conventional underframes—see page 27—all LMS standard coaches had separate, usually wood framed bodies mounted on a steel underframe. The underframe design first appeared in 1923 and hardly changed at all, except for developing different lengths as years passed by. It was directly derived from final MR style and is depicted at Figure 2.

The underframe itself was built from mild rolled steel channel sections and plates riveted together. The solebars had the channel section facing outwards and trussing was made of 'L' section rolled steel. Bogies were also made from rolled steel channels, angles and plates. They were of single bolster design fitted with laminated side bearing springs and had bolster springs of helical coil type. The four wheel bogie was of 9ft 0in wheelbase and the six wheel of 12ft 6in wheelbase. Slight changes in this general specification were to be found in the electric multiple unit coaches.

The underframe headstock was fitted with non-automatic screw couplings and generally had round headed buffers. Long coaches (62ft and above) had oval buffers. All LMS standard coaches except 50ft kitchen cars, were electrically lit and thus the underframes all carried dynamos and battery boxes. Most coaches were vacuum fitted only with two vacuum cylinders. However, some coaches were dual fitted with vacuum and Westinghouse air brakes for through working. Gas cylinders and other ancillary equipment were also fitted to the underframes of such vehicles as dining cars and kitchen cars.

In the middle 1930s, welded construction was introduced to save weight and increase strength. This technique initially appeared in the pioneer Stanier 69ft sleeping cars (D1926, Volume II) and became an alternative standard method of construction. The underframe design remained basically the same but the welded construction made it possible to preserve a flush top to the underframe and enable the steel floor to be welded directly to it. By bringing the teak body pillars right down to this very strong substructure it became possible to dispense with the use of bottom side members for the coach body. The bottom of the teak pillar was bolted direct to a steel box bracket welded to the underframe.

The LMS standard underframe seems to have been all but identical to the final MR style—it being well nigh impossible to detect the difference between them in pictures. The four wheel bogie was probably also derived from the MR but the six wheel bogie was more of an LNWR speciality†. However, MR and LNWR bogie design was so very similar by 1923, especially in appearance, that there was probably little to choose between the two sorts. What does seem clear is that LMS coach and bogie design seemed to owe very little to any of the companies except the LNWR and MR.* Like the underframe, the LMS standard four wheel bogie changed scarcely at all and in spite of its single bolster design it was an extremely good riding unit. Recent experience of riding in the residual survivors of LMS design coaches confirmed this latter fact.

The standard LMS underframe was built in a variety of lengths but the vast bulk of designs were made for the 57ft length which was the final LNWR standard and was also, latterly, a length which the Caledonian and Midland Railways had used. Regardless of length, all LMS underframes were substantially identical and shared common truss rod dimensions (Fig. 2). Longer chassis were adopted for more specialised stock and the following list summarises the principal utilisation of the various lengths, other than the 57ft standard variety:

69ft	Period III 12 wheel Sleeping Cars.
68ft	All Kitchen/Dining Cars and pre-Stanier 12 wheel sleeping cars.
65ft	Period III vestibule first dining coaches and third class sleeping cars.
62ft	Later versions of Period III corridor brake composites.

†Some of the early 12-wheel dining and sleeping cars were built with LNWR pattern bogies – see Volume II.

*It should, however, be recorded that the final Caledonian Railway coaches were 57ft vehicles with angle trussed underframes.

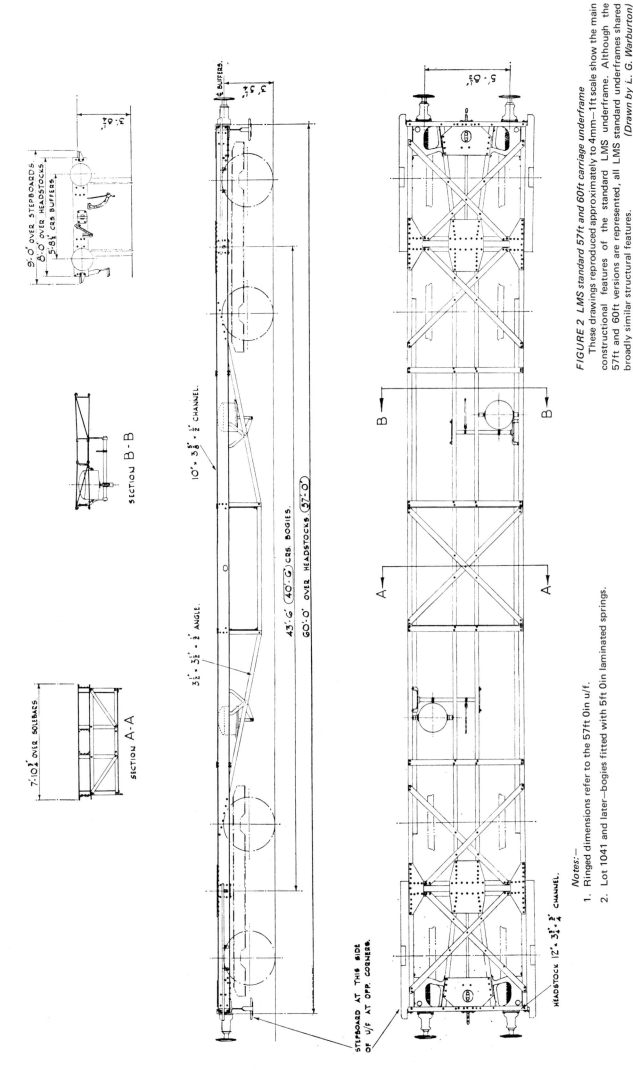

FIGURE 2 *LMS standard 57ft and 60ft carriage underframe*
These drawings reproduced approximately to 4mm—1ft scale show the main constructional features of the standard LMS underframe. Although the 57ft and 60ft versions are represented, all LMS standard underframes shared broadly similar structural features.
(Drawn by L. G. Warburton)

Notes:—
1. Ringed dimensions refer to the 57ft 0in u/f.
2. Lot 1041 and later—bogies fitted with 5ft 0in laminated springs.

SECTION B - B

SECTION A - A

22

60ft	Period I third class sleeping cars, Period II vestibule third class dining coaches, most designs of corridor composites and brake composites (except for the earlier Period I all-door designs) and many TPO vehicles. This was the most common alternative length for gangwayed coaches after the 57ft variety.
59ft	Some electric driving motor coaches.
58ft	Some electric multiple unit stock.
54ft	Non-corridor stock for the LT&S and Cathcart Circle services plus a few batches for general service.
51ft	One batch only of non-corridor composites for the Cathcart Circle services.
50ft	Most passenger full brakes and kitchen cars.

The LMS also built some articulated coaches and for the gangwayed vehicles, Stanier designed a centrally trussed lattice type underframe. This was first tried out as far as is known on corridor third brake No. 5844. The 1937 general service coaches were articulated by a single pivot 'male and female' joint, but for the experimental diesel articulated train (Volume III) and the 1939 'Coronation Scot' stock, the 'LMS type' of articulation was utilised. This basically made use of a double pivot and enabled a slightly longer distance between bogie centres to be achieved without the throw-over on curves exceeding the loading gauge although still within the maximum distance between wheels permitted by points locking bars. Three basic kinds of articulated locomotive-hauled stock were built. In 1937 there were introduced some gangwayed open articulated pairs in the Central Division—mainly for excursion use—and at the same time there was built a batch of three coach units of non-corridor stock. These were articulated on the same principle but had conventionally trussed underframes. Finally there were the 1939 'Coronation Scot' coaches which had centrally trussed frames like the 1937 vestibule pairs but had the later type of articulation. The full history of the LMS articulated experiment has survived in contemporary documents and is given in Volume III.

BODY CONSTRUCTION

Apart from the all-steel vehicles, LMS coaches were generally built with wood frames. From grouping until 1930, coach bodies were timber framed (usually teak) and timber panelled in mahogany. Panel joints were capped by raised wooden beading strips on the outside of the coach while coach ends were made from tongue and groove matchboarding arranged vertically from roof to headstock. Coach roofs were teak framed and covered with longitudinal boards which were then concealed with canvas and fitted with longitudinal end to end rainwater strips. All external mouldings, cornices and so forth were also made from timber.

The later method of construction involved a change to steel outside panelling. From 1930, steel took the place of wood for sides and ends but roofs, window framing, cornices and so on remained as they had always been. However, metal framed or frameless droplights entirely replaced wood framed droplights except in the outside doors. From the start of the Stanier period, steel panelling was introduced for the roof and cornices while outside window mouldings ceased to be used. However, the coaches retained their timber framing except that, as already remarked, when welded underframes came into general use, the bottom side member was omitted. Little further change seems to have taken place except that increasing use seemed to be made of steel components for other parts of the coach such as cantrails, corner pillars and so forth.

It was in 1923 that the celebrated Derby mass-production technique was introduced into the building of coaches and, fortunately, full details of its principles have survived. It was later introduced at Wolverton. Although materials changed during the 1930s, the basic method of assembly remained fairly constant and the great majority of Wolverton and Derby built coaches were constructed to these principles.

Fundamentally, the building of an LMS coach depended on the prefabrication in quantity of all the standard basic coach units (sides, ends, roofs &c.). This was first made possible by the introduction of limit gauges into Derby Works by R. W. Reid, the Midland and then LMS carriage superintendent, in 1923. By this means and the overhauling of the saw mill, it became possible to use jigs for cutting out components instead of laboriously marking out each one separately. All components were machine-cut, then inspected and gauged for accuracy. The use of well-seasoned timbers all but eliminated shrinkage problems and the main task became to ensure that the design of components was such that they could be incorporated into as many different varieties of coach as possible. This enabled numerically larger production runs of components to be made before setting up the jigs and tools for a different unit. It was the use of this method that enabled the LMS to dispense with all its other carriage works although the number of coaches built was considerably greater than anything either Wolverton or Derby had tackled before.

Once the pre-cut units had been checked for accuracy, they were fabricated with a minimum of hand tools into basic coach units—sides, ends, roofs, doors, partitions, seats and so forth. The fabrication process took place simultaneously on a variety of different components in various parts of the works so the final coach assembly involved little more than the fitting together of a minimum number of finished units. In the assembly of the units themselves, extensive use was made of power tools such as jig drills, magazine fed screwdrivers, compressed air cylinders for forcing tenons onto mortices and the like. All doors were fitted into standard cast iron openings. By this means, complete sides and ends could be assembled simultaneously.

Roof construction was equally mechanised. The roof was built on a floor level jig with adjustable pillars for the various coach sides. The cantrail was dropped on to the jig, the roof profile timbers—already pre-drilled &c.—were fixed and the roof boards, canvas, water strips and cornices added.

The main floor framing was built on the underframe direct. One bottom member was fixed to a solebar, the cross bearers clamped into it and then the other bottom side member fixed to the cross bearers. This was clamped tight by means of a portable ball bearing clamp which ran along the full length of the underframe and was fitted with handwheels to enable the second bottom side member to be pulled up tight. Pre-cut floor boards were then fitted and the whole time for a single coach floor assembly was one working day.

Plate 30 Wooden bodied coaches under construction at Wolverton Works during the 1920s. Note the number of mass-produced standard components assembled on various parts of the shop floor.

Plate 31 Interior view of a pre-war Stanier coach under construction—type of vehicle unidentified. The coach visible through the window is the Duke of Sutherland's private saloon—now preserved at the National Railway Museum.

Plate 32 A post-war side corridor coach at Derby Works with the framing erected on the under-frame but before the addition of side panels. The vehicle is typically Period III in style, being of composite timber and steel construction. The end framing and each of the sections of side framing between the door openings were prefabricated before erection on to the frames. The coach was a corridor brake third to Lot 1448 (D2123).

The coach erection was simplicity itself. Erection roads had platforms round them at coach floor level to dispense with scaffolding. The underframe was brought in and the coach floor laid as described. The prefabricated ends were then fitted into the endboard tenons by compressed air cylinders. The complete side units, minus bottom panelling, were similarly added and finally the complete roof was lowered onto the coach by means of two hand cranes running the length of the erecting roads. Power clamps were applied inside the cantrails to pull the roof down onto the tenons. The whole operation after the floor had been laid took about one hour.

Interiors were similarly mass-produced using jigs and standard patterns for each and every component even down to picture frames on the compartment walls. Little if any handwork was done on any of them and the work was of a high order.

As far as has been ascertained, few significant changes in assembly procedure were made when steel panelling was first introduced. However, as has been stated, increasing use was made of steel for other parts of vehicles too as time went by and this led to a common policy of prefabricating and erecting the complete coach framework before adding outside panelling.

Plate 33 The method by which steel panelling was applied to Period III stock. The vehicle is one of the 1937 vestibule articulated coaches–see Volume III.

Plates 34-35-36 Various stages in the erection of the pioneer Stanier 69ft 12-wheel sleeping cars to D1926. Note particularly the steel box brackets, welded direct onto the under-frame, thus dispensing with the need for a bottom side member for the coach body. Note also the continued use of prefabricated sections of side framing as during the wooden bodied period. The main difference in body erection during Period III was that the whole of the framework was erected before the side sheeting was applied.

Plate 37 Detail view of the welded version ▶ of the LMS standard six-wheel bogie. Note the heavy framing above the centre axle linking the two swing planks of the bolster, thus enabling it to function as a single unit but effectively doubling the amount of springing available. Coaches fitted with this bogie were supremely comfortable to ride in.

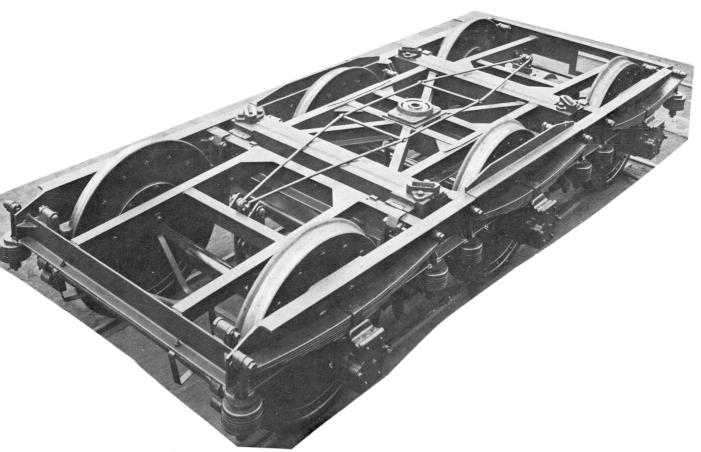

ALL-STEEL COACHES

The principal exceptions to conventional coaches were the various 'all steel' vehicles. For the most part these were built by outside contractors and in the case of the Period I vestibule coaches and full brakes (see p. 167), they were almost certainly ordered to assist the steel industry at the time. The open coaches were designed principally for use on long distance weekend trains and excursion workings.

The coaches were built in the form of a long tubular girder. The underframe formed the bottom boom and the cantrails, purlins and roof sheets the top boom. The body side plates formed webs connecting upper and lower booms and were stiffened by pressed channel section pillars riveted to them. The whole structure was very light but extremely rigid. The coaches were practically fireproof and much stronger than the equivalent wooden vehicles. None of them had conventional truss rods but all carried a somewhat rudimentary support for the battery boxes and electric light regulator.

The coaches were built by various outside contractors (see Volume III) and the designs varied in detail between the batches. Some were heavily riveted; others were of a more flush sided nature. Some had rounded side/end corners–as on modern BR stock but less emphasised–and so on. These variations in detail were, according to the surviving records, devised to gain practical experience in this country of the methods adopted by the various contractors in the construction of similar vehicles for use overseas. Thus, all had insulating lining material except the Cammell-Laird coaches which were given a free-air space between the inner and outer lining of the coach.

Most vehicles were finished inside in the standard LMS style utilising mahogany veneers but some were steel throughout in which case special colour schemes were used. Seats were covered with black or fawn York velvet and the brass fittings were finished in Venetian bronze.

Following on these twin-window vestibule coaches and full brakes, the next steel coaches were some corridor brake firsts and brake thirds during Period II. They could be identified from their Period II contemporaries by the deeper than normal eaves panelling and the lack of conventional truss rod framing. The coaches were again built in the form of a hollow box girder using both roof and floor as strengtheners–hence the presence of the rather deeper eaves section which was an essential part of the structural form. These coaches too had metal roof panelling.

The final pre-war steel coaches were the 1939 'Coronation Scot' trains but these were specialised vehicles and are considered in detail in Volume III.

During the war, virtually all coach construction ceased and a considerable backlog of overdue vehicle replacement had to be cleared immediately hostilities ceased. This left little time for further experimental work and the LMS embarked on a massive coach construction programme utilising basically pre-war patterns and ideas–not that the coaches were in any way inferior because of this fact. However, by 1949 the immediate shortages had been overcome and Derby works presumably felt free to experiment again with steel construction. Although no recorded evidence has been located, the experiment was presumably encouraged by the Railway Executive since one must assume that consideration was being given at this time to the designing of new BR standard stock. The outcome was the appearance of the 60ft corridor composites to D2159, the design for which had appeared in 1947, and these vehicles may safely be stated to be the last expression of pure LMS design ideas although not the last LMS pattern coaches to be built. The slightly altered profile has been alluded to on page 19 but the construction too had several points of interest, especially since it more or less established BR standard coach construction methods.

The steel body shell was welded directly to the underframe which was carried on standard LMS pattern welded bogies. However, the underframe, although similar to the LMS pattern was designed with slightly lighter section solebars and truss rods. Furthermore, the truss rods, although still of the conventional angle section were also fitted to the central longitudinal chassis members as well as to the solebars. Sides, ends and roof were prefabricated units of light skeleton structure to

Plate 38 The construction of the 'porthole' CKs to D2159 at Derby in 1949. These vehicles were of 'all steel' construction and the side, end and roof sections were prefabricated before erection on to the underframe. This picture gives a good impression of the changed profile of this batch with the rather sharper radius between side and roof.

which were welded the steel outer panels. All the main body assembly was welded together and the timber floor was fixed direct to the underframe. Interior finishing was of conventional woodwork and veneered surfaces but in order to reduce corrosion from interior condensation, circulation air spaces were left between the interior finishing panels and the steel structure of the coach. An innovation inside the coach at least from the LMS/LMR point of view, was the elimination of sharp corners from the compartment and corridor ceilings by introducing ceilings of an arch type. These blended at the corridor partition into a common through pocket in which the coach wiring was carried. Many of these vehicles remained in service until at least 1967/8.

Plate 39 Period I 'two-window' FO No. 3716, later 7414. This coach exhibited a transitional seat end design from the Midland style to the LMS standard pattern of Figure 3. The ornate panel decoration between the windows did not last long after Grouping.

Plate 40 Interior of 56-seat open third No. 6260, later 8071. This was a member of the Metropolitan C & W batch to Lot 185 and was given all metal interior finishing. The seat end design, although rendered in pressed steel is still of standard LMS pattern—see Figure 3. Note the 'cranking' of the seat end to provide more gangway width at shoulder level—a feature of all LMS open coaches with two-and-two rather than two-and-one seating.

COACH INTERIORS

Regrettably, less information has survived about LMS coach interiors than one would have liked. Nevetheless, it is possible to reconstruct an abbreviated story of the development of ideas. Figures 3a/3b give some of the more common interior designs.

At all times the LMS made extensive use of timber finishing. Throughout its history the company laid strong emphasis on the use of 'selected Empire timber' and this may have had suitable patriotic overtones for the publicity department. However, the important point seems to be that timber finishes lent themselves admirably to the mass-production technique. Interior panels, window frames, tables, seats and the like could all be mass produced. In consequence, the interiors of LMS coaches, especially the Period II examples, showed far less change than one might expect from the outside styling.

Vestibule stock

Early vestibule stock was particularly consistent. Kitchen/dining cars, vestibule dining coaches and general service open stock all had common seat designs, variations being principally in the width of the seat depending on whether the coach seated two-and-one or two each side of the gangway. First class seats were generally a little softer (!). The seat end design remained unchanged for almost 10 years (Fig. 3a/b) and its wing ended style owed a great deal to its Midland predecessors. In centre gangway coaches, the seat-ends were shaped to give a greater width to the gangway at seat back level than at the seat itself. This gave extra elbow room for passengers walking through the coach but enabled the widest possible seat to be achieved.

Plate 41 The characteristic Period III open first style—see Figure 3. The picture is of the first class portion of the vestibule articulated coaches—see Chapter 12. The offset gangway is very clear and the doorway is surmounted by a class indicator board. The LMS monogram in the luggage rack supports was not always present in Period III coaches, being replaced by a plainer design of support—see Figure 3.

Tables were fitted between the seats in all open coaches and a reading lamp was often located on the wall over the table. Pullman type table lamps were occasionally used in dining cars. Three bulb 'electroliers' or single unit fixtures were spaced down the centre of the ceiling which was enamelled white for greater reflectivity. Interior veneers were generally mahogany stained to a very dark shade, although first-class coaches often had silver grey wood veneers instead. The double floors were felt insulated and had a strip carpet down the gangway.

Upholstery was provided in various patterns. Unfortunately the contemporary accounts do not give much idea about the colours adopted. It would seem that traditional red and black velvet was very popular but fawn and blue patterned moquettes were increasingly used as time went on. Seat antimacassars in the first class cars were unbleached holland embroidered with the LMS monogram.

The Stanier coaches witnessed little change in seat size but the general styling was modernised to the typical 'boxy' style so favoured in the 1930s. Both classes of accommodation retained wooden seat ends—presumably for their harder wearing properties—but open firsts became much 'softer' in appearance (Fig. 3a/b). From the many black and white pictures of LMS interiors it seems that there was little standardisation in upholstery colour but that patterned moquette, sometimes of rather bold design, had, by this time, become almost universal. The shade of wood veneering was also lightened and the lamps and other fittings were somewhat more 'streamlined' in their styling.

Plate 42 (*left*) The typical Period III open third finish—again an articulated coach. Extra width at shoulder level in Period III coaches with 2 + 2 seating was gained by inclining the whole seat end from the armrest level rather than 'cranking' the end as was the case in pre-Stanier coaches.

Plate 43 (*below*) When Period III third class coaches had 2 + 1 seating, as in the case of this composite dining car No. 241, the seat end supports were vertical.

FIGURE 3a LMS standard coaches—interior cross sections

These cross-sections reproduced approximately to $\frac{3}{8}$in—1ft scale are typical of most LMS coaches of the periods concerned but the diagrams to which the original works drawings relate are quoted in brackets:

  I   Period I non-corridor first class compartment (54ft Lavatory Composite D1765, Lot 130).

  II Period I non-corridor third class compartment (57ft Third Class Brake D1703, Lot 356).

 III Period I/II vestibule stock (first or third)—centre gangway types had 'cranked' seat ends—see plate 24d (60ft vestibule dining coaches to Lots 491/519 of D1721 and D1722).

 IV Period III vestibule Stock showing third class seat design (LHS) and first class seat design (RHS). Centre gangway thirds had the seat end angled-in above the armrest level.

  V Period I corridor first class half compartment showing the partition arrangement opposite the sets (57ft corridor first D1747, Lot 246).

 VI Period II corridor third class compartment (60ft corridor third D1782, Lot 551).

(Drawn by D. Jenkinson)

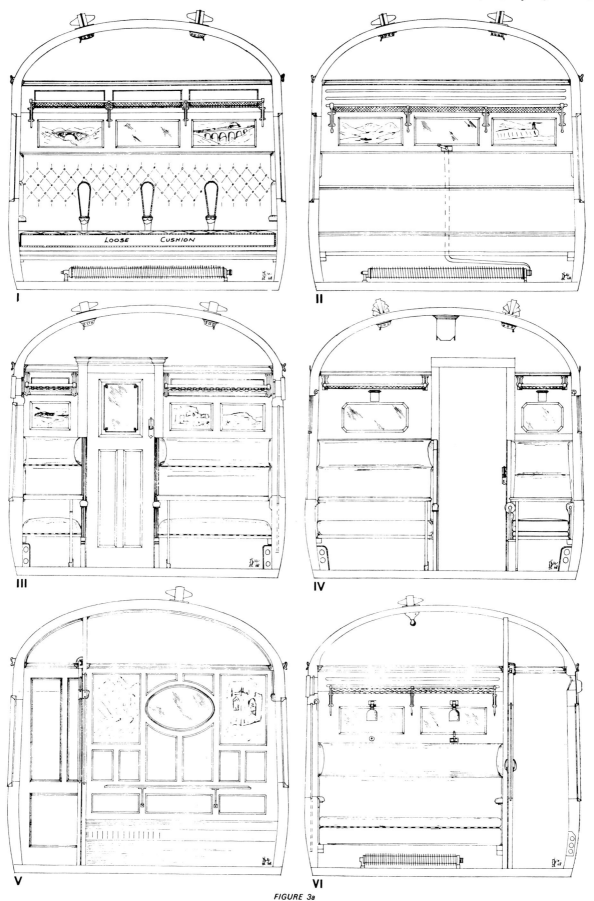

FIGURE 3a

I

II

III

DROPLIGHT   FIXED LIGHT

IV

V

FIGURE 3b

PREVIOUS PAGE: FIGURE 3b
LMS standard coaches—interior longitudinal sections

These sections also at $\frac{3}{8}$in—1ft scale match the cross sections in Figure 3a except for the corridor first which is omitted in order to include both types of Period III seat end design:

I Period I non-corridor first class.
II Period I non-corridor third class.
III Period I/II vestibule stock (first or third class).
IV Period II corridor third class.
V Period III vestibule stock showing third class seat design (LHS) and first class seat design (RHS).

(Drawn by D. Jenkinson)

Plate 44 Interior of 'two-window' style Period I coach. Note the difference in framing between the fixed light (LHS) and the drop-light (RHS). The scenery through the window is a fake as is proved by the Midland clerestory coach just visible through the Stones ventilators!

Most LMS open carriages were designed to carry luggage as well as passengers. There was a considerable space beneath the seats which was achieved by fitting the steam radiators close to the sides of the coaches beneath the windows and covering them with perforated brass guards. The system hardly changed for over 30 years except for the less ornate guards over the radiators by the time of the BR standard coaches which used the system. Supplementary net racks for smaller luggage were also fitted inside the coaches and these mostly made use of supports in whose design was incorporated the LMS monogram.

Large racks for heavier luggage were fitted inside the entrance vestibules which also contained toilets with hot and cold water supply. Later Stanier pattern excursion coaches tended to dispense with the luggage shelves, even though the coaches were often used for main line work as well.

Compartment and Corridor stock

During early years, third class compartments were characterised by the extensive use of crimson and black figured velvet upholstery and mahogany veneers. Fittings were brass. First class compartments were generally trimmed with blue cloth on the top sides and American cloth on the under surfaces. They were usually panelled in walnut and had Venetian bronze fittings. First class compartments were also fitted with carpets—often with the letters 'LMS' incorporated in the design.

There does not seem to have been any real difference between the furnishing of corridor and non-corridor stock at this time. Third class compartments had no armrests in either case but the first class areas did, frequently with headrests as well. Seating was six a side in non-corridor thirds and four a side in the corridor equivalents; first class compartments were four and three respectively. There was, however, one batch of non-corridor coaches (Cathcart Circle stock—Volume II) which was given five a side first class seating without armrests.

All compartments were electrically lit, first class compartments usually rather better than the thirds—for example four 12 candle power lamps per compartment instead of three. Extra courtesy lights were often placed over the first class seats, and ceilings in both types of compartments were enamelled white. Steam heating was generally employed but electric stock was, of course, electrically heated.

When the LMS introduced its twin-window style corridor firsts and first brakes in 1927, many improvements were made, quite apart from the obvious one of improving the outlook and eliminating the outside compartment door and its attendant draughts.

Plates 45-46 Two contrasting compartment interiors of LMS 15933–see also Volume III, the first design of semi-open coach to D1707. All three compartments were, in fact, slightly different in upholstery, veneers and decorative motifs. Note the very wide double doors to the compartments. In both cases, the view through the window is a fake.

Plate 47 Corridor view inside Period II coach No. 15556. The compartments of these coaches seated two per side and were very similar to those on the 1928 luxury stock.

The first change was to increase the compartment size from 7ft 3in to 7ft 6in between partitions and this gave more leg room. Inside panelling was now rendered in silver/grey wood veneering relieved by olive green mouldings. Upholstery was in Persian pattern moquette and seats were fitted with embroidered antimacassars with the company monogram. Specially made Wilton rugs were fitted in the coaches and the floors were covered with thick felt to deaden the sound. Removable tables were also provided and all compartments had bell pushes to summon the attendant. Fittings were satin brass.

This more opulent trend was continued in the single window first class coaches of 1928/29 with two a side seating. These were the semi-open firsts and the Period II first brakes. In these coaches, all compartments were differently finished both in upholstery and in the wood veneer employed. In photographs these coaches look to have been supremely comfortable and seem also to have been of less sombre appearance than earlier vehicles. These coaches appear to have introduced the double sliding door to the compartment.

By the time Period III corridor coaches appeared, first class compartment design seemed to have reached its ultimate expression except for the increasingly varied nature of upholstery materials, the more modern fittings and the generally paler shades both of wood and upholstery. Seats became a little softer and deeper and were built both two a side and three a side

The former were regarded as 'luxury' finish and confined to the more important trains. After the war, the compartment size was reduced from 7ft 6in to 7ft 2in in order to fit six into a 57ft body length. One wonders why the LMS did not use a 60ft length for its full firsts as it had long done for its composites.

Plate 48 First class half-compartment of LMS BCK No. 9318, see Volume II. Note the luxury two per side seating and the still very dark wood veneers of this 1932 coach. Ash trays and luggage racks both display the LMS monogram and the seating is 'softer' than earlier first class compartments.

Plate 49 Third class half-compartments of 9318, see Volume II. These coaches set the style for Stanier-pattern third class corridor coach compartments, and apart from lighter wood finishes, the design remained largely unchanged until after Nationalisation.

Plate 50 Interior view of a typical Period III first class compartment in a side corridor coach. Interestingly, the coat hooks on either side of the window seem to be of an almost pure Midland Railway pattern.

Plate 51 Corridor view of Period III coach No. 4298 (picture dated 1939). By this time, wood finishes had become lighter in shade. Note the corridor carpet at the first class end only.

Plate 52 This typical Period III third class compartment is of coach M4858 of the 1947/8 batch to D2117. It shows the shorter element sliding window ventilators but otherwise little changed from the pre-war version.

Until 1930, third class passenger accommodation in compartment and side corridor stock seems to have been rather neglected. Not until 1929 were outside doors abolished and even this was only in a few 'two-window' composites. It was the advent of Period II coaches that saw the final abolition of outside doors to all compartments and this went with an increase in length of third class compartment from 6ft 0in to 6ft 6in between partitions. At the same time, the Period II third class compartment retained its traditional four a side seating (Fig 3a).

With the advent of the Period III coach, the third class passenger was given a completely new standard of travel—comparable in many ways with the emancipation of the third class passenger in the 19th Century by the Midland Railway in the person of James Allport. Stanier is justly remembered for his magnificent stock of locomotives but the third class LMS passenger had equal cause to remember the LMS CME of the 1930s.

From 1932 onwards, all side corridor third class compartments were built with three a side seating with armrests, courtesy lights and single large windows. Apart from the slightly firmer springing of the seats and the folding nature of the armrests, they were little different from their contemporary three a side firsts. By the time of the 1939—45 war, the Stanier corridor third was so widespread that one could claim that the LMS almost certainly led the field as far as the British scene was concerned. Moreover, many of the more modern Period I and II coaches were converted to three a side seating and generally refurbished to match the Stanier coaches. So good, in fact, were the LMS thirds that after the war, some of the 'Coronation Scot' cars were actually *upgraded* to first class when they re-entered service!

The design of third class compartments changed little from 1933 onwards. The only major alteration was to reduce the size from 6ft 6in to 6ft 3in which allowed slightly improved toilet facilities to be provided. This remained the standard dimension apart from the 1939 'Coronation Scot' coaches which reverted to 6ft 6in and were the ones which were temporarily upgraded. These coaches are considered in greater detail in Volume III.

One wishes that one could be equally enthusiastic about the non-corridor stock. Right until the end, LMS non-corridor stock remained virtually unchanged. In fairness, however, it became increasingly confined to short distance suburban working where maximum seating capacity was of the essence. Inter-district and medium distance workings were increasingly handed over to older gangwayed coaches.

Upholstery in Stanier compartment and corridor coaches seems to have been as varied as it was in the open stock. No specific details can be given beyond the general statement that colours became lighter and patterned finishes more common.

Sleeping Cars

The design of LMS sleeping cars seems to have derived from that of the LNWR and, of course, the first 50 or more first class coaches were basically LNWR designs brought up to date. The first 10 were slightly more old fashioned than the remainder which were the vehicles which initially established the post-group trend. However, both types set the style, as it were, for the LMS Sleeping Cars.

To reduce vibration and noise, India-rubber body blocks were fitted between body and underframe and hair felt was inserted between the double floors. Inside the compartments, walls above the dado, together with the ceilings, were enamelled in white, while wood veneers were mahogany or walnut. All wall angles were rounded for ease of cleaning and beds were metal framed with loose spring mattresses and separate hair stuffed mattresses.

Plate 53 Interior of 'port hole' brake first No. M5077. These coaches had several features similar to the later BR standard coaches—upholstery material (bluish grey), ash trays, window ventilators. The letters BR (M) appeared on the carpet in succession to the LMS of pre-1948 vehicles.

Particular attention was paid to those small ancillary details calculated to make a good impression on the class of passenger for which the coaches were designed. Apart from hot and cold water supplied to each compartment wash basin, drop writing tables, mirrors, brush and comb racks, glass holders and shelves were additional fittings. All compartments were single but eight could be utilised to form four twin berth compartments by unlocking the interconnecting doors. Windows were fitted with rolling shutters which gave rather a snug appearance when they were lowered. Other fittings included bedhead lights and electric fans, both of which could be regulated from a switchboard near the bedhead, and loose bedside rugs were provided as a finishing touch. Not surprisingly, these very fine coaches lasted for many years, not becoming extinct until 1962.

Until 1928 the third class railway traveller in this country had to take what rest he could in his compartment if he was misguided enough to wish to travel at night. In that year the LMS, LNER and GWR pioneered third class sleeping cars, the LMS vehicles being 60ft coaches to D1709. There was nothing particularly revolutionary about the design itself, the coaches being rather like a corridor third and styled inside to match. However, above the seats was a fold-away top bunk which enabled each compartment to be converted for night use into a four berth sleeping area. Full bedding was not provided but pillows and rugs could be obtained. The idea was basically that of a modern European couchette coach. For through coach working, this convertible idea was combined with six orthodox first class sleeping compartments in the composite sleepers of 1930/31.

By the middle 1930s the older sleeping cars were thought to compare unfavourably with the newer Stanier types then being built. As a result of this, the third class compartments of many of the third class and composite sleepers were converted to a fixed berth arrangement while the LNWR styled 68ft first class coaches were modernised. The LMS records refer to this as being an air conditioning operation but it is felt that the 'air conditioning' was of the type to be described below, rather than the more generally understood present day interpretation of the term.

The Stanier sleeping cars again set new standards of comfort much as their contemporary day coaches had done. The first class cars were built to the maximum dimensions allowed by the loading gauge (9ft 2¼ins over the body). They were fitted with recessed door handles to allow for this extra width and were made a foot longer than the earlier coaches, thus becoming the largest non-articulated coaches ever built by the LMS or any of its constituents. The interiors retained all the conveniences of the earlier cars but the extra width enabled the provision of a slightly longer bed. They were also given much brighter interiors in which considerable use was made of plated metal fittings.

Plate 54 First class compartment of non-corridor composite coach No. 16502 (D1849). This was one of the first Stanier non-corridor coaches. Note the 'LMS' woven into the corner panel of the carpet.

Plate 55 Third class compartment of 16502.

Plate 56 Interior view of the 1951 built non-corridor first class coach No. M10124, again featuring certain BR style details.

Plate 57 This picture shows the interior of a compartment in first class sleeping car No. 350 (D1705) which went to America with the 'Royal Scot' tour train in 1933. Compared with the earlier LNWR and LMS sleeping cars, this vehicle exhibited considerably brighter decor, albeit still with plenty of polished woodwork. Note the use of the 'air conditioning' control above the bedhead, replacing the wall fan of earlier cars.

Plate 58 Close-up view, ▶ showing panel and other detail, of Period I BFK No. 18564, later 5035, to D1654. This is a corridor side view of the coach later fitted with LNER type bogies–see Volume II.

A further innovation in these cars was the provision of a combined heating and ventilation system under the individual control of the passenger. This seems to have been referred to by the LMS as air conditioning. All the compartments were fitted with a punkah louvre type air vent which enabled the passenger to adjust the volume, direction and temperature of the incoming air. The post-war batch of these coaches with slight further improvements, was with the odd exception, still in service as late as 1968, many being finished BR Blue/Grey. Several are now privately preserved.

Stanier also introduced the first fixed berth third class sleeping cars to the LMS which may have been a GWR inspired importation. These singularly handsome cars again represented a major step forward in passenger amenity and the earlier versions were altered to match them as nearly as possible. As with the earlier sleeping cars, the basic principle of the Stanier pattern first and third class cars were combined in the 69ft composites.

The final improvement in sleeping cars came after the war when, in 1951/2, the first twin berth sleeping cars for third class use were built. They were mounted on the 65ft chassis of the pre-war thirds but were given the wider body of the Stanier 12 wheel sleeping cars. They were pure LMS designs and most were still in service as late as 1968. Apart from the twin berth arrangement they were every bit as well equipped as the matching firsts sharing such features as carpeted floors, reading lamps, passenger controlled heating/ventilation and so forth. They were additionally interesting as being, with their Eastern Region contemporaries, the first British third class sleeping cars to be provided with fully made up beds.

LMS design sleeping cars tended to be less standardised in their furnishings than did day coaches and almost every batch exhibited some changes or innovations compared with their predecessors. The above general outline of sleeping car interiors only covers the main trends and additional details for individual batches of cars are given in Volume II.

Chapter 3 - Livery, Painting and Finishing

Introduction; body colours; lining details; insignia styles; insignia placing; summary of styles;
special liveries; painting methods; paint specifications; interior finishing

UNLIKE that of locomotives, LMS coach livery was very standardised and for the most part, generalisation is readily possible. Coaches were usually repainted every six or seven years, except during the war, so it is also possible to make reasonably accurate deductions as to the probable repainted styles of various coach types from the building dates and the known style of painting at the time when coaches were due for shopping. With the exception of obsolete and obsolescent pre-group stock due for early scrapping, the following livery summary applies equally to all the coaches taken over by the LMS in 1923.

BODY COLOURS

The standard LMS body colour was crimson lake, being basically the ex-MR shade. This colour has been discussed at length elsewhere so the argument will not be repeated here. The shade may have become a little darker as the years went by but until 1946 the nomenclature never changed. In this year, the LMS changed the name to maroon although whether there was any noticeable change in the actual colour is conjectural.

In 1956/7 when BR adopted an all-red coach livery, a definite attempt was made to revert to the pre-war MR/LMS shade and careful matching of painted panels indicates that this was achieved, especially when BR coaches were newly ex-works. At the same time, BR never reverted to calling the shade 'crimson lake' and it was always referred to as 'BR locomotive hauled stock maroon'. However, as the shade is more recent in history than LMS red, it will probably help readers to visualise the colour more readily.

Coach ends were painted crimson until about the close of 1936 when, except for the driving ends of motor driving trailers, black ends were adopted and remained standard from that date. Chassis and all ancillary details were black but the roof colour varied a little. Until the Stanier period, roofs were generally painted in MR style which was lead grey between the rainstrips and black between rainstrips and cantrail. All-steel coaches often had a metallic roof finish. From 1933 to the outbreak of war, new Stanier pattern coaches generally had a metallic aluminium type paint finish on the roof and this treatment was also specified for repainted pre-Stanier coaches (see p. 50). Unfortunately, roof tops quickly became dirty in service assuming an overall muddy grey shade and it is not, therefore, possible to be more precise about their colour. Most available pictures are of ex-works new coaches so these do not assist greatly in assessing the colour for repaints.

The post-war painting drawings specify grey as the roof colour but its introduction cannot be exactly date. It probably started during the war years and continued until the abandonment of LMS coach livery some two years after nationalisation. The final batches of LMS design coaches were usually turned out from new in BR crimson and cream, or plain crimson livery, although a few coaches were, at first, given some of the early experimental BR liveries (other details not known)

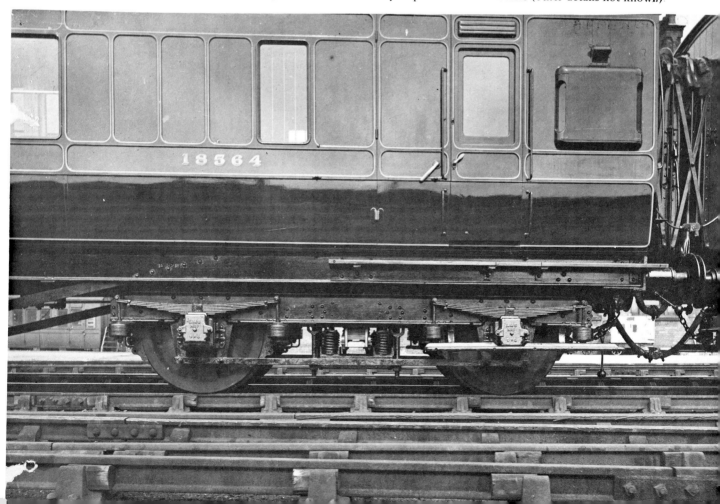

Plate 59 Unidentified Period I 'twin window' open third to D1692 (fitted with experimental American type equalised beam bogies) showing Period I panel and lining detail.

LINING DETAILS

Until the close of 1933/early 1934, all coaches were fully lined out in Midland style. All raised beading was painted black and was edged in 3/8in gold (gangwayed stock) or 3/8in pale yellow (non-gangwayed stock). The gold or yellow lines were edged each side with 1/16in vermilion lines. The lining followed the physical outline of the beading (square cornered in the case of pre-group stock with this variety of beading) and all three colours appeared on the beading itself and not on the main body panels. Coach ends were unlined but detail work (steps, pipework etc) was generally picked out in black. Pre-group coaches were fully panelled and beaded ends (as opposed to the LMS type matchboard ends) usually had the end beading painted black without lining which was the old MR practice.

This fully lined livery continued in use during the whole of Period II and the first year or so of Period III and was thus applied to many coaches with steel panelling and no beading. In this case, pseudo 'beading' in paint was applied to the coach side and appeared in two main variants; high and low waisted.

Plate 60 Kitchen side elevation of kitchen car No. 312. These cars all showed typical Period I "pseudo" panelling on a steel clad vehicle. They also typify the pre-1928 insignia placing, with the running number repeated twice. Car 312 became 30002 in 1933.

Plate 61 Period II non-corridor composite to D1734 No. 3096 (later 16363). This shows the Period II livery style (without waist panel) and the post-1928 insignia placing with only one running number. In this view, the running number is in the enlarged 'stretched scroll' figures.

Steel panelled stock with high waist built before the end of 1928 was given imitation waist panelling in order to match the fully beaded orthodox Period I coaches. It was generally given rounded corners further to simulate raised beading but one or two batches of coaches were given a slightly simplified style with square corners (e.g. some 'all steel' open thirds).

With the introduction of low waisted stock in 1929, waist panelling was abandoned and this was also reflected in the imitation 'beaded' livery of flush clad Period II and early Period III coaches. Even when the coach type retained a high waist—e.g. some sleeping cars and all non-corridor stock—the coaches were not given painted waist panelling after 1928 if they were flush clad. Needless to say, high waisted *wood* panelled stock, which continued to be built in small quantities until 1930, retained waist panelling and full lining.

Examples of the lining shades and some of the dimensions during the full livery period are depicted in the Panels on page viii and in Figure 1 (page 6).

From 1934 onwards, the LMS adopted a simplified lining scheme. This took the form of a single horizontal ½in yellow line just below the cantrail, a similar ½in line above the tops of the windows and two ½in yellow lines separated by a 1in wide black line just below the windows. The yellow shade was changed to a darker chrome yellow hue and with this simplified livery, there was no distinction in lining colour between gangwayed and non-gangwayed stock, yellow being universal.

During the war, all lining was discontinued if coaches were fully repainted but this practice was not common, retouching of existing paintwork being the more usual procedure. The simple lining was reintroduced from 1945 onwards and from 1946 the colour was changed from yellow to straw—an even paler shade than the 1923-33 pale yellow lining colour.

The simplified livery was applied to all repainted stock and in the case of wood panelled, fully beaded coaches, the single yellow lines were applied centrally along the upper and lower beading strips of the eaves panel and the yellow/black/yellow line was applied along the upper beading strip of the waist panel. This livery with straw lining continued in use until about the end of 1949. Panel E (page viii), and with Figure 1, (page 6) illustrate the simplified livery and insignia placing.

Plate 62 Period III open third No. 8929 to D1904 shows the fully lined livery as applied to some early Stanier coaches. Note particularly the post-1933 running number rendered in unshaded gold sans-serif figures.

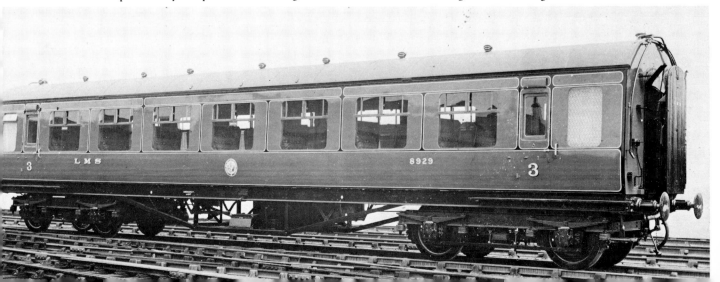

Plate 63 Standard 60ft open first to D1917 illustrates the typical Period III simple livery in its earliest form with unshaded sans-serif figures and the coach end still painted red with details picked out in black.

INSIGNIA STYLES

Lettering

From 1923 until Nationalisation, the letters LMS and any other descriptive wording—KITCHEN CAR, SLEEPING CAR &c.—were applied to the coach side in somewhat elongated serif characters, 4in high. The basic colour was gold leaf until about 1934/5 and chrome yellow after this date. At all times the letters were shaded in pinkish white to the left blending to dark red/brown below the characters. They were shadow shaded to the right and below in black. From 1946 onwards, a very few coaches were given block style lettering 6in high in straw paint edged with black. This was not widespread but would, presumably, have become the standard treatment. At the same time, the branding of dining cars was changed to 'RESTAURANT CAR' if given this block style of letter.

The lettering 'ROYAL MAIL' on GPO vehicles was in 10in high serif characters, coloured as for the letters LMS (Fig 4). *Note:* Smaller lettering about 3in high, was used on many pre-group coaches with shallow depth waist panels but not often, as far as can be ascertained, on LMS standard vehicles.

Numbering

Several styles of running number were adopted by the LMS but the changes generally coincided with coach styling changes as well.

1923-28 Small scroll figures in gold leaf some 3in high were employed, shaded to match the serif 'LMS' described above. They just lasted to the start of Period II designs.

1929-32 During Period II, a stretched out scroll type figure the same height as the serif 'LMS' was employed, retaining the same colour scheme as before. Wolverton Works refers to this design as the 'bastard' style and claims that the figures were handpainted not transferred. These figures remained in use only until the 1932/3 renumbering and were, in consequence, confined mainly to Period II coaches and the few Period III coaches which were built before the renumbering. They were also placed on the coaches of the 'Royal Scot' train which toured America in 1933. These latter coaches were renumbered before the tour and are thought to be the only vehicles which had their post-1932 numbers in the 'stretched' scroll style of figure.

Plate 64 Period III non-corridor third No. 12194 to D1906, illustrates the simple LMS livery in perhaps its most common form with shaded sans-serif numbers (now in chrome yellow) and black painted coach end. On this example, as with many coaches, the insignia were placed well in from the coach ends.

THE COMET

THE MANCUNIAN

LONDON (EUSTON)

EUSTON

III

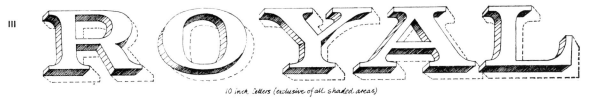

10 inch letters (exclusive of all shaded areas)

body colour yellow or gold

shading white, blending through pink and crimson to brown

black shadow

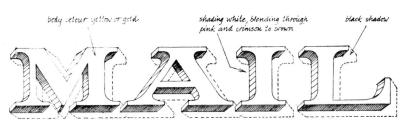

IV

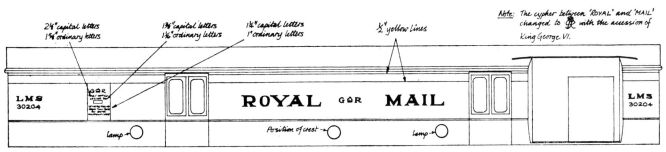

pillar box red background colour to letter box

LMS 30204   ROYAL   G◊R   MAIL ← 10 inch letters   LMS 30204

Position of crest

4 inch letters and figures

Upper inscription on letter box reads: POST OFFICE LETTER BOX

Lower inscription on letter box reads: LETTERS POSTED HERE MUST BEAR AN EXTRA HALFPENNY STAMP

yellow/black/yellow line along waist

2¼" capital letters
1¾" ordinary letters

1¾" capital letters
1½" ordinary letters

1½" capital letters
1" ordinary letters

½" yellow lines

Note: The cypher between 'ROYAL' and 'MAIL' changed to G◊R with the accession of King George VI.

LMS 30204   G◊R   ROYAL   G◊R   MAIL   LMS 30204

lamp   Position of crest   lamp

FIGURE 4 *LMS coaches—miscellaneous livery drawings*

I   Coach headboards—1935 and later:—These boards reproduced at ½in—1ft scale were 12ft 6in long, 6in deep and carried 5in high letters in black on a white ground. The width of the letters was adjusted to suit the name of the train or service. The boards were either mounted on the roof (Period I/II and early Period III stock) or on the eaves panel (later Period III stock). Some Period III coaches had mounting brackets in both locations.

II   *Coach destination boards*: Upper: 1923-33 pattern; black letters on white ground
　　　　　　　　　　　　　　　　　　　Lower: 1933 and later; black letters on deep cream ground
　　These boards were 2ft 4in long and usually fixed to brackets on the eaves panel close to an entrance door.

III   *Lettering 'Royal Mail'*:—¾in—1ft scale. These letters were 10in high but the drawing also gives the correct general shape, colour and shading details for all types of serif LMS coach lettering. The shading detail is also generally accurate for carriage running numbers. The original from which this drawing was prepared is the only official LMS insignia drawing which has been located by the authors.

IV   Layout of lettering etc., on Royal Mail vehicles c. 1935/6 Scale $\frac{1}{8}$in—ft.

(Drawn by D. Jenkinson)

Plate 65 This view of a D1705 sleeping car No. 3792 (later 342) shows the full livery and pre-1928 layout of the descriptive wording. After 1928, coaches with a proper waist panel still carried the descriptive wording over the LMS emblem but the 'LMS' itself moved to the position of the left hand running number in this view.

Plate 66 Typical insignia layout on a Stanier 12-wheeler. Note the descriptive wording flanking the emblem. The diner is to D1900 and externally was all but identical to the D1923 version at Plate 21.

Plate 67 Period III FO No. M7544 to D1917 shown in close-up. Note the post-war pattern of insignia and the large figure '1' on the window. The date of this picture is probably 1948.

1933-40 The 1932/3 renumbering introduced new sans-serif coach numbers still 4in high. For a year or so they were applied in plain gold figures but from about 1934/5 onwards they became chrome yellow and were shaded to match the serif pattern 'LMS' and remained thus. In general the shaded style of block figures seems to have been introduced at or shortly after the time of change to simple livery and the change from gold leaf to chrome yellow colour approximately coincided with the similar change in lining shade. Vitually all new coaches and renumbered pre-1933 coaches received this style of sans-serif number and the style itself may have been introduced to enable the operating staff, during the renumbering period, to distinguish more readily between the renumbered coaches and those with original numbers. There were, of course, odd exceptions like the case of the 1933 'Royal Scot' train (page 44).

1940 onwards From this period, reversion was made to scroll type figures generally similar to the 1923-28 type but about 4in high, chrome yellow in basic colour and having flat topped '3s'. For economy reasons, residual supplies of sans serif numerals were probably used up on repaints but most, if not all newly constructed vehicles were given scroll pattern figures. They continued in use after Nationalisation until the onset of BR livery, frequently being given an 'M' prefix in 1948/9. In 1946 a sans-serif style of figure, 4½in high in straw edged with black was introduced to match the 6in high straw coloured 'LMS' mentioned above but only saw limited use, being confined to the few coaches given the experimental 1946 sans serif insignia.

Full colour samples of the shaded sans-serif numbers are incorporated in Panel Q, (page ix).

Passenger Class Numbering

Most LMS coaches carried the figure '1' or '3', as appropriate, on the outside of carriage doors. These were always 8in high and again rendered in gold (changing to chrome yellow in about 1934/5), with blended red shading, shadow shaded black. Throughout the 1923-47 period these figures were of scroll pattern but in 1940, or thereabouts, the 's' was changed to a flat topped version. In this form it was applied to all new and repainted coaches. As with lettering and numbering, there was a short-lived 1946 sans serif version in straw with black edging which again only saw limited use.

After the war, it was general to affix a figure '1' centrally on the windows of all first class compartments (including the appropriate corridor side windows). The colour of this figure was white or cream and it seems to have been a sort of adhesive label some 6in—8in high (details uncertain).

Very few LMS coaches were placed in service without class branding. Those that were turned out minus figures on the doors were usually 'neutral' vehicles (i.e. for first *or* third class use) and included such coaches as composite diners, unclassed vestibule coaches and so forth. There were not very many of them. After Nationalisation, of course, the present practice of labelling only the first class areas of the coach was introduced.

The LMS Emblem

The circular LMS emblem—it was not a true coat of arms in the heraldic sense—was used continuously on coaching stock from 1923 to 1947. It was nominally 14in in diameter and the lettering and surrounds were gold until 1934/5 when they became yellow coloured. There was also a post war 'straw' version (Panel P). The principles underlying the use of the device do not seem to have been at all clear but the following observations are correct as far as they go.

The emblem was never used on non-corridor stock (except for some open electric stock) or on corridor coaches with a full complement of compartment doors. It was always applied to vestibule stock and specialised gangwayed stock (Kitchen Cars, Dining Cars, Sleeping Cars &c.). It was generally used on the later types of side corridor stock which had no compartment doors but there were numerous exceptions to this practice, generally third class coaches.

INSIGNIA PLACING

The placing of the insignia on the coach side was relatively straightforward and only two methods were adopted, most details of which are incorporated in Figure 1 (page 6).

From 1923 to 1928, the letters 'LMS' appeared in the coach waist panel as near to the centre of the vehicle as possible. The exact configuration of the vertical beading dividers in the waist panel rarely affected the insignia placing and often the 'LMS' was off-centre in relation to the specific panel in which it appeared. The LMS emblem, if present, was located immediately below the LMS and midway between the lower waist beading, or pseudo beading, and the solebar.

During the same period, the running number appeared twice on the coach side, located towards each end of the vehicle and always in the waist panel—real or simulated. The precise placing of the numbers was a little variable. They were rarely located at the extreme end of the coach side, there generally being at least one compartment, or equivalent, 'outside' the running numbers. Running numbers were almost invariably placed 'inside' the end doors of vestibule coaches.

Descriptive wording during 1923-8 appeared in full in the waist panel thus:'LMS SLEEPING CAR' and was located so that the whole inscription was as near central as possible. The emblem was placed centrally beneath the descriptive wording.

From 1928 onwards, slight changes were made in this scheme. These coincided with the first Period II coach designs with low waists and this revised placing remained unaltered for the rest of the company's lifetime. The 'LMS' was now placed towards the left hand end of the coach and the running towards the right hand end. In fact, they occupied much the same places as had the two running numbers during 1923-8. With Period II and III coaches, the insignia was placed just below the waist lining—full or simplified—but it remained in the waist panel of coaches which had this feature, whether or not the livery was simplified or full.

The LMS emblem was still located as near to the centre of the coach side as possible. On Period II and III coaches it was placed midway between windows and solebar but the descriptive wording, if any, now flanked the emblem. At the same time, high waisted Period I and pre-group specialised vehicles continued to carry their descriptive wording in the waist panel surmounting the LMS emblem. This was also true of the Period II high waisted steel panelled composite sleeping cars which had no waist panel.

At all times, passenger class figures were placed centrally on the lower door panels, midway between lower waist beading and solebar on Period I coaches and usually midway between door handles and solebar on the remainder (see Figure 1).

SUMMARY OF STYLES

As can be seen, most changes in livery approximately coincided with changes in coach styles and although there are exceptions to this pattern which are duly noted in the relevant chapters, it seems useful to give the following generalised summary of the livery of *new* coaches. Repainted pre-group coaches generally followed the same principles as far as possible.

Period I   Full livery, red ends, grey and black roofs, original insignia placing, small scroll type running numbers.
Period II   Full livery, red ends, grey and black roofs, final insignia placing, 'stretched' scroll type running numbers .
Period III (1933–4) Full livery, red ends, metallic roof finish, final insignia placing, unshaded sans-serif running numbers.
Period III (1934–9) Simple livery, red ends (1934-6), black ends (late 1936 onwards), metallic roof finish, final insignia placing, shaded sans-serif numbers. Insignia shade changed from gold leaf to chrome yellow.
Period III (1940–9) Simple livery (with straw lining from 1946 onwards), black ends, grey roof finish, final insignia placing, small scroll numbers with flat topped '3', flat topped '3' on outside doors, figure '1' on first class windows.

Wartime repainting was unlined and after Nationalisation, the LMS lettering and circular emblem were omitted but an 'M' prefix was often added to the running number, often in matching style.
*(below)

SPECIAL LIVERIES

The LMS employed few special coach liveries. The most well known were the 'Coronation Scot' liveries of 1937 and 1939. The 1937 style was blue and silver and the 1939 style was red and gold, each version with its own lettering style.

The other distinctive livery was that applied to the three-car diesel articulated unit (see Volume III). This was cream above the waist and bright red below the waist, the two colours being separated by a black line.

No evidence has been located of any other LMS coach liveries nor of any experimental liveries during 1923. It seems that, as with locomotives, so with coaches, Derby would brook no argument about their colour! The decision to adopt the MR coach livery as the LMS standard was taken early in May 1923 and actually *preceded* the decision to adopt the Midland Railway locomotive livery as well.

PAINTING METHODS

The painting and finishing of LMS coaches was a somewhat complicated procedure and, perhaps surprisingly, involved rather more stages and considerably more time in shops than the procedure for finishing locomotives. The technique varied with the type of coach (steel or wood panelled) and, accordingly, the two will be considered separately. It should be noted that the details given below apply to new and fully repainted coaches *only*. In many other cases, coaches were given an intermediate 'rub down and re-varnish' between general repaints. The details given also apply to fully repainted pre-group coaches except for old vehicles with a limited life expectancy of up to four years. The latter, if due for repaint, were painted to a rather similar but less thorough specification. The details given are those issued by the Carriage and Wagon Department at Derby in September 1935. Paint mixes are referred to by numbers, the full specifications being given on pages 50 and 51.

Steel Panelled Coaches (New or completely repainted)

Before assembly of the coach and prior to painting, all body and roof panels had the oil and grease removed with cotton waste and were then 'washed' with a 4:1 mixture of Methylated Spirit and Phosphoric Acid. Galvanised steel panels were similarly washed but with a rather more sophisticated mixture (Mix 1). The following day, all panels were painted with steel primer (Mix 2). Steel details (e.g. roof struts) were painted with bauxite (Mix 3) and wooden body framing was painted with lead colour paint (Mix 4). All key sheeting for floors was given two coats of Venetian Red bitumastic paint.

The backs of plywood panels which formed the ceilings of the compartments were painted with protective white paint (Mix 5) as was the back of the deal lagging which formed the interior surface of brake vans.

Pre-assembly work on the underframe and bogie consisted of the removal of rust and mill scale from the components by scraping or wire brush which process was immediately followed by coating the part concerned with bauxite (Mix 3) and a second coat of bauxite (Mix 3A). All parts of the underframe of non-welded coaches were painted before assembly but painting was not carried out before assembly in the case of underframes of welded construction. After welding, the weld itself was thoroughly cleaned and then coated with a primer for welded joints (Mix 6). After this, the complete underframe was painted in similar manner to the individual components of the non-welded underframe.

After assembly the insides of body and roof panels were painted with bauxite (Mix 3). Any new panels fixed to repaired coaches were, in addition, given two coats of steel primer (Mix 2) before fixing.

The exterior finishing procedure laid down in the paint schedules assumed that for repainted vehicles, the whole of the earlier paint coat had been burnt off or other 'suitable arrangements' made for the areas not so treated. Emphasis was also laid on the importance with steel coaches of removing all rust, scale &c. before repainting—using panel 'wash' if need be. Once the vehicle was prepared for painting/repainting, the daily sequence was as follows:

---

*Note

The authors have, regrettably, been unable to locate many usable drawings of LMS insignia. The little information which has survived is appended at Figure 4. Fortunately, the heights and placement of the various insignia *were* recorded and the perusal of photographs in this book together with Figure 1 will clarify this chapter. In addition, Panel O gives a good idea of the colour of the LMS insignia shading.

Day 1	One coat of steel primer (Mix 2).
Day 2	Brush filling (Mix 7) applied over joints and screw holes, stopped up with hard stopping (Mix 8) when the brush filling was dry.
Day 3	Repeat Day 2.
Day 4	Faced down with stone blocks and water. Stopped up with hard stopping where necessary.
Day 5	Faced down with composition rubbing blocks and water, left for at least four hours and afterwards given one coat of lead undercoat (Mix 9).
Day 6	One coat of brown undercoat (Mix 10).
Day 7	One coat of undercoat for lake (Mix 11)
Day 8	One coat of standard LMS lake (Mix 12).
Day 9	One coat of lake glaze (Mix 13).
Day 10	Lined in black, yellow and red*, (Mixes 14–16) and transfers applied.
Day 11	One coat of exterior finishing varnish over the whole body.
Day 12	Coach allowed to harden.
Day 13	Varnish flatted with pumice dust and water, second coat of varnish applied over the whole body.
Day 14	Coach allowed to harden.
Day 15	Varnish flatted again with pumice dust and water, third coat of varnish applied over the whole body except the ends.
Note: *	It is not known why red lining colour was specified in 1935. All available evidence indicates that this colour was omitted when the fully lined style of painting was terminated in 1933/4–but see note at end of chapter.

During the above painting process, the roof was, after treating with steel primer, given two coats of metallic roof paint (Mix 17). At the same time, the complete chassis (including bogies and wheels) was painted with black enamel, lettered in white and then varnished. Battery boxes were painted with acid resisting black varnish. Door droplights were painted lake and varnished after being treated with wood primer (Mix 18).

Finally, the coach was allowed to harden for at least two more days after completion of all painting and before entering service was sparingly wax polished.

Plate 68 This view of BCK No. 6792 (formerly 9485) was almost certainly taken at the time the vehicle was renumbered. Both numbers are painted (temporarily) on the right hand compartment window. The picture also shows one of the many locations adopted on LMS coaches for the short destination boards (see Figure 4-II). The coach itself is to D1850.

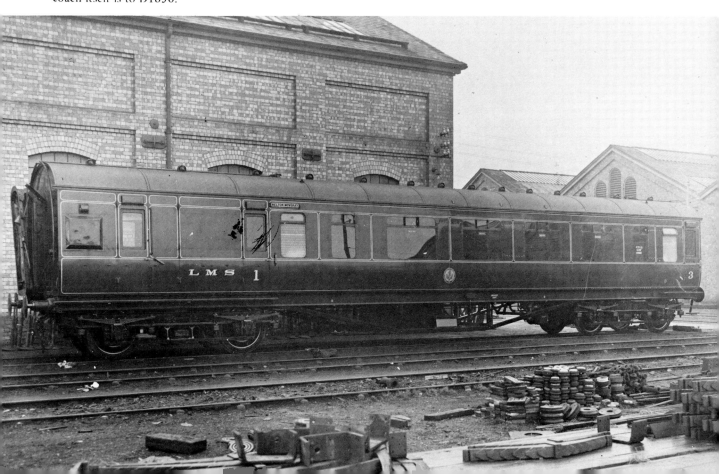

Wood Panelled Coaches

By 1935, the LMS had ceased to make wood panelled coaches so the 1935 paint schedules refer solely to repainted vehicles. However, the procedure used was in all probability very little different to that employed during the building of wood panelled coaches. As far as can be deduced, the chassis was treated exactly as described for steel coaches and the differences apply solely to the body treatment. The schedules again assume that the whole of the previous paint was burnt off before repainting:

Day 1	One coat of wood primer (Mix 18) over the whole body.
Day 2	One coat of a mixture of equal parts of brush filling (Mix 7) and lead undercoat (Mix 9) over the whole body.
Day 3	Two coats of brush filling (Mix 7) over the whole body except the ends. The coach was stopped up with hard stopping (Mix 8) at a convenient stage.
Day 4	Rubbed down with stone blocks and water.
Day 5	One coat of lead undercoat (Mix 9) plus further hard stopping (Mix 8) as necessary.
Day 6	Faced down with composition rubbing blocks and water, left for at least four hours and then given one coat of undercoat for lake (Mix 11).
Days 7—14	As for steel coaches Days 8—15.

With wooden coaches, repainted roofs were given two coats of metallic roof paint (Mix 17) which represented a change in colour for many coaches from their original black/grey scheme (see page 41). If the roof needed repairing, the old canvas was removed, any repairs to the wood completed and all bare wood then treated with wood primer (Mix 18). Jointing paste was then applied and the new canvas stretched on. It was treated with a 50/50 mixture of boiled linseed oil and jointing paste and then covered with *three* coats of metallic roof paint (Mix 17). Presumably, when new, wood/canvas roofs had been similarly finished (except for the colour of the roof paint itself) during the 1923-32 period.

PAINT SPECIFICATIONS

Mix 1—Zinc Wash for galvanised panels

Methylated Spirits	6gal
Toluol	3gal
Spirits of Salts	½gal
Carbon Tetrachloride	½gal

Mix 2—Steel Primer

Oxide of iron in oil, type R, red shade	88lb
Zinc Oxide white in oil	2lb
Aluminium powder (fine varnish powder)	10lb
Raw linseed oil	10lb
Mixing varnish	26lb
Genuine Turpentine	16-20lb
Liquid Drier	Not more than 4lb

Mix 3—Bauxite Paint

Boiled linseed oil	8lb
White Spirit	6-10lb
Liquid Drier	2-4lb
Bauxite residue in oil	82lb

Mix 3A—Bauxite Paint (2nd coating)

Mixture No. 3	100lb
Black in oil	6lb

Mix 4—Lead Colour

Note: This mixture was the standard LMS lead colour for wagons and was intended to match British Standard Colour No. 32. Slight adjustments were permissible for matching purposes.

Zinc White, composite pigment in oil	112lb
Boiled linseed oil	60lb
Black in oil	3-4lb
Liquid Drier	2-5lb
Mixing Varnish	19lb
Ultramarine blue in oil	3-4lb

Mix 5—Protective White Paint

Protective white paint paste	112lb
Paste Driers in oil	Not more than 4lb
White Spirit	4-8lb
Boiled linseed oil	8-12lb

Mix 6—Primer for welded joints

Mixture No 2	80lb
Aluminium powder (fine varnish powder)	10lb
Mixing varnish	10lb

Mix 7—Brush Filling

Enamel filling	112lb
Gold size, type A (dark)	4-7lb
Mixing varnish	4-7lb
Genuine Turpentine	14-18lb
Raw linseed oil	Not more than 4lb

Mix 8—Hard Stopping

Enamel filling	112lb
Gold size, type A (dark)	4 parts This to be added to the filling to bring to required consistency
Genuine Turpentine	1 part

Mix 9—Lead colour undercoat

Protective white paint paste	112lb
Liquid Drier	9-12lb
White Spirit	26-30lb
Black in oil	9-10lb
Raw linseed oil	4lb

Mix 10—Brown undercoat

Oxide of iron, in oil, type R, red shade	100lb
Liquid Drier	4-6lb
Mixing varnish	26-30lb
Genuine Turpentine	12-14lb

Mix 11—Undercoat for Lake

Mixture No. 10	95lb
Black in oil	5lb

Mix 12—Standard LMS Crimson Lake

Standard LMS Lake (paste form)	12lb
Mixing varnish	4lb
Genuine Turpentine	3-5lb
Liquid Drier	1-3lb

Mix 13—Lake Glaze

Mixture No. 12	75lb
Exterior finishing varnish	25lb

Mix 14—Black lining colour

Drop black in turpentine	78lb
Gold size, type B (light)	18-20lb
Genuine Turpentine	6-8lb
Raw linseed oil	8-10lb
Liquid Drier	Not more than 4lb

Mix 15—Yellow lining colour

Note: This mixture was intended to match British Standard Colour 56 and adjustments to quantities were permissible for matching purposes.

Lemon Chrome in oil	18-20lb
Orange Chrome in oil	2-3lb
Zinc White, composite pigment in oil	15-20lb
Genuine Turpentine	2-5lb
Liquid Drier	6-10lb

Mix 16—Red lining colour

Vermilion substitute in oil	100lb
Gold size, type B (light)	8-12lb
Genuine Turpentine	6-8lb
Liquid Drier	Not more than 4lb

Mix 17—Roof Paint

Protective white paint paste	56lb
Thickened linseed oil	4lb
Boiled linseed oil	7lb
Mixing varnish	7lb
White Spirit	8-12lb
Black in oil	8lb
Aluminium powder (fine varnish powder)	7lb
Liquid Drier	Not more than 4lb

Mix 18—Wood Primer

Mixture No. 9	80lb
Aluminium powder (fine varnish powder)	10lb
Mixing varnish	10lb

INTERIOR FINISHING

The ceilings and compartments of new coaches were painted white, receiving three coats of undercoat and one finishing coat of gloss white enamel or eggshell gloss white enamel, depending on the type of coach. Repainted ceilings varied from receiving a simple touching up coat to a complete repaint involving burning off the old coat.

Interiors of brake vans, when new, were given one coat of knotting prior to any painting. Ceilings and sides down to 14in from the ceiling were then painted white as for compartment ceilings. The remainder of the interior was painted terra cotta (two coats) followed by terra cotta varnish. The terra cotta shade was mixed as follows:

Zinc White, composite pigment in oil	112lb
Venetian Red in oil	38lb
Vermilion substitute in oil	14lb
Yellow ochre in oil	38lb
Orange Chrome in oil	28lb
Liquid drier	9lb
White Spirit	8-12lb
Boiled linseed oil	16-20lb

The terra cotta varnish shade was a 9:1 mixture of the above paint and Mixing Varnish. Repainted coaches were given the same colour scheme, the number of coats depending on the state of the vehicle.

The interior finishing of compartments was mostly concerned with the preparation and finishing of the various wood veneers involved. The type and colour of the wood filler used varied according to the nature of the veneer, but could generally be obtained by a judicious blending of the three standard fillers, brown, walnut and white. The schedules laid down that only three types of wood *stain* were to be used, namely Vandyke crystals or Mahogany crystals (both water soluble) and Acid Brown (spirit soluble). Sanding down of, the wood finishes was always done with grade 0 or grade 1 sandpaper. New work underwent the following stages of preparation and finishing:

1st Process	Water stain applied to the bare wood and allowed to dry thoroughly.
2nd Process	Sandpapered, treated with wood filler and allowed to stand at least six hours.
3rd Process	Where matching up was necessary, a second coat of water stain was applied.
4th Process	One coat of spirit stain followed by sandpapering. The stain was mixed as follows:

Methylated Spirit	1gal
Acid Brown	sufficient to produce the required shade.
Genuine Orange Shellac	4 oz

5th Process	First coat of cellulose lacquer applied and allowed to stand overnight.
6th Process	Sandpapered and matched if necessary with a further coat of spirit stain.
7th Process	Second coat of cellulose lacquer applied and allowed to stand overnight.
8th Process	Third coat of cellulose lacquer applied and allowed to stand overnight.
	Note: First class compartments had a fourth coat of cellulose lacquer applied.
9th Process	Bodied up with levelling solution mixed 3:1 with cellulose lacquer and a small amount of thinners added.
10th Process	Finished with the mixture described in the ninth process.
11th Process	Burnishing carried out as and when necessary, using reviver obtained from the Derby paint laboratory.

In general, interiors of repaired coaches were cleaned down with a weak solution of soda water and then brought back with reviver. Sometimes, if a finish had been damaged or had 'sunk' it was brought back with a 4:1 mixture of levelling solution and cellulose lacquer. If it was necessary to strip wood right down, the area had to be treated as new wood.

Finally, toilets were treated in yet a different way and the following procedure was employed:

Day 1	One coat of wood primer for Scumblegrain, Duck Egg Green shade, applied by spray.
Day 2	One coat of Buffer Coat, Duck Egg Green shade, applied by spray.
Day 3	One coat of Scumblegrain, Duck Egg Green shade, applied by brush and stippled.
Day 4	Two 'mist' coats of cellulose lacquer, applied by spray.
Day 5	Finished by flatting with soap and water, using a mild abrasive if necessary.
	Note: Polished wood in toilets was treated as for the wood veneers in compartments.

Addenda

Since this work was first published, evidence has been examined which proves that a fourth variety of the circular LMS emblem was provided for use with the blue painted 'Coronation Scot' sets of 1937. This emblem was identical to the normal version but with lettering and surrounds rendered in silver. Very few transfers could have been made—almost certainly one batch only—for only 27 coaches were painted in this style.

We have also established that with the advent of the simple livery in 1934, first class sleeping cars and dining cars continued to have the new style lining rendered in gilt with vermilion edging. This would undoubtedly explain the presence of red lining colour in the 1935 schedules—see page 49. On these coaches, the gilt version of the circular emblem continued in use, as did the use of gilt insignia.

Chapter 4 - Train Formations and Coach Working

Express Workings; Dining Cars; Sleeping Cars and Mail services; The coaches used;
Medium Distance and Excursion workings; Suburban and Local workings

WHEN analysing the formation of LMS passenger trains, it is important to remember that the company was never particularly addicted to the operation of set train formations for long distance working. Set formations were more common for suburban working and short distance inter-district operation but there was little sacrosanct about even this class of traffic. Thus when describing LMS trains one can only discuss the matter in general terms.

Express Workings

LMS express workings varied from massive regular formations of 16 coaches or more to quite lightly loaded trains. In general, the pre-group picture altered surprisingly little. Thus, for example, the heaviest tasks were usually to be found on the ex-LNWR lines while the Midland Division tended to perpetuate the shorter and more lightly loaded formations. The nature of the workings changed little in the early years and it was some time before rationalisation of services such as the running of Heysham boat trains to Euston instead of St. Pancras, began to be seen. The West Coast Joint Stock became wholly LMS owned as did the M&GSW element of the Midland-Scottish Joint Stock. Only the M&NB stock remained in shared ownership and this perpetuated the anomalous M&NB designation until 1928 when the coaches were divided between the LMS and LNER. However, since only two coaches (both SLFs) had been built after 1922 specifically for the M&NB services and both of them eventually came to the LMS, the effect of the division of the ex-M&NB stock was negligible as far as the LMS was concerned.

Plate 69 This nostalgic view of the 'Royal Scot' dates from the early 1930s and illustrates the variety of types of coach to be seen even on the most prestigious LMS trains. From the foreground backwards can be identified the following types before the detail becomes unclear: Period II BFK to D1717; Early Period III BTK to D1851; RC to D1743 (LNWR styled); Period II Semi-RFO to D1719. The picture also shows the very characteristic carriage headboards—see Figure 4-I.

TABLE 4a SELECTED LMS EXPRESS TRAIN FORMATIONS

Note: The formations given below are only a representative sample of pre-war LMS trains as it would be impossible to give a complete coverage. Most of them have been extracted from the LMS passenger train marshalling books of the 1930s but some are based on the personal observation of enthusiasts. All formations are given in the down direction (where applicable) with locomotive to the left. The numbers adjacent to the name of the train refer to the footnotes.

Train	Approx Date	Formation
The Royal Scot [1]	c. 1938	BTK/TK/TO/RTO/RK/Semi-RFO/BFK/TO to Glasgow RTO/RK/Semi-RFO/TO/BTK to Edinburgh
The Coronation Scot	1937-9	BTK/RTO/RK/RTO/RTO/RK/RFO/FK/BFK
The Night Scot [2]	1938	BG/SLF/SLF/SLF/RF/RCO/SLT/SLT/CK/TK/TK/BG
The Mid-Day Scot [3]	1934	BG/TK/RTO/RT/Semi-RFO/BFK/to Glasgow BTK/Semi-RFO/RT/BTK/to Edinburgh CK/BG to Aberdeen TK/BFK to Whitehaven
The Royal Highlander [4]	1934	BG/ /CK/SLC/BG/ /TK/CK/SLC/BG/ /BG/ /SLC/ /RC

Key: a. Glasgow
Key: b. Aberdeen
     c. Inverness
     d. Dundee
     e. Oban(FO)
     f. Crewe only

        a   , b   c   d   e   f

Train	Approx Date	Formation
The West Coast Postal [5]	1934	BG//BG//POT//BG//POT/POT//POS/POS//POS/POS/POS/POT

Key: a. Liverpool
     b. Manchester
     c. Preston
     d. Stranraer
     e. Perth(SO)
         Aberdeen(SX)
     f. Aberdeen (one only
         to Perth (SO))
     g. Glasgow

        a b c d   e   f   g

Train	Approx Date	Formation
Thames-Clyde Express [6]	1938	BTK/TK/TO/RTO/RK/RCO/CK/BFK
Thames-Forth Express [7]	1938	BTK/TK/TK/RTO/RF/CK/BTK
St Pancras-Glasgow [8] night express	1938	BG/BG/CK/SLF/SLT/TK/TK/BG
The Irish Mail [9]	1934	BG/POS/POT/POS/POS/BG/BG/SLF/SLT/BTK/CK/

                          a   b   b a a

Key: a SO   CK/BTK/TK/BG/BG . . . . all to Holyhead
     b SX   c b   b
     c MFO   plus: BG(SX) for Birkenhead
                                   TK(SO) for Crewe
                                   BG/BG(SO) for Manchester and Hereford

Train	Approx Date	Formation
The Comet (Down) [10]	1934	BTK/TK/RTO/RF/CK/BFK to Manchester BTK/CK/CO/RTO/RK/RFO/BFK to Liverpool BCK to Birkenhead
The Comet (Up) [11] (ex-Manchester)	1934	TK/RTO/RF/CK extra coaches BFK/CK/RF/RTO/TK/BTK the main set TK/BCK to Birmingham
The Merseyside Express [12]	1934	BTK/CK/BFO(lounge)/RFO/RF/CK/CK/RTO/RK/RTO/ BTK to Liverpool TK/BFK to Southport
The Pines Express [13]	1939	TK/TO//BTK/CK/BTK//BCK/RCO/RT/BTK//BCK//BCK

Key: a extra coaches
     b Manchester—
        Birmingham set
     c Main train
     d Through coach
     e GWR through coach

        a   b   c   d   e

Train	Approx Date	Formation
The Peak Express [14] The Palatine	c. 1937	BTK/TK/TK/RT/RFO/BFK
1005 Glasgow-Aberdeen (1520 return)	1938	BTK/TK/CK/RT/RCO/CK/TK/BTK to Aberdeen BTK/CK/BTK to Perth (northbound only)
0800 Glasgow-Oban [15] (1715 return)	1938	BTK/CK to Callander RT/RCO/TK/BTK/CK/BTK to Oban
1015 Inverness-Kyle of Lochalsh [16] (1735 return)	1938	CK/CK/RU/TO/TO/BG

Footnotes

1. Standard formation—strengthened when necessary.
2. The RF/RCO inserted at Carlisle (northbound only). Often loaded heavier than this.
3. Formation given ex-Euston. The Aberdeen and Whitehaven coaches came off at Crewe and were replaced by through coaches from Plymouth to Glasgow. The train also carried a TK for Barrow (FSO), detached at Crewe.
4. This train ran in very similar formation for many years. There was no southbound 'Royal Highlander' at the time as the balancing workings of the coaches were too complex.
5. Formation given ex-Euston. During the journey there was considerable re-marshalling by addition/detachment of coaches.
6. The standard set, augmented by extra TKs on Saturdays. Conveyed through coaches for Leeds only (northbound) and for Bristol (southbound). There was also an extra BG(southbound) from Glasgow. Train reversed at Leeds so the BTK was always at the leading end when departing from either London or Glasgow.
7. The standard set. Up to four extra TKs (SO) in summer. Train reversed at Leeds (see note 6).
8. This was the 2130 St Pancras-St Enoch train. The leading BG was for Kilmarnock. During the journey the train picked up various through sections from Bristol and Leeds. The 2115 St Pancras-Edinburgh train was somewhat similar except for the replacement of the SLF/SLT by a single SLC.
9. This was the down train. The SLT contained facilities for serving light refreshments. The Birkenhead coaches came off at Chester and the Manchester/Hereford coaches at Crewe. The passenger carrying portion of the up train was identical but the complement of vans was slightly different.
10. Extra TK(SO) for Manchester and extra TK(MFO) for Birkenhead.
11. The up Comet did not carry a Liverpool portion.
12. This was the down train and carried an extra TK(FO). At times of peak traffic this train loaded to 15 or even 16 coaches. The up train ran less the leading BTK/CK and had a modified Southport section viz: BCK(SO)/BFK/TK/TK(MFO). The lounge brake was replaced by a BTK during Christmas and Easter weeks and the BTK/CK pair did not run on Saturdays.
13. An observed southbound formation at Birmingham (New Street) in March 1939.
14. Typical lightweight Midland Division trains—often with through sections added.
15. BCK added at Callander from Edinburgh to Oban. In the reverse direction, the Oban-Edinburgh portion was BCK/TK/BCK(SX) and the Callander-Glasgow section was two TKs(SO).
16. Usually carried odd vans (outward). The coaches seem to have been remarshalled for the return trip thus: TO/CK/RU/CK/TO/BG.

Plate 70 This view of a southbound express at Oxenholme c. 1934 shows a typical LMS cavalcade of the inter-war years. There are examples of Period I, II, and III coaches, not to mention an 'all-steel' open third and an ex-LNWR double ended brake composite fourth from the rear. There do not appear to be any catering vehicles in the twelve coach train. Another interesting feature is that half the coaches are brake ended and at least four of the brakes are composites. The locomotive is Royal Scot 4-6-0 No. 6138 'The London Irish Rifleman'.

The most noticeable post-1922 change was the increasingly widespread use of open stock for third class passengers on express services. Until 1939, the LMS built open gangwayed stock almost on a 'one for one' basis with side corridor types and in so far as anything typified an LMS express train, the greater proportion of open coaches vis à vis that found on other lines might well be said to be the main characteristic. This matter is considered in more detail in Chapter 9.

The LMS laid down precise marshalling instructions for all its passenger services. These filled quite substantial sized booklets and space permits only a few examples to be given. They are listed in Table 4a.

From the details in the Table, a few generalisations can be drawn. First class accommodation tended to represent some 20—30 per cent. of the capacity of the train in terms of vehicles (not counting diners) and was usually marshalled towards one end of the formation. This was generally the London end for those trains operating from the capital city. The dining cars were usually positioned between the first and third class areas of the train, although in several instances, e.g. the 'Royal Scot', some of the bigger formations were, in effect, two trains in one with two sets of diners, first class sections &c. Short through portions attached to the major trains were located at whichever end was more convenient from the point of view of traffic working. For the most part, these through sections contained the only first class seats which were located away from the main first class areas.

A study of contemporary working instructions reveals that the LMS, in its heyday, provided a considerable number of through workings to smaller traffic centres off the main trunk routes, although the company did not favour the 'slip' coach method of operation. A single through coach would almost invariably be a corridor brake composite of which the LMS built very many (see Volume II). Typical through portions consisting of more than one coach might be CK + BTK or TK + CK + BTK or, possibly even TK + BCK. It seems to have been somewhat more rare for open stock to have been utilised on these through portions than on the main train itself.

Plate 71 This train leaving St. Pancras behind 4-6-0 No. 5570 'New Zealand' is composed mainly of Stanier coaches in simple livery, but the first vehicle, probably a strengthener, is a Period II open third in full livery. The date of the picture is probably 1938/9, but may just be post-war.

Plate 72 This impressive shot taken at Bushey troughs c. 1939, shows a 17 coach train headed by a red streamlined 4-6-2 No. 6225 'Duchess of Gloucester'. The train itself is 'The Royal Scot' and the leading seven coaches are the Edinburgh portion. The ten coach Glasgow section at the rear is wholly made up from Period III coaches but as can be seen, the Edinburgh section, apart from the Period III kitchen car, is formed from Period I and II coaches. The leading two vehicles are a BFK to D1717 and a semi-RFO to D1707. Behind the kitchen car are marshalled a Period I unclassed open diner (D1706) and three Period II fully panelled 60ft coaches. The Glasgow formation cannot be identified. (Photomatic)

Dining Cars

Little generalisation can be made about the use of dining cars. The LMS was the greatest user of dining cars in Britain and built a considerable variety of vehicles in order to satisfy the various different needs of its patrons. The simplest form of refreshment vehicle was the Tea car for light corridor service and the like. These coaches were not LMS-built vehicles but were generally similar to pre-group corridor thirds. A small number of LMS standard Buffet Cars was, however, built (see page 80). These seem to have been somewhat experimental and were not widespread; the growth of buffet type facilities being more of a post-nationalisation phenomenon. The most common LMS type of single-unit dining vehicle was the composite kitchen dining car. The LMS built some 30 of these coaches in addition to the many pre-group examples of the genre such as the handsome ex-LNWR and ex-MR coaches or the equally distinctive ex-Pullman vehicles taken over in Scotland. Many of the pre-group coaches were originally first class cars but by the 1930s had become classified as 'common' diners—i.e. for first *or* third class use (BR code RU). They were in particular demand at weekends and in holiday periods.

Where the services demanded more than one vehicle, there was a little more consistency in approach. First class kitchen diners, of which the LMS built very many, were almost always marshalled with a 42 seat vestibule third class diner and, sometimes, with two of these coaches. Third class kitchen diners generally ran with a vestibule composite or, somewhat more rarely, a full vestibule first diner. The respective seating capacities of these combinations were usually as follows: RF + RTO: 24F + 42T; RT + RCO: 18F + 48T; RT + RFO: 42F + 30T.

Continuing up the scale, where even more meals were envisaged, the full kitchen car was employed. This type of vehicle was very rare before the grouping but the LMS built very many of them. This policy was probably allied to the building of large quantities of open stock already mentioned on page 55. The kitchen car was marshalled between, at the very least, a full vestibule first and a full vestibule third diner. Sometimes two vestibule third diners would be provided while in many instances the semi-open firsts (see page 9) were marshalled next to a kitchen car. Typical kitchen car formations and seating capacities would therefore include the following: RTO + RK + RFO: 42F + 42T; Semi-RFO + RK + RTO + RTO: 18F + 84T. Kitchen cars were also used widely in excursion trains which, when formed as they often were from open stock, lent themselves readily to the insertion of one or two kitchen cars somewhere in the formation.

For a more detailed account of LMS dining car services of the 1930s, readers are referred to the *Railway World* for January/February 1968 and February/June 1969.

Sleeping Cars and Mail services

Sleeping car and mail services were fairly straightforward. Apart from the notable example of the 'Night Scot' (Table 4a), there seems to have been no other regular LMS train composed mainly of sleeping cars. The most usual policy was to provide a certain number of sleeping cars (probably one or two each of first and third class) supplemented by side corridor third class accommodation. It was, however, somewhat rare to find much first class accommodation, other than the sleeping cars themselves, in LMS sleeping car trains. Composite sleeping cars seem to have been used almost exclusively on an individual basis as single through coach workings to various small centres or as the sole sleeping car in an otherwise fairly normal train. As through coaches they would generally run attached to a convenient main line overnight service for the bulk of the distance involved.

The third class sleeping cars were first introduced on September 24, 1928, on the following routes: Euston to Aberdeen, Edinburgh, Glasgow, Holyhead, Inverness and Stranraer; St Pancras to Edinburgh and Glasgow. The charge for berth reservation was 6/- (30p) (between England and Wales) or 7/- (35p) (between England and Scotland). Compartments were reserved for ladies only if necessary—and where this was possible by grouping four bookings for ladies together—and preferences for upper or lower berths were granted as far as possible.

Turning now to mail services, a few points can be made. The celebrated "West Coast Postal' service (Table 4a) was, of course, an entirely non-passenger train comprised of mail vans and full brakes. However, it was not entirely typical of mail workings on the LMS. A much more common solution seems to be that represented by the 'Irish Mail' (Table 4a), where the train formation was a combination of passenger and mail coaches. Of course, a considerable mail traffic was also handled by normal trains—generally utilising luggage compartments or by adding an extra full brake or two to the normal formation (particularly overnight services). It should be noted that only where TPO facilities were necessary, were specially designed mail coaches incorporated in the formation. Even so, these vehicles ranged pretty far and wide, penetrating well into the more remote areas of Scotland and Wales.

The coaches used

With regard to the vehicles used on LMS express services, it was, as has been mentioned, somewhat rare for the LMS to build coaches for a specific service and the most usual policy for the newest vehicles to be rostered immediately to the most important services. Thus, for example, the palatial Period II corridor thirds to D1782 were immediately put in service on the 'Royal Scot' train as had been the luxury lounge brakes and semi-open firsts (page 9) a year or so before. However, as these coaches were superseded by later stock, they became more widely scattered through the system. Similarly on the Midland Division, as new dining cars were built during the 1930s so the older Midland cars were either scrapped or relegated to lesser workings. In general, Scotland seemed to get less than its share of new gangwayed coaches, especially diners, but this may have been because many of the services operating into Scotland were formed from vehicles based south of the border.

The LMS only introduced complete set trains for the 'Coronation Scot' services of 1937 and afterwards. These were of unusual interest and are covered in detail in Chapter 13. However, in 1933, the company sent a set of coaches on exhibition to North America which seems to have escaped much notice. It was a collection of vehicles assembled for the Chicago World Fair of 1933 and was aimed at showing off LMS locomotive and coaching practice. The engine was a member of the Royal Scot class while the train, masquerading as the 'Royal Scot' set, was in fact made up from typical examples of LMS type coaches. Being purely an exhibition train, its formation in terms of vehicle types bore little resemblance to a typical LMS express least of all the 'Royal Scot' itself! The coaches themselves were an interesting mixture of all three periods of LMS design, the Stanier era having just commenced, and the details were as follows:

Period II	57ft Corridor brake first No. 5005 (D1717)
Period I	(LNWR styled) 68ft First class sleeping car No. 350 (D1705)
Period III	65ft Third class sleeping car No. 585 (D1863)
Period I	(Single window) 57ft First class lounge brake No. 5003 (D1741)
Period II	57ft Corridor/vestibule Car No. 1030 (D1719)
Period III	60ft All-electric kitchen only car No. 30073 (D1855)
Period II	60ft Vestibule third class dining coach No. 7764 (D1795)
Period III	57ft Corridor brake third No. 5465 (D1851)

All the coaches were, of course, in fully lined livery and carried their new (i.e. 1932/3 series) running numbers in the 1930-32 stretched scroll type characters. As far as is known, no other LMS coaches were renumbered using this style of figure.

Medium Distance and Excursion workings

Between the extremes of long distance express and short distance local and suburban workings was a range of medium distance services and excursion workings of such variety that it almost defies analysis in the space available. Basically, these services made use of short sets of gangwayed stock formed into what the company called 'Inter-Corridor' sets. These were generally formed either BTK/CK/BTK or BTK/CK/TK/BTK although in many cases two composites or an odd open coach would find their way into the set. Such three- or four-coach sets would also be used—possibly in pairs— to provide, say, an additional express train, often with a dining car set inserted for good measure. Alternatively, one such inter-corridor set might form a through section attached, intermediately, to some other long distance working. For example, the Lancashire-Scotland services via the Midland route frequently utilised a three- or four-coach set which was attached at Hellifield to the main train—except on summer Saturdays when it expanded to a full train of somewhat indeterminate formation.

Excursion workings often employed open stock throughout, although some examples included the odd side corridor composite or composite brake. Kitchen cars could be inserted if necessary in such excursion sets. There were also, however, many excursion workings which employed non-corridor stock, often without either lavatory or refreshment facility.

It is not readily possible to generalise about the coaches used in these intermediate services. Both pre-group and LMS standard coaches of side corridor type were to be found in the inter-corridor sets, sometimes a mixture of both. It was, however, more usual to find the older stock in such sets rather than the very latest coaches, although the latter did some-times appear. Most vestibule excursion sets were of mainly LMS standard stock since open stock was more of an LMS development than a pre-group feature. Table 4b gives some fairly characteristic examples of LMS medium distance workings of the 1930s.

Note: The English trains listed are based mainly on contemporary observation by enthusiasts during the 1930s. The Scottish details have been extracted from official records. In some cases pre-group coaches can be identified. These are indicated thus:

(W) — LNWR coach
(M) — Midland coach
(S) — N. Staffs coach
(Y) — LYR coach

Train Type	*Formation*
Typical Euston-Wolverhampton sets:	BTK/CK/RF(W)/TO/CK/BTK
	BTK/TK/FK/RCO/RT/TK/BTK
	BTK/RTO/TO/RK/RFO/FK/BTK
	BTK/CK/FK/RFO/RT(W)/TO/BTK
Typical Western Division 'Inter-Corridor' sets:	
Holyhead, Manchester & Liverpool	BTK(W)/CK(W)/BTK(W)
London and Rugby	BTK/CK(W)/CK(W)/BTK
Crewe and Llandudno[1]	BTK(W)/CL(W)/CL(W)/BTK(W)
Typical Western Division 'Extra Trains' for excursion and other work:	BCL(W)/TL(W)/TL(W)/FL(W)/TL(W)/BCL(W)
	BT(S)/4 × T(S)/C(S)/BT(S)
	BCK(W)/4 × TO/BTO
	BCK(W)/3 × TK(W)/2 × CK(W)/BTK(W)
	BTO/7 × TO/BTO
Typical Central Division Extra or Excursion sets:	BTO/4 × TO/RK/4 × TO/BCK(Y)
	BT(Y)/C(Y)/6 × T(Y)/BT(Y)
Typical 'London Rd & Buxton' set:	BTO/CO/FO/FO/CO/BTO
Typical Midland Corridor sets:	BTK/CK/TK(W)/BTK(M)
	BTK(M)/TK/TK (W)/BFK(M)
	BTK/TK/CK/BTK(M)
	BTK(W)/CK/TO/BTK
Typical Midland Division Excursion sets:	BCL(M)/4 × TL(M)/BCL(M)
	BT(M)/4 × TL(M)/BT(M)
	BCK(M)/6 × TO/BTO
	BCK(M)/4 × TO/TO(M)/2 × TO/BTO
Typical Scottish sets:	
Carlisle-Perth	BTK/TK/TK/CK/CK/TK/BTK
Carlisle-Stranraer[2]	RU/BTK/CK/BTK
Dundee-Glasgow/Perth	BTK/CK/BTK to Glasgow plus non-corridor Inter-District set to Perth
Edinburgh-Perth	TK/BCK/BTK/BCK/TK
Glasgow-Stranraer[3]	BTK/CK/BTK/BG
Inverness-Aberdeen	TK/CK/TK/BG
Perth-Inverness[4]	RU/TK/CK/BG via Carr Bridge plus CK/BG via Forres
Wick/Thurso-Inverness[5]	TK/CK/BG from Wick plus BCK/TK from Thurso

1. The mixture of corridor/non-corridor stock was not uncommon.
2. This would often be added to a through boat train working from England.
3. Sometimes an Inter-Corridor set plus diner would be used, depending on the time of service.
4. Such a set would almost always run with through coaches from further south to supplement the seating.
5. A dining car would often run attached to such a train between Helmsdale and Inverness.

Suburban and Local workings

LMS locomotive-hauled stopping services were operated by a variety of non-corridor coaches together with older pattern (usually pre-group) gangwayed vehicles. Non-corridor stock was generally of suburban type but the LMS built a reasonable quantity of lavatory stock for the longer distance inter-district workings. This was a direct continuance of pre-group practice where the non-corridor lavatory type vehicle was a favoured type for services other than for purely suburban commuting purposes. With the exception of the London, Tilbury & Southend line, the North London services and the Cathcart Circle services of Glasgow (see Volume III), little effort was made by the LMS to introduce standard non-corridor coaches in set formations. Thus, local trains tended to be a somewhat indiscriminate mixture of pre- and post-group stock. Nevertheless, it was quite common to assemble 'sets' of coaches in the various districts and brand them as such on the coach ends. Euston-Bletchley-Northampton sets were unaccountably branded as 'Euston and *Watford* set No. X'. However, locally formed sets were frequently made up from non-matching stock of various ages, sometimes including gangwayed coaches. Suburban formations varied considerably from area to area. Many of the Midland Division London area services were formed of three-coach sets often in pairs, while at Euston six, later seven, coach sets were the rule. In contrast, 11 coach sets were used on LTS services.

The non-corridor LMS standard lavatory stock was, theoretically, introduced as an attempt to provide new inter-district sets but the coaches themselves rarely ran in set trains, often being used as one-for-one replacements of roughly comparable pre-group vehicles. This one-for-one replacement of old stock was quite a common feature of LMS operating practice, noticeably so in the case of first class and composite coaches. This was to ensure that the first class passenger was given the first benefit of better accommodation and often resulted in local trains formed basically from pre-group third class coaches but with LMS standard first class or composite coaches in place of the older type equivalents.

By the 1930s, non-corridor stock seems to have started to go out of favour for the longer distance inter-district services. No non-corridor lavatory coaches were built by the LMS after 1930, except for four vehicles for the LT&S services, and the use of older inter-corridor sets on medium distance stopping services gradually increased. Even so, the mixture continued as before and one could often see even non-lavatory stock in quite long distance workings. Non-corridor stock was also extensively used for excursion working (because of its carrying capacity) and was often mixed indiscriminately with vestibule stock.

The actual formation of local trains was equally variable. The main differences were found between the Divisions. Thus, the Midland Division tended to employ a basic two-coach unit of brake third plus composite and augment it where necessary. The Western Division and many districts in Scotland, preferred slightly more third class space in their basic

Plate 73 A 15 coach Euston-Manchester train approaching Tring c. 1946 behind 4-6-0 No. 5552 'Silver Jubilee'. The train itself is two-thirds composed of Period III stock, but among the earlier coaches can be identified a Midland clerestory corridor, a Period I 'twin-window' vestibule and, probably, at least one ex-LNWR coach.

Plate 74 The 10.25 a.m. Euston-Windermere train ascends Camden bank in 1946 behind rebuilt Royal Scot No. 6116 'Irish Guardsman'. In spite of the fact that the LMS was then 23 years old, the first ten coaches are a really interesting mixture viz: LNWR corridor composite c. 1910; LNWR corridor brake c. 1910; LMS Period I composite; LMS Period II vestibule third; LMS Period I vestibule third; LMS Period I composite (or third); LNWR full brake; two LNWR corridors of 1913 vintage and a Period III brake!

formations and tended to utilise a three-coach unit of brake third, composite, brake third. The ex-LYR areas preferred even more third class seats and it was by no means rare in this division to have a first/third ratio of something like one composite to every six or seven third class coaches.

Of course, much variation reflected the nature of the districts in which the trains were operating and one should not assume that the Midland Division had no services with a high proportion of thirds or that in Lancashire there were few first class travellers. Quite the contrary, in fact, since the Central Division was responsible for running some of the high class Club trains as well as its predominantly third class suburban services. Thus, as might be expected, the proportion of third class accommodation bore a strong correlation to the amount of industrialisation in the operating areas of the LMS.

For branch services, the LMS, like other companies, often employed push-pull trains, referred to by the company as motor-fitted trains. Many of the vehicles used were of pre-group origin but the company also built its own motor-fitted stock. Apart from the extra vacuum fittings and the windows in the driving ends of the coaches, the vehicles were all but indistinguishable from conventional non-corridor stock. The usual formations, involving two coaches, were driving trailer third and composite or driving trailer third and third. Many services were operated by a single driving trailer third and locomotive.

The LMS did not have a large network of electrified lines but for the London Suburban (ex-LNWR), Liverpool-Southport and Mersey/Wirral lines, there were built several sets of electric multiple-unit stock. The electrified Manchester, South Junction and Altrincham lines were also operated by LMS-pattern vehicles. All the electric coaches and their associated set formations are considered together in Volume III.

Plate 75 This BR vintage picture taken at Carlisle towards the end of steam services still shows a typical LMS local train. It is composed of three Period III corridors (two brake thirds and a composite) but with a non-corridor third as a strengthener. This type of working was very characteristic of later LMS and early BR practice for stopping trains, other than purely suburban services.

Part Two

Non-Passenger Coaching Stock

Chapter 5 – Introduction and NPCS Livery

GENERAL ASPECTS

The uninitiated could be forgiven for presuming that the term 'non-passenger coaching stock' should apply to all those vehicles which did not actually carry passengers. However, this interpretation would not be strictly accurate since the LMS divided its non-passenger carrying stock into those coaches which were actually included in the passenger diagram book proper (the full brakes and GPO vehicles – see Volume III) and those which it put in the official 'non-passenger' diagram book. It is this latter group with which the rest of this first volume is concerned.

The definition of non-passenger coaching stock vehicles referred to their ability to run in passenger trains. Thus, all they needed to have were automatic brakes and/or 'through pipe', together with running gear, axle journals, oil boxes, springs, drawgear etc such as to permit them to run at 'passenger train' speed. Thus, the non-passenger diagram book includes many vehicles which, in terms of styling, would be just as much at home in the freight stock book – but equally, by one of those paradoxes which only railway management can explain, the freight book also included vehicles of a NPCS nature! We have taken the formal non-passenger book as our blueprint for the ensuing chapters.

Our information is based on surviving official records but since the vehicles do not readily fall into the Period I/II/III classification of the conventional passenger carrying carriages, we shall deal with them by generic types. However, for the record, we also include at Table 5 an index of all LMS designed NPCS in diagram page number order, noting the chapter in which they later appear. In our detailed treatment, we have slightly re-organised the 'batting order' to keep together the broadly similar types in terms of utilisation.

TABLE 5: INDEX TO NON-PASSENGER COACHING STOCK

Livery

With the exception of the rail-carried milk tanks, all LMS passenger rated vehicles were normally given crimson lake livery. Until the introduction of the simplified lining style on normal coaching stock, the non-passenger equivalent was regularly given some form of lined treatment. It is not easy to generalise about the lining adopted since so much depended on the type of vehicle involved, though it does appear that some kind of deliberate effort was made to conform with customary LMS carriage painting practice wherever possible.

Thus, if the vehicle bodywork exhibited 'coach-style' panelling – eg the fully panelled horse boxes to D1878 or the first Stanier luggage and parcels vans to D1870 – it was normal to give them what amounted to the complete passenger livery (lined in yellow not gold), whereas such vehicles as outside framed milk vans or theatrical scenery vans were given yellow lining on the edge of the raised framing but the black seems to have been omitted. In many cases, very simple yellow lining (more or less round the edges of the main side panels and doors only) or no lining at all was applied. These latter treatments were most usually given to those vehicles with pronounced 'freight stock' visual lines. In all cases, underframes and running gear were black and roofs usually grey or metallic silver, the latter usually being the case for the roofs of metal clad vehicles from the Stanier period.

After the 1934 livery simplification, most stock became plain crimson without lining, save for the 42ft Stanier luggage and parcels vans which, because of their general configuration, mostly came out in the proper simplified carriage livery with horizontal lining, much as the first batch had come out fully lined – above. There were also a few 'special' treatments reserved for some perishable traffic vehicles. These are considered in the detailed chapters. It should also be mentioned that it was not uncommon in later years for NPCS to be turned out with varnish and lettering applied *direct* to the undercoat colour, thus giving a rather brown appearance to the vehicle.

The insignia adopted during the first ten years or so generally matched that given to conventional carriages. The 3in scroll numerals were all but universal and the seriffed 'LMS' was usually of matching height rather than the 4in version used on passenger coaches. It was also slightly less 'stretched' in form. After the 1934 livery changes, the running numbers usually appeared in sans serif characters and a $3\frac{1}{2}$in version of the seriffed 'LMS' also began to appear – again less elongated in shape than the 4in version which continued in use on most of the conventional coaches and some NPCS. Towards the end of the LMS period, much NPCS began to appear with 'freight' style lettering and numbering, usually rendered in plain yellow, sans serif and without shading.

It is not possible to generalise about the placing of insignia. The pictures in the remaining chapters show some of the variations but it is felt most probable that there were other schemes as well.

The principal exceptions to the above very general outline were the milk tanks. Before the war, these carried the distinctive owning company liveries on the tank itself, the underframe below the sole bar being black and lettered in plain sans-serif freight type markings. Headstocks and sole bars were regularly painted to match the tank colour. We once thought these to have been lettered white – and stated as much – but it now seems that yellow was used on many (all?) milk tank chassis and the restored example at the NRM (repainted under the direction of one of the authors) has been given yellow insignia. We have been unable to determine whether white lettering was also used on some milk tanks but it is possible.

Chapter 6 – Livestock Vehicles

The LMS built only two types of non-passenger livestock vehicles, namely horse boxes, of which there were seven varieties and prize cattle vans for which two diagrams only were raised. All were four-wheel vehicles.

The first LMS horse box was to D1878 and was characteristic of MR designs. It had a fully panelled exterior with matchboard ends and was given full livery. The interior arrangement set the style for all subsequent diagrams. There was a half compartment for the groom at one end, a luggage compartment at the opposite end and between the two was the accommodation for the horses, of which three could be carried.

D1878 was succeeded by a series of diagrams of almost identical appearance but with varying arrangements of such matters as brakes and lighting which was the reason for the many diagrams (D1879/1952/1956/1972). All shared the same basic body shape as D1878 and retained the 12ft 6in wheelbase. However, on all four diagrams, the body style exhibited horizontal planking rather than the panelling of D1878. All had matchboard ends.

In 1938, an example from D1972 was converted to 16ft 0in wheelbase and this seems to have been the prototype for D2125, a post-nationalisation diagram which was built with the new longer wheelbase. It continued to have the 21ft long fully planked body of its predecessors and the standard LMS horse box profile. The final diagram (D2181) was a complete break from the previous types. It is difficult in some ways to see why this Diagram was included in the LMS book at all for the running numbers were in the LNER series and basically the design emanated from the LNER to ER Diagram 9. The first 25 were built at York in 1954 but 120 were built at Earlestown in 1955.

Prize cattle vans, sometimes referred to as Special cattle vans, were very similar to horse boxes but unlike the majority of horse boxes, the first LMS prize cattle vans to D1876 were built with straight sides. Dimensionally they were very similar to the horse boxes but had no luggage space–the cattle compartment being correspondingly longer. The second diagram for this category of livestock (D1877) was identical in layout to D1876 but had the horse box profile with horizontal side planking and matchboard ends. One batch of this version was built as late as 1952. These were 24ft vehicles running on 15ft 6in wheelbase.

TABLE 6: SUMMARY OF LIVESTOCK VEHICLES

Horse Boxes:—For variations in brakes/lighting, etc., see notes at foot of table. All had 12'6" wheelbase unless noted otherwise.

Diag	Lot	Qty	Date	Built	Wt	Dimensions (L x W x H)	Running Numbers	Withdrawals First	Last
1878	232	*49	1926	Derby	10T	21'x8'6½"x12'0⅛"	42000-42048	2/54	10/61
1879	436	60	1929	Derby	10T		42099-42158	12/57	13/62
	493	100	1930/1	Derby	10T	21'x8'6½"x12'0⅛"	42159-42258	11/58	13/62
	584	100	1931/2	Derby	10T		42259-42358	1/59	10/62
	657	50	1932/3	Derby	10T		42359-42408	1/59	13/62
1952	part 854	3	1935	Derby	10T	21'x8'6½"x12'0⅛"	42521-42523	9/62	13/62
1956	317	50	1927/8	Derby	10T		42049-42098	6/56	8/61
	696	50	1933	Derby	10T		42409-42458	3/62	13/62
	748	25	1934	Derby	10T	21'x8'6½"x12'0⅛"	42459-42483	10/62	13/62
	749	25	1934	Derby	10T		42484-42508	9/62	13/62
	part 854	12	1935	Derby	10T		42309-42520	9/62	13/62
1972	1040	20	1937	Derby	10T	21'x8'6½"x12'0⅛"	42524- 42543†	12/62	3/66
	1088	30	1938	Derby	10T		42544-42573	5/63	3/66
2125	1452	20	1948	Derby	10T		42574-42593	12/63	3/66
	1534	30	1948/9	Derby	10T	21'x8'6½"x12'0⅛"	42594-42623	7/63	—
	1502	40	1950	Derby	10T	(16'0" wheelbase)	42624-42663	1/64	3/66
	1582	26	1950/1	Derby	10T		42664-42689	2/64	—
2181	1662	70	1954	Earlestown	12T		2391-2460‡	not	
	1664	30	1955	Earlestown	12T	24'x8'3"x12'3"	2461-2490‡	known	
	1675	20	1955	Earlestown	12T	(16' 0" wheelbase)	2491-2510‡		

* Possibly 50 built but only 49 renumbered—the only panelled horse boxes.
† 42536 converted to 16'0" wheelbase in 1938.
‡ Many of these were allocated off the London Midland Region with the appropriate regional prefixes, etc. An LNER design with LNER series number.

Diagram differences, other than dimensional:
D1878 Gas lit, automatic vacuum and hand brake, Westinghouse through pipe.
D1879 Oil lit, automatic vacuum and hand brake, Westinghouse through pipe.
D1952 Electrically lit (Stones inductor alternator system), automatic vacuum and hand brake only.
D1956 Gas lit, automatic vacuum and hand brake only.
D1972 Electrically lit (Stones Lilliput single battery system), automatic vacuum and hand brake only.
D2125 Electrically lit (Stones O.L. system), automatic vacuum and hand brake only.
D2181 Electrically lit, automatic vacuum and hand brake only.

Prize Cattle Vans:—All with automatic vacuum and hand brake and all fitted with Westinghouse through pipe.

Diag	Lot	Qty	Date	Built	Wt	Dimensions (L x W x H)	Running Numbers	Withdrawals First	Last	Remarks
1876	227	27	1926	Ntn. Heath	10T		43800-43819	5/55	12/60	All gas lit.
	318	15	1927	Derby	10T	21'x8'0"x 11'8¼"	43820-43834	7/56	8/61	
	377	15	1928	Derby	10T	(12'6" wheelbase)	43835-43849	6/57	1/61	
1877	463	10	1930	Derby	10T		43850-43859	5/59	13/62	All oil lit except Lot 855 (gas).
	598	10	1931	Derby	10T	24'x8'6½"x12'0⅝"	43860-43869	4/61	13/62	
	855	5	1935	Derby	10T	(15'6" wheelbase)	43870-43874	12/63	3/65	
	1638	25	1952	Earlestown	10T		43875-43899	12/63	—	

Horse Box – D1878

This design was based on the Midland predecessor and was the only LMS version to display the fully panelled body styling. They were built to LMS Drawing Nos 6290 (body) and 6291 (underframe). Basic details are given at Table 6 and the full 1923-1933 number correlation was as follows:

New No.	Old No.	New No.	Old No.	New No.	Old No.
42000	545	42016	4671	42032	5323
42001	759	42017	4675	42033	5374
42002	832	42018	4689	42034	5671
42003	907	42019	4701	42035	5894
42004	915	42020	4708	42036	6017
42005	916	42021	4710	42037	6228
42006	919	42022	4741	42038	7881
42007	2912	42023	4742	42039	7882
42008	3088	42024	5064	42040	7891
42009	3089	42025	5108	42041	7892
42010	3158	42026	5167	42042	7915
42011	4212	42027	5183	42043	7916
42012	4326	42028	5228	42044	7917
42013	4417	42029	5242	42045	7918
42014	4454	42030	5287	42046	7919
42015	4535	42031	5294	42047	7920
				42048	7921

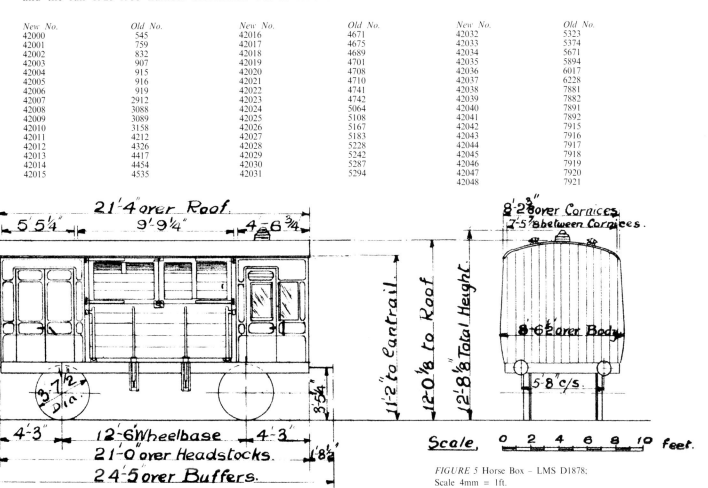

FIGURE 5 Horse Box – LMS D1878;
Scale 4mm = 1ft.

Plate 76 Exterior view of the first D1878 Horse Box No. 545, later 42000. Note the general resemblance to contemporary coaching stock practice, including the fully lined livery.

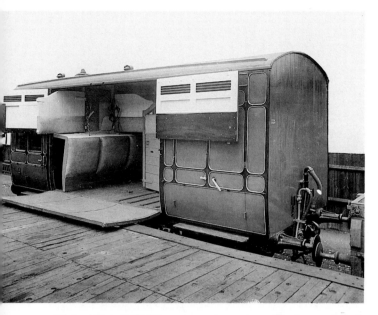

Plates 77 and 78 These two views show interior and further close-up body details of this very attractive looking design. In particular, they both emphasise the considerable degree of protection offered to the horses in transit. Most of the time, these were racehorses and thus of considerable value.

Horse Box – D1879

The horse boxes to D1879 were by far the most numerous of the many LMS-built vehicles of this type. Their construction came in the middle of the broadly identical D1956 version (below), hence the interruption in the 1933 number series of the latter type. The two diagrams differed solely in respect of the oil lamps and Westinghouse through pipes on D1879 and both versions were built to the same works drawing, as indeed were the three vehicles to D1952: Drawing No.11/72. The LMS probably favoured the Westinghouse version at the time owing to the frequent routing of horse boxes over 'foreign' lines, many of which retained air brakes for some time after the grouping. Oil lighting was also preferred because of its lack of dependence on replenishment gas supplies at more remote locations. We do not have a picture of this particular type but it was externally identical to Plate 80. Summary details are in Table 6 and the full 1933 renumbering details were as follows:

New No.	Old No.	New No.	Old No.	New No.	Old No.	New No.	Old No.	New No.	Old No.
Lot 436		42149	3850	42199	3925	42251	7171	42301	3671
42099	1037	42150	3896	42200	3982	42252	7179	42302	3673
42100	1038	42151	3899	42201	4008	42253	7187	42303	3674
42101	1053	42152	3919	42202	5850	42254	7192	42304	3698
42102	1092	42153	3942	42203	5861	42255	7525	42305	3703
42103	1096	42154	3947	42204	5870	42256	7537	42306	3722
42104	1102	42155	3981	42205	5877	42257	7543	42307	3724
42105	1109	42156	3993	42206	5879	42258	7884	42308	3735
42106	1116	42157	3999	42207	5895			42309	3754
42107	1177	42158	4002	42208	5901	**Lot 584**		42310	3756
42108	1188			42209	5902	42259	1024	42311	3773
42109	1202	**Lot 493**		42210	5920	42260	1120	42312	3784
42110	1206	42159	1106	42211	5929	42261	1269	42313	3787
42111	1218	42160	1111	42212	5935	42262	1300	42314	3806
42112	1220	42161	1172	42213	6235	42263	1310	42315	3837
42113	1228	42162	1215	42214	6239	42264	1389	42316	3842
42114	1247	42163	1361	42215	6243	42265	1407	42317	3865
42115	1248	42164	3356	42216	6248	42266	1417	42318	3873
42116	1278	42165	3380	42217	6251	42267	1493	42319	3878
42117	1301	42166	3383	42218	6253	42268	1499	42320	3882
42118	1302	42167	3389	42219	6254	42269	1502	42321	3885
42119	1307	42168	3397	42220	6707	42270	1506	42322	3909
42120	1341	42169	3408	42221	6726	42271	1509	42323	3914
42121	1436	42170	3436	42222	6731	42272	1516	42324	3915
42122	1460	42171	3452	42223	6734	42273	1517	42325	3922
42123	1489	42172	3457	42224	6739	42274	1525	42326	3926
42124	3448	42173	3477	42225	6743	42275	3377	42327	3931
42125	3527	42174	3503	42226	6744	42276	3391	42328	3936
42126	3551	42175	3512	42227	6756	42277	3392	42329	3940
42127	3572	42176	3519	42228	6775	42278	3398	42330	3941
42128	3581	42177	3552	42229	6784	42279	3416	42331	3943
42129	3590	42178	3652	42230	6798	42280	3439	42332	3957
42130	3619	42179	3656	42231	6815	42281	3466	42333	3961
42131	3665	42180	3691	42232	6817	42282	3473	42334	3990
42132	3699	42181	3695	42233	6820	42283	3483	42335	3995
42133	3701	42182	3718	42234	6821	42284	3497	42336	4006
42134	3726	42183	3730	42235	6822	42285	3498	42337	5824
42135	3734	42184	3745	42236	6853	42286	3509	42338	5864
42136	3744	42185	3753	42237	6858	42287	3514	42339	5903
42137	3760	42186	3758	42238	6868	42288	3522	42340	5923
42138	3767	42187	3772	42239	6871	42289	3525	42341	5924
42139	3781	42188	3777	42240	6873	42290	3574	42342	5937
42140	3791	42189	3829	42241	7125	42291	3585	42343	5944
42141	3798	42190	3830	42242	7127	42292	3588	42344	6007
42142	3799	42191	3852	42243	7129	42293	3589	42345	6008
42143	3800	42192	3856	42244	7139	42294	3591	42346	6009
42144	3814	42193	3866	42245	7141	42295	3628	42347	6231
42145	3833	42194	3870	42246	7143	42296	3629	42348	6238
42146	3836	42195	3881	42247	7145	42297	3640	42349	6240
42147	3844	42196	3886	42248	7147	42298	3657	42350	6244
42148	3845	42197	3901	42249	7151	42299	3661	42351	6246
		42198	3908	42250	7161	42300	3664	42352	6286

42353	6717	42366	5511	42381	5574	42396	5628
42354	6719	42367	5512	42382	5575	42397	5631
42355	6722	42368	5514	42383	5576	42398	5632
42356	6724	42369	5515	42384	5578	42399	5634
42357	6733	42370	5519	42385	5580	42400	5638
42358	6737	42371	5520	42386	5581	42401	5642
		42372	5521	42387	5587	42402	5643
Lot 657		42373	5525	42388	5589	42403	5649
42359	5501	42374	5531	42389	5597	42404	5653
42360	5503	42375	5533	42390	5601	42405	5654
42361	5504	42376	5534	42391	5602	42406	5665
42362	5505	42377	5536	42392	5603	42407	5668
42363	5507	42378	5569	42393	5606	42408	5669
42364	5508	42379	5571	42394	5620		
42365	5510	42380	5573	42395	5626		

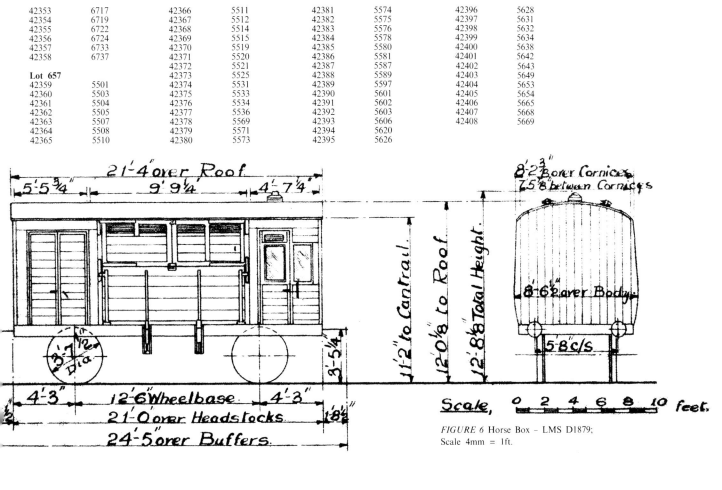

FIGURE 6 Horse Box – LMS D1879;
Scale 4mm = 1ft.

Horse Box – D1952

Three vehicles only were built to this diagram in 1935 as part of the final Lot issued for D1956 (below). They marked the change from gas to electric lighting, being fitted with experimental apparatus, and were followed, chronologically, by the main batch of electrically lit horse boxes to D1972 (below). Summary details are given in Table 6 and this small group was built after the 1933 renumbering. Our only copy of this diagram is unsuitable for reproduction, but the vehicles were identical in appearance to D1956 (below).

Plate 79 Horse Box No. 42522 to D1952 taken c1938. (G. Y. Hemmingway)

Horse Box – D1956

This diagram represented the non-Westinghouse pipe and gas-lit version of the D1879/D1952/D1956 series of horse boxes and was in effect the prototype of the whole group, the initial Lot 317 to this diagram being the first to be built. Production then switched to D1879, further construction of D1956 not being resumed until after the 1933 renumbering. Summary details are given in Table 6 and the 1933 renumbering details of Lot 317 were as follows:

New No.	Old No.	New No.	Old No.	New No.	Old No.
42049	1086	42065	1437	42082	5939
42050	1099	42066	3639	42083	5946
42051	1121	42067	3813	42084	6234
42052	1132	42068	3838	42085	6236
42053	1160	42069	3849	42086	6237
42054	1167	42070	3854	42087	6241
42055	1186	42071	3857	42088	6245
42056	1198	42072	3861	42089	6741
42057	1231	42073	3864	42090	6781
42058	1234	42074	3945	42091	6799
42059	1250	42075	3968	42092	6812
42060	1260	42076	4612	42093	6869
42061	1270	42077	4622	42094	7350
42062	1292	42078	4627	42095	7359
42063	1322	42079	4703	42096	8133
42064	1395	42080	5922	42097	8160
		42081	5926	42098	8174

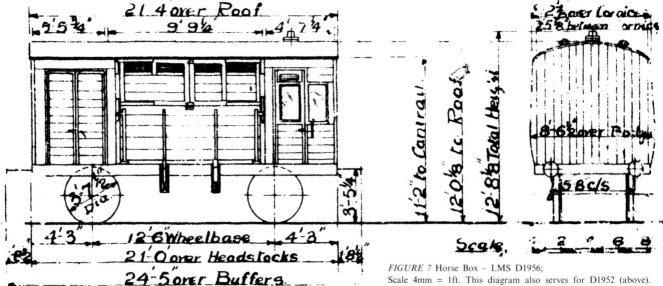

FIGURE 7 Horse Box – LMS D1956;
Scale 4mm = 1ft. This diagram also serves for D1952 (above).

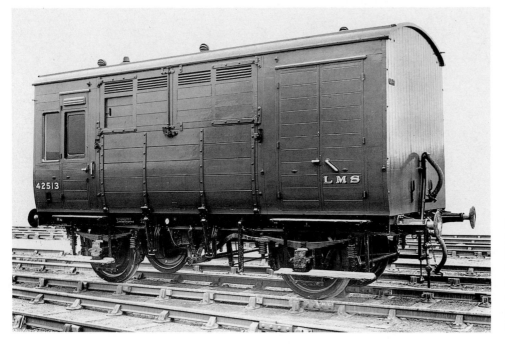

Plate 80 This view shows No. 42513 of Lot 854, newly built in 1935. Note the use of shell pattern roof ventilators and unlined livery – both conceivably being part of the increasing Stanier influence.

Horse Box – D1972

This 1937 diagram was raised for the electrically lit horse boxes which were otherwise identical in body style to the previous three diagrams. For some unknown reason, however, the quoted drawing numbers on the diagram differed from their immediate predecessors. They had the 1933 series numbers from the outset and were always plain crimson in LMS days. It was No. 42536 from this diagram which was converted to 16ft wheelbase in July 1938. Summary details are in Table 6.

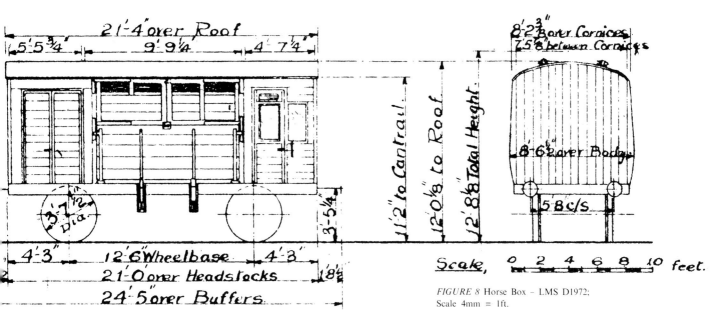

FIGURE 8 Horse Box – LMS D1972;
Scale 4mm = 1ft.

Plate 81 Our only picture of D1972 shows No. M42560 at St Rollox in May 1948. The vehicle has plain crimson livery and the letters 'L' and 'S' have been deleted to leave the new 'M' prefix – the BR form of identity. (A. G. Ellis)

Horse Box – D2125

This diagram was the 16ft wheelbase continuation of the LMS design series, not introduced until BR days, though obviously based on the 1938 rebuild (above). It was otherwise identical to D1972 and built to Drawing No. 6525G. Summary details are in Table 6.

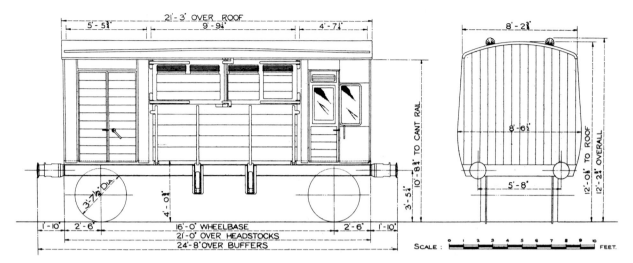

FIGURE 9 Horse box – BR (LMR)
D2125; Scale 4mm = 1ft.

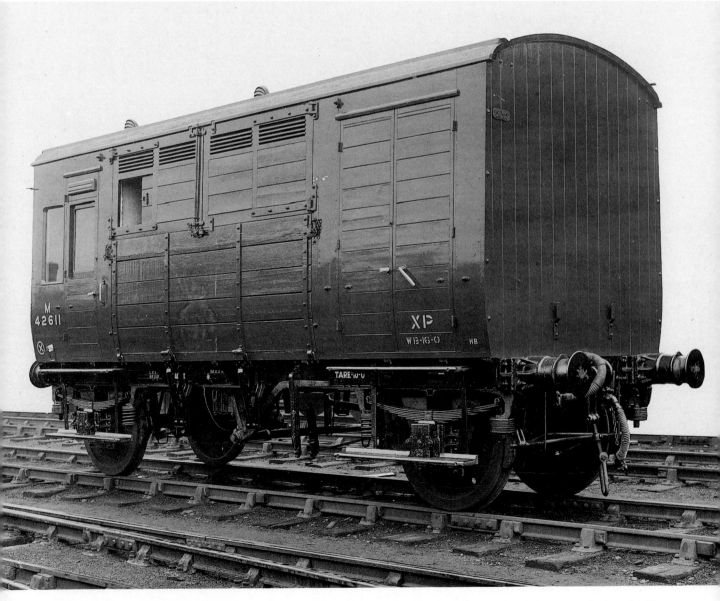

Plate 82 This view shows No. M42611 of Lot 1534 immediately prior to entering service in 1949. It displays LMS wagon-pattern insignia but carries the plain BR crimson livery.

Plate 83 No. M42684 was one of the final examples of D2125 to be built – in 1951. It is seen here at Doncaster in September 1964 in the plain BR red livery with correct BR style insignia. (J. Johnson)

Horse Box – D2181

As mentioned in the introductory section, these 120 vehicles, built in 1954-5, were of LNER design. They were, however, built for the LMR and were included in the former LMS diagram book, so for completeness we include them here. Their BR running numbers, being in the LNER series, always carried an 'E' suffix to denote their region of design.

FIGURE 10 Horse Box – BR (LMR)
D2181; Scale 4mm = 1ft.

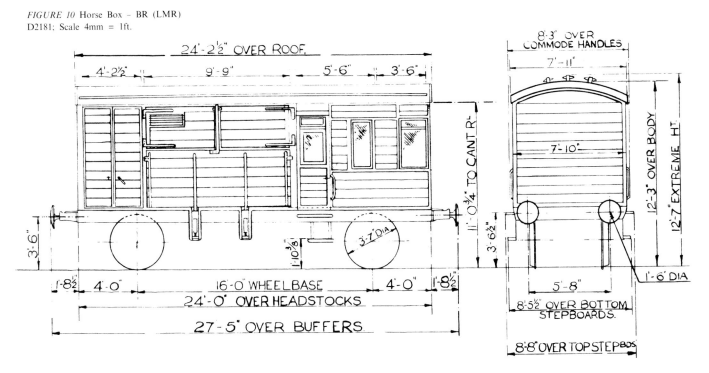

Plates 84 and 85 One of the authors happened upon this well-preserved example of D2181, No. M2466E, at Willesden in July 1964. Its more utilitarian shape and different arrangement of the groom's compartment was in marked contrast to the normal LMS design. (R. J. Essery)

Prize Cattle Van – D1876

Prize Cattle Vans were used mostly for the conveyance of pedigree bulls and high value cattle. This was useful traffic but not as widespread as that in horses, most cattle going in normal cattle wagons! There were thus only two LMS designs of PCV and this, the first of them, was of largely MR inspiration and displayed more 'freight vehicle' styling than the contemporary horse boxes. In consequence, as explained in Chapter 5, when new they carried the 'full' pre-1933 livery in its most simple form – ie fine yellow lining confined to panel and door edges only plus some embellishment of the main hinges. Summary details are given in Table 6 and the 1933 renumbering details are as follows:

Lot 227		Lot 318		Lot 377	
New No.	*Old No.*	*New No.*	*Old No.*	*New No.*	*Old No.*
43800	6713	43820	826	43835	1869
43801	6714	43821	831	43836	1870
43802	6721	43822	892	43837	1871
43803	6742	43823	896	43838	1872
43804	6747	43824	897	43839	1873
43805	6750	43825	900	43840	1874
43806	6793	43826	909	43841	4931
43807	6802	43827	924	43842	5627
43808	6804	43828	1045	43843	5647
43809	6810	43829	1075	43844	5667
43810	6847	43830	1082	43845	5677
43811	6849	43831	1390	43846	5681
43812	6850	43832	1510	43847	5692
43813	6856	43833	1805	43848	5701
43814	6857	43834	8164	43849	7106
43815	6859				
43816	6870				
43817	6872				
43818	6875				
43819	6876				

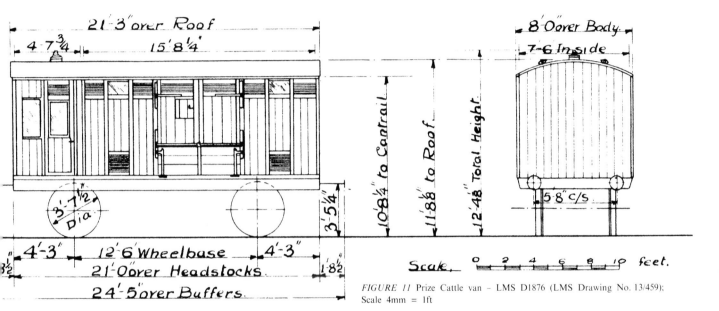

FIGURE 11 Prize Cattle van – LMS D1876 (LMS Drawing No. 13/459); Scale 4mm = 1ft

Plate 86 This ex-works view of No. 1805, later 43833, gives a very clear impression of the 'full' livery applied to the D1876 vehicles when new. It rather seems as if the hinges and strapping have been picked out in black.

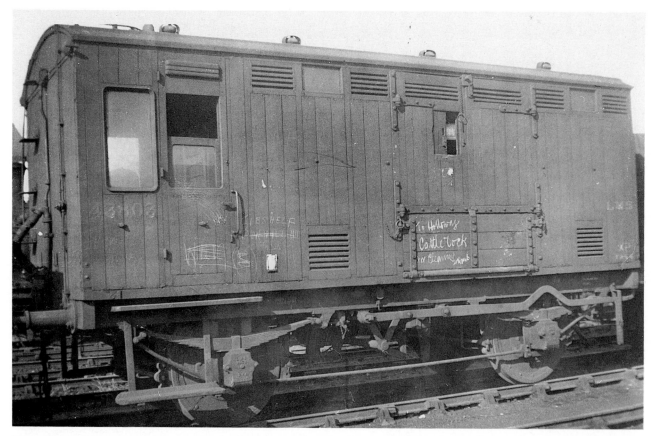

Plate 87 No. 43803, an early example of Lot 227, was in rather unkempt plain crimson livery when photographed at an unknown location just prior to Nationalisation. The flat topped '3s' of the numerals suggest a post-1945 repaint. (Authors' Collection)

Prize Cattle Van – D1877

This diagram shared the basic internal layout of D1876 but introduced the more curvaceous 'horse box' body styling along with 3ft increases in body length and wheelbase. The first two lots came out before the 1933 renumbering and also before the change from full livery. They may therefore have been lined out as D1876 but we cannot confirm this. The 1936 and 1952 batches were given 1933 series numbers and plain red livery (LMS and BR respectively) from new, and the long interval between the final two lots may have been indicative of the declining nature of this form of traffic. The summary details are in Table 6 and the 1933 renumbering details for Lots 463 and 598 are as follows:

Lot 463				Lot 598			
New No.	Old No.	New No.	Old No.	New No.	Old No.	New No.	Old No.
43850	5185	43855	5254	43860	3465	43865	3658
43851	5186	43856	5270	43861	3490	43866	3713
43852	5209	43857	5333	43862	3507	43867	3747
43853	5212	43858	5338	43863	3606	43868	3788
43854	5249	43859	5366	43864	3621	43869	3795

FIGURE 12 Prize Cattle Van – LMS D1877 (LMS Drawing No. 11/208);
Scale 4mm = 1ft

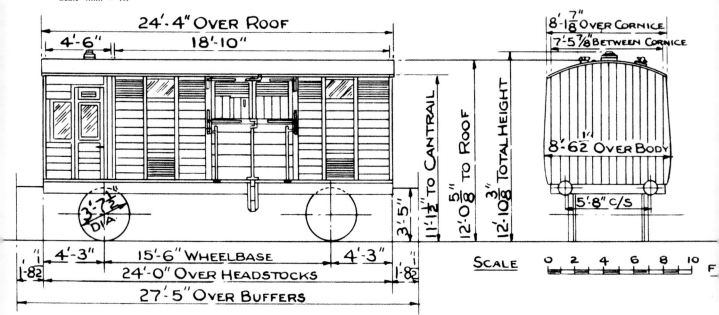

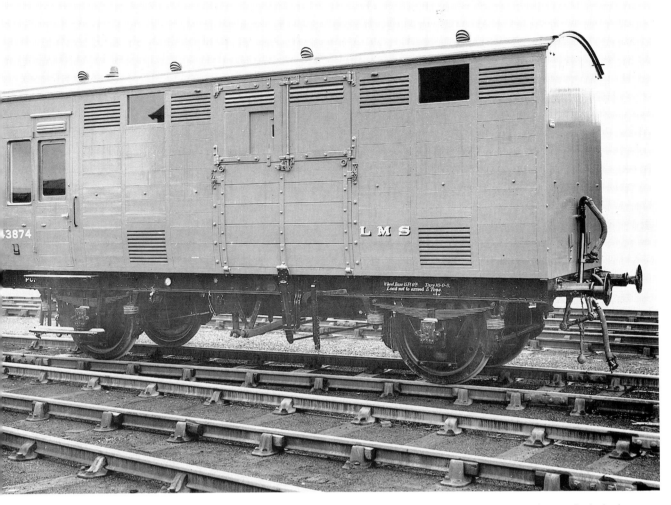

Plate 88 Official view of No. 43874 from Lot 855, ex-works in 1935 in plain crimson livery and coach style transfer insignia.

Plate 89 This September 1964 view shows No. M43877 of the 1952 series at Stranraer, now carrying its BR 'SCV' ('Special' Cattle Van) markings and plain red livery. (D. F. Tee)

Chapter 7 – Covered Combination/Carriage Trucks

This family of mainly four and six-wheel vehicles embraces stock which was variously called 'Motor Car Van' and 'Aeroplane Van' in the diagram book as well as the normal CCT reference. With odd exceptions, most of the vehicles were around 30ft long over headstocks, there being variations of a few inches, and were carried either on six-wheel or very long wheelbase four-wheel chassis. The principal exception was one diagram issued as an 'Aeroplane Van' which was a bogie vehicle (see below).

Two six-wheel diagrams were issued under the CCT reference (D1871/1872). D1871 was a 30ft vehicle on a 21ft 6in wheelbase chassis while D1872 was a 30ft 5in design on a 21ft 0in wheelbase chassis. Later lots of D1872 had 30ft 1in bodies but retained the 21ft wheelbase. Both varieties were outside framed and bore a strong resemblance to the Midland design from which they must have originated.

Many of these vehicles, of both diagrams, were later converted to departmental use and this went along with slight modifications to the bodywork. Outside steps were removed, end doors were boarded up and so forth. They were prohibited from passenger train use in February 1959 and this instruction probably heralded their general downgrading for other purposes. The third CCT diagram in the LMS diagram book was D1929. This was a 30ft 5in four-wheel vehicle with a 19ft 0in wheelbase. One hundred and twenty-five were built during the middle 1930s and the vehicles presented a cleaner external appearance. Unlike the six-wheel CCTs, they were vacuum fitted only. Curiously, however, the diagram book rates them at 8T carrying capacity rather than the 6T of the six-wheel designs.

The bulk of the remaining vehicles in this section were classified as Motor Car Vans. The first of these was D2032 which was a variant of the D1872 CCT considered above. Twenty-five were built and they were 30ft 1in vehicles with a high arch roof and 20ft 0in wheelbase, six-wheel chassis. These vehicles were built in 1925 as part of the same lot as some of the D1872 CCTs. The next Motor Car Van was a hideously ugly experimental design which appeared in 1925 to D1868 (later altered to D2042). One only was built, of steel construction and, judging from the fact that it was not repeated, one must presume that even though it had a long life it was not entirely successful.

The most numerous LMS design Motor Car Van was D2026. These vehicles first appeared in 1938 and some were built as late as 1956. They were 30ft 5in vehicles on a 19ft 0in wheelbase four-wheel chassis. They had a sort of GWR 'Fruit D' appearance and one naturally speculates if Stanier had any influence on the design. The design was classified CCT by British Railways.

The final design to be considered here is the above-mentioned 'Aeroplane Van'. Six were built to D1880 at Derby and Wolverton on second-hand underframes. From the bogie style and other features, the underframes were clearly of Midland origin. The design was extremely distinctive and built to the extreme limit of the loading gauge. The lettering on the solebar indicated that the wheels must not exceed 3ft 6in diameter on the tread–one is not entirely surprised!

TABLE 7: SUMMARY OF COVERED COMBINATION TRUCKS AND ALLIED VEHICLES

Diag	Lot	Qty	Date	Built	Wt	Dimensions (LxWxH)	Running Numbers	Withdrawals First	Last
Covered Combination Trucks									
1871*	111	25	1926	Wolverton	12T⎫	30'0"x8' 5¼"x12'4¼"	35030-35054	2/57	4/63
	123	75	1926	Wolverton	12T⎭		35055-35128‡	2/57	4/64
1872*	part 35	5	1925	Wolverton	12T⎫		35025-35029	2/59	4/62
	363	20	1928	Derby	12T		35129-35148	9/56	7/62
	406	50	1928/9	Wolverton	12T		35149-35198	4/55	6/68
	532	50	1930	Wolverton	12T⎬	30'5"x8'5¼"x 12'4½"	35199-35248	5/55	5/63
	594	100	1931/2	Wolverton	12T		35249-35348	2/55	5/65
	661	25	1932	Wolverton	12T		35349-35373	11/57	7/65
	746†	50	1934	Wolverton	12T⎭		35374-35423	12/56	6/66
	747†	50	1934	Wolverton	12T		35424-35473	8/57	4/64
1929	860	100	1935	Wolverton	12T⎫	30'5"x8'7¾"x12'10"	35474-35573	9/61	Some extant
	999	25	1937	Wolverton	12T⎭		35574-35598	4/65	early 1970s

* Fitted with automatic vacuum and hand brake, also Westinghouse through pipe. Six-wheel vehicles.
† 30'1" over headstocks.
‡ One withdrawn before 1933.

Motor Car Vans									
2032	part 35	25	1925	Wolverton	12T	30'1"x8'5¼"x12'9½" (six-wheeled)	35000-35024	4/54	4/64
2042	85	1	1925	Derby	not known	33'0"x8'6½"x12'1¼" (four-wheeled)	37200	—	4/65
2026	1154	150	1938	Met-Cammell	12T⎫		37000-37149	6/63⎫	Many
	1636	30	1951/2	Earlestown	12T	30'5"x9'0⅞"x12'10"	37298-37327	6/68⎬	extant early 1970s
	1770†	35	1956/7	Swindon	12T		37200-37234	9/60⎭	
	1773†	10	1956	Swindon	12T⎭	(four-wheeled)	37235-37244		

† GW not LMS series Lot numbers.

Aeroplane Vans									
1880	299	1	1927	Derby	17T⎫	39'6"x9'1"x13'0"	44300*	—	1/42
	407	5	1929	Wolverton	17T⎭	(bogie vehicle)	44301-44305	6/45	6/68

* Later allocated CCT No. 37067

Covered Combination Truck – D1871/1872

Because of the general similarity of these two designs, as already noted, it is logical to consider them together. First, however, a brief word about the CCT classification in LMS parlance is called for. The more usual description of this type of vehicle is 'Covered *Carriage* Truck', but the LMS preferred the word 'Combination' – essentially in recognition of the various *combinations* of uses to which this versatile type could be put as well as carrying road vehicles. As long as they had end doors, both designations referred to the same type of vehicle for all practical purposes!

The summary of vehicles concerned is at Table 7 and the only significant difference between the diagrams was the nature of the end doors, full height on D1871 but with a transverse bottom 'flap-down' section on D1872. The latter type was also built on second-hand underframes, mainly of LNWR but sometimes of MR origin, hence the slight differences in overall length and wheelbase between the two diagrams. We cannot give the 'split' between the LNWR/MR chassis for D1872, though pictorial evidence – eg Plates 93 and 96 – suggest that Lot 594 may have been the ex-MR examples. It should also be noted that Lot 35 of D1872 was shared with D2032 (below), the latter type being classified as a Motor Car Van.

There was clearly a considerable need for this type of vehicle in early LMS days and the availability of hundreds of serviceable six-wheel chassis from older redundant passenger stock soon after grouping no doubt made the whole process of building D1872 very economical. By far the bulk of the CCTs to both diagrams emerged before the 1933 renumbering and a full list of this renumbering is given below:

D1871

Lot 111

New No.	Old No.
35030	7220
35031	7259
35032	7288
35033	7376
35034	7378
35035	7380
35036	7397
35037	7403
35038	7404
35039	7411
35040	7415
35041	7418
35042	7449
35043	7450
35044	7459
35045	7461
35046	7465
35047	7470
35048	7506
35049	7512
35050	7519
35051	7533
35052	7598
35053	8138
35054	8188
35055	5590
35056	5591
35057	5594
35058	5595
35059	5596
35060	5600
35061	5618
35062	5622
35063	5625
35064	5629
35065	5630
35066	5636
35067	5641
35068	5644
35069	5645
35070	5648
35071	5650
35072	5660
35073	5691
35074	5834
35075	5838
35076	5843
35077	5859
35078	5862
35079	5863
35080	5896
35081	5897
35082	5905
35083	5906
35084	5907
35085	5908
35086	5909
35087	5910
35088	5969
35089	5978
35090	5985
35091	5986
35092	6325
35093	6334
35094	6369
35095	6415
35096	6536
35097	6555
35098	6589
35099	6640
35100	7102
35101	7104
35102	7105
35103	7230
35104	7235
35105	7247
35106	7267
35107	7278
35108	7284
35109	7310
35110	7322
35111	7943
35112	7944
35113	7945
35114	7946
35115	7947
35116	7948
35117	7949
35118	7950
35119	7951
35120	7952
35121	7953
35122	7954
35123	7955
35124	7956
35125	8117
35126	8152
35127	8170
35128	8180

D1872

Lot 35 (part)

New No.	Old No.
35025	4739
35026	4740
35027	4693
35028	5163
35029	5180

Lot 363

35129	1688
35130	1795
35131	1813
35132	1821
35133	1823
35134	4347
35135	4444
35136	4691
35137	4712
35138	4823
35139	4920
35140	5111
35141	5194
35142	5198
35143	5238
35144	5239
35145	6578
35146	6580
35147	6599
35148	6690

Lot 406

35149	801
35150	802
35151	884
35152	887
35153	890
35154	891
35155	904
35156	906
35157	908
35158	911
35159	914
35160	920
35161	922
35162	923
35163	927
35164	928
35165	929
35166	930
35167	931
35168	932
35169	933
35170	934
35171	935
35172	936
35173	937
35174	938
35175	943
35176	4834
35177	4837
35178	4848
35179	4850
35180	4857
35181	4859
35182	4866
35183	4867
35184	4868
35185	4869
35186	4888
35187	4890
35188	4896
35189	4898
35190	4900
35191	4908
35192	4909
35193	4911
35194	4916
35195	4918
35196	4927
35197	4936
35198	5134

Lot 532

35199	658
35200	4152
35201	4161
35202	4164
35203	4173
35204	4357
35205	4360
35206	4364
35207	4370
35208	4372
35209	4373
35210	4374
35211	4381
35212	4382
35213	4386
35214	4388
35215	4389
35216	4390
35217	4397
35218	4418
35219	4419
35220	4428
35221	4432
35222	4433
35223	4435
35224	4436
35225	4437
35226	4441
35227	4457
35228	4463
35229	4469
35230	4472
35231	4475
35232	4493
35233	4495
35234	4548
35235	4610
35236	4626
35237	5516
35238	5656
35239	5657
35240	5659
35241	5694
35242	5699
35243	5741
35244	5802
35245	6268
35246	6610
35247	6645
35248	7101

Lot 594

35249	657
35250	659
35251	665
35252	669
35253	676
35254	677
35255	678
35256	680
35257	682
35258	686
35259	687
35260	698
35261	699
35262	700
35263	706
35264	709
35265	712
35266	713
35267	714
35268	716
35269	717
35270	720
35271	731
35272	4154
35273	4352
35274	4354
35275	4355
35276	4358
35277	4359
35278	4361
35279	4362
35280	4363
35281	4366
35282	4371
35283	4375
35284	4376
35285	4377
35286	4379
35287	4380
35288	4383
35289	4384
35290	4385
35291	4391
35292	4396
35293	4400
35294	4402
35295	4404
35296	4406
35297	4407
35298	4408
35299	4409
35300	4414
35301	4425
35302	4429
35303	4430
35304	4438
35305	4446
35306	4447
35307	4448
35308	4449
35309	4452
35310	4462
35311	4464
35312	4467
35313	4468
35314	4477
35315	4483
35316	4488
35317	4489
35318	4492
35319	4502
35320	4523
35321	4593
35322	4594
35323	4597
35324	4613
35325	4616
35326	4623
35327	4624
35328	4625
35329	4799
35330	4801
35331	4815
35332	4860
35333	4977
35334	5012
35335	5169
35336	5588
35337	5633
35338	5655
35339	5658
35340	5661
35341	5662
35342	5680
35343	5682
35344	5711
35345	5729
35346	5735
35347	6264
35348	6553

Lot 661

35349	4217
35350	4434
35351	4479
35352	4534
35353	4810
35354	4833
35355	4839
35356	4840
35357	4841
35358	4842
35359	4870
35360	4882
35361	4894
35362	4904
35363	4926
35364	4940
35365	4948
35366	4967
35367	4970
35368	4976
35369	4991
35370	4994
35371	5001
35372	5056
35373	5065

The general configuration followed the traditional Midland body style but it is mildly surprising that they continued to be built unchanged, well into the 1930s when most LMS carriage building had undergone considerable modernisation. In this, a parallel can be seen with the former Southern Railway which went on building many CCTs to a basic SECR design until BR days. We guess that in both cases, economy of cost was the driving force.

They lasted well but in 1959, a note appeared on D1871 to the effect that this type was no longer to work in passenger trains. They were mostly a few years older than D1872, though paradoxically, their underframes were newer which one would have thought would be the critical factor; even so, they were not finally to vanish for another five years or so. Furthermore, even after the last of D1872 had been withdrawn from BR capital stock in 1966, examples of both diagrams continued in departmental use for at least another 20 years and for all we know (written in 1990) there may still be a few lurking about! Thus, mindful of the needs of modellers, we have included two BR departmental views to supplement the ex-works and 'in traffic' examples.

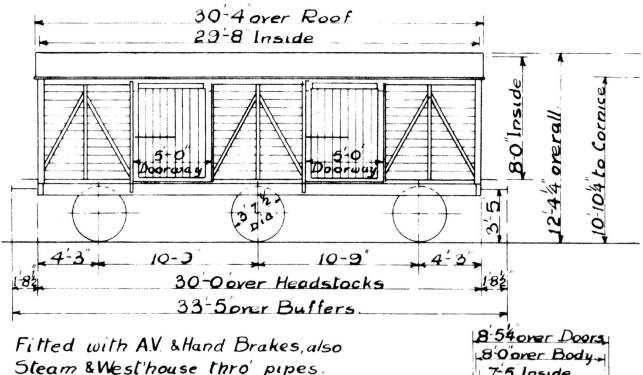

30'-4 over Roof
29'-8 Inside

5'-0" Doorway   5'-0" Doorway

3'-7½" Dia.

8'-0" Inside
12'-4¼" overall
10'-10¼" to Cornice

3'-5"

4'-3"   10'-3"   10'-9"   4'-3"
1'-8½"   30'-0 over Headstocks   1'-8½"
33'-5 over Buffers.

Fitted with A.V. & Hand Brakes, also Steam & West'house thro' pipes.
Capacity = 6 Tons.
Tare = 12 Tons.

FIGURE 13 Covered Combination Truck – LMS D1871 (LMS Drawing No. W1/945); Scale 4mm=1ft.

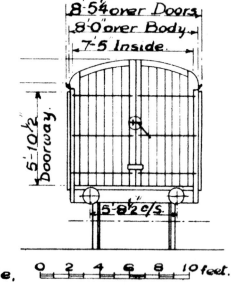

8'-5¾" over Doors.
8'-0" over Body.
7'-5 Inside.

5'-10½" Doorway.

5'-8½" c/s.

Plate 90 No. 5595, later 35058, of D1871, ex-works at Wolverton when new, clearly shows the full height end doors of this diagram and the fully lined paint scheme first given to these useful vehicles. Note the LMS 'wagon-style' buffer shanks and steel underframe. For some reason, it is branded to carry 8 Tons, not the 6 Tons of the official diagram.

Scale, 0 2 4 6 8 10 feet.

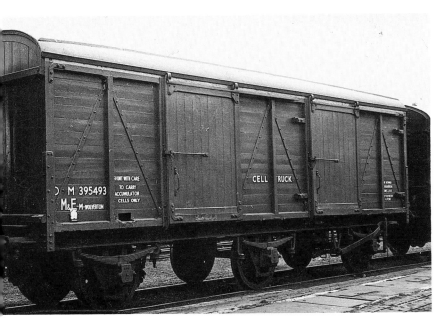

Plate 91 By amazing coincidence, this view shows the same vehicle as the previous picture, now modified to cell truck No. DM395493 for departmental use at Wolverton in 1965. The sides remain more or less unchanged but the end doors have been replaced by solid planks. The hole in the side of the vehicle above the LH wheel set was to allow any liquid spillage to escape from the floor inside, which was lead covered on these conversions. (R. J. Essery)

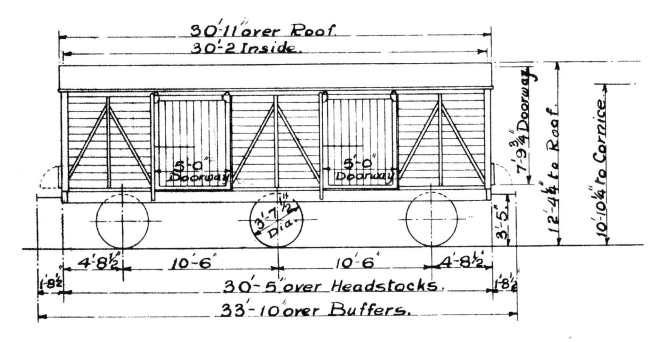

Fitted with A.V. & Hand Brakes, also West'house & Steam Thro' Pipes.
Capacity = 6 Tons.
Tare = 12 Tons.

✳ 5 vehicles Nos 35025-9 incl.
 Pr. Lot 35-1928.

FIGURE 14 Covered Combination Truck – LMS D1872 (LMS Drawing No. 13/1096); Scale 4mm=1ft.

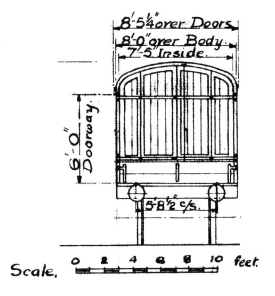

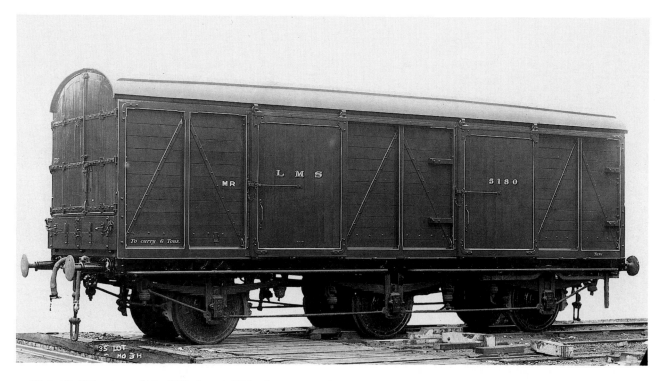

Plate 92 This view of No.5180, later 35029, shows one of the very early D1872 vehicles, the last of Lot 35 in fact, and clearly reveals its ex-LNWR chassis. It also shows the different arrangement of the bottom end-door on this diagram. It seems likely that this drop-down flap was considered rather more practical in terms of the end-loading of road vehicles directly from the loading bay.

Plate 93 No. 5735 (later 35346) was built in 1932 as part of Lot 594. It is seen here brand new, ex-works and clearly by this time, full lining had been abandoned for this type, even in advance of the livery change. The underframe is now ex-MR, the buffer bodies and axleguards (plus absence of tie-bars) being the main visual clues. This variant seems to have been rather less common than those with ex-LNWR chassis but may have embraced the whole of Lot 594 (see also Plate 96). On the original print, 8 Tons can again be seen marked as the load limit.

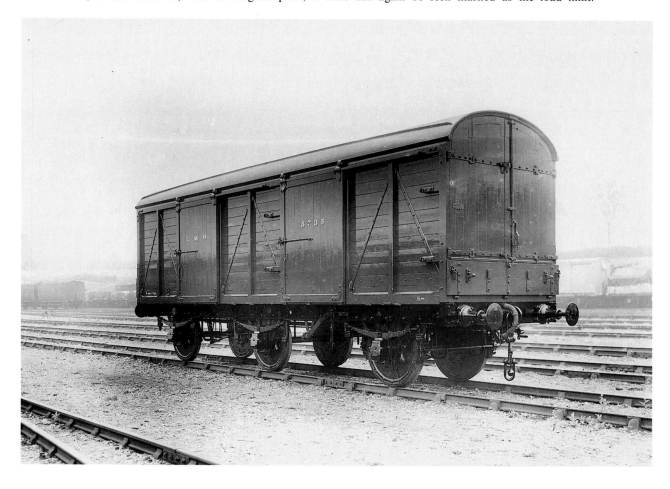

Plate 94 We believe this D1872 vehicle to be in the LMS 3515x series, thus being from Lot 406. It was clearly in unlined crimson when seen at Renfrew in August 1946. Again note the ex-LNWR chassis: clearly identified by its outside mounted axleguards, round-bar tie rods and long brake lever. It has, however, lost its full length side-steps. (A. G. Ellis)

Plate 95 The supply of ex-LNWR underframes lasted until, at least, the end of Lot 746, built in 1934. This is No. M35423 at Wolverton in April 1967, shortly after withdrawal. (Authors' Collection)

Covered Combination Truck – D1929

This starkly utilitarian, but by any standards far more modern style of CCT, was the last LMS essay in this field – perhaps surprisingly, given the obvious use which the company made of the type. This time, though the body remained much the same general size and shape as its predecessor, save for having but one pair of hinged side doors rather than two single sliders, it was of far cleaner design and mounted on a thoroughly modern long wheelbase four-wheel steel underframe which would have looked by no means out of place amongst the modern four-wheelers of the 1980s and 1990s, now so familiar.

Fortunately, we have a good spread of views of the type which lasted well into the 1970s, though we cannot offer a date for the last withdrawal. As far as we are aware, they were always plain red (LMS and BR in turn), although the first LMS insignia were slightly variable. We append two official views, from which it would seem that Lot 860 of 1935 had the correct unshaded sans-serif carriage pattern numerals but that some (maybe all) of Lot 999 received the pre-1933 shaded scroll numerals in 1937 (using up old transfers?) with the insignia positioning 'reversed'. Whether these pictures typify the whole of each batch we cannot say, but a further picture, also appended, shows an example of Lot 860 in 1938 with shaded sans-serif numerals in a third position. We think it unlikely that a full repaint would have been given to such a vehicle within three years but a re-arrangement of insignia without repainting is possible.

Summary details of the design are given in Table 7.

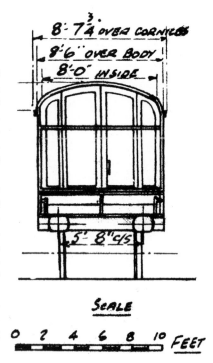

SCALE

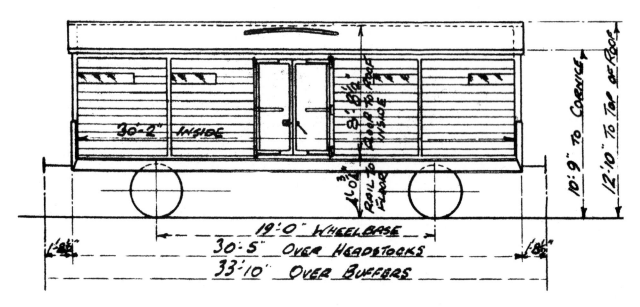

FIGURE 15 Covered Combination Truck – LMS D1929 (LMS Drawing No. 2102/2102A); Scale 4mm=1ft

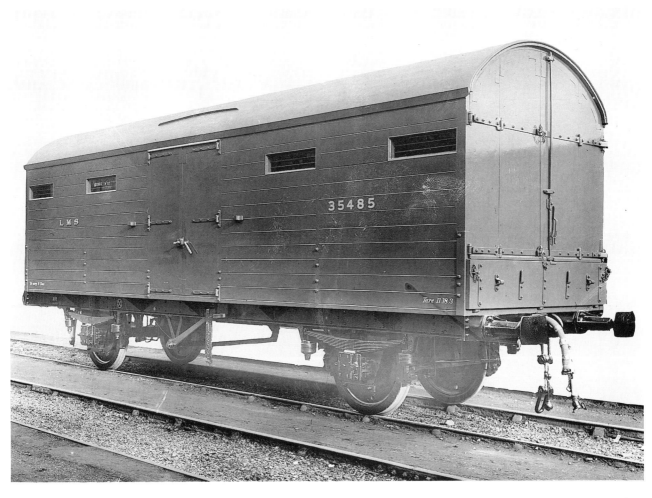

Plate 97 No. 35485 of Lot 860, ex-works in 1935 in plain crimson livery with the smaller NPCS-style 'LMS' and conventional unshaded sans-serif carriage numerals.

Plate 98 No. 35590 of Lot 860, ex-works in 1937 with the pre-1933 style numerals and 'reversed' insignia positioning.

Plates 99 and 100 No. 35493 was a Lot 860 example with shaded sans-serif numerals when photographed in October 1938. The insignia are now at a much lower level and again 'reversed'. We also offer a close-up of the brake gear for the benefit of modellers. (A. E. West)

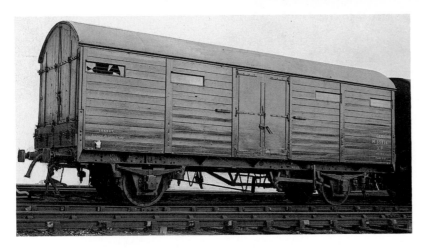

Plate 101 in BR days, the marking of the D1929 series of CCTs also varied slightly. This is No. M35556, soon after Nationalisation still displaying its LHS markings in LMS style. (Authors' Collection)

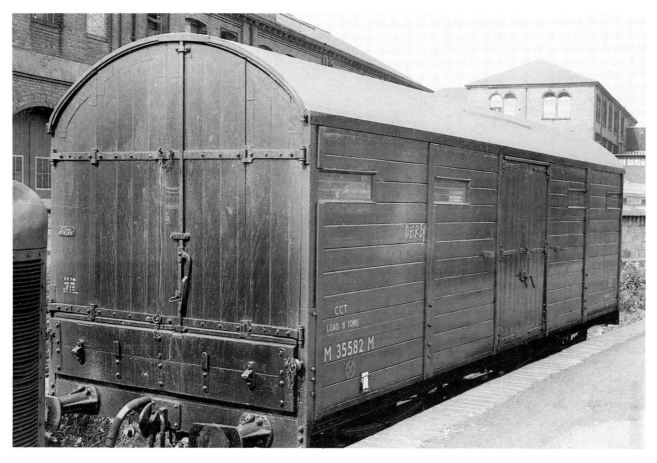

Plate 102 Conventional BR markings were seen on maroon-painted No. M35582M at Derby in September 1964. (R. J. Essery)

Plate 103 This final view of D1929 shows an end-door modification, which we think was not universally applied, along with Eastern Region 'ownership' markings on the running number: E35510M at Washwood Heath in October 1964.

(Authors' Collection)

Motor Car Van – D2032

This design, in effect a modified CCT with higher 'arched' roof, was built as part of Lot 35 (D1872 – above) but from the diagram dimensions, appears to have used yet another variety of second hand underframe, the stated 20ft wheelbase being different from either D1871 or D1872. We say 'appears' because this is one of very few LMS coaching stock designs for which we have been unable to trace a single photograph of any kind. Judging from the diagram, however, they were probably a combination of something like the roof profile of D2026 (below) with the body style of the outside framed D1872 (above) with extra door bracing.

They lasted until 1964 but, as with D1871, an instruction that they were not to work in passenger trains was issued in September 1958. Summary details are given in Table 7 and the 1933 renumbering details are as follows:

Lot 35 (part)

New No.	Old No.		
35000	4631	35013	4707
35001	4666	35014	4711
35002	4669	35015	4715
35003	4672	35016	4730
35004	4674	35017	4731
35005	4682	35018	4732
35006	4683	35019	4733
35007	4685	35020	4734
35008	4687	35021	4735
35009	4695	35022	4736
35010	4699	35023	4737
35011	4702	35024	4738
35012	4704		

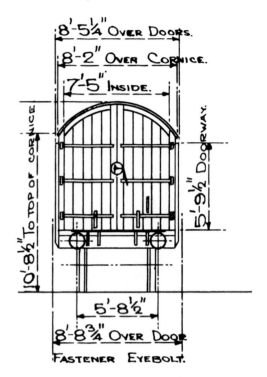

FIGURE 16 Motor Car Van – LMS D2032 (LMS Drawing No. W2/1206); Scale 4mm=1ft.

FITTED WITH A.V. & HAND BRAKE.
Also WESTINGHOUSE PIPE & THRO'
STEAM PIPE.
CARRYING CAPACITY:- 6 TONS.
CODE:- M.R.

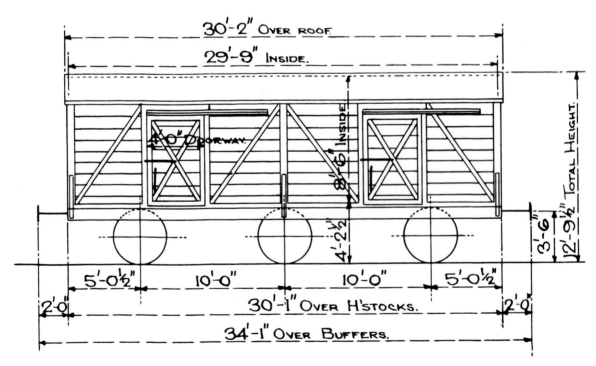

Motor Car Van – D2042

Originally allocated D1868 in the freight stock book, this extraordinary and experimental 'one-off' was later put into the NPCS book as D2042, probably when rebuilt to the form shown at Figure 17. Built in 1925 as No. 500, conceivably as part of the LMS 'all-steel' experiments of the mid-1920s, it became No. 37200 under the 1933 scheme. When this number was wanted for the Swindon-built Lot 1770 of 1956 (D2026 – below), the van was again renumbered M34999. It remained a solitary example but, for a prototype, it must be considered as having had a good innings, not being withdrawn until it was 40 years old. As the pictures reveal, the vehicle was subject to a major side-door modification (date unknown but probably quite soon after building), and the diagram appended shows it in this later form.

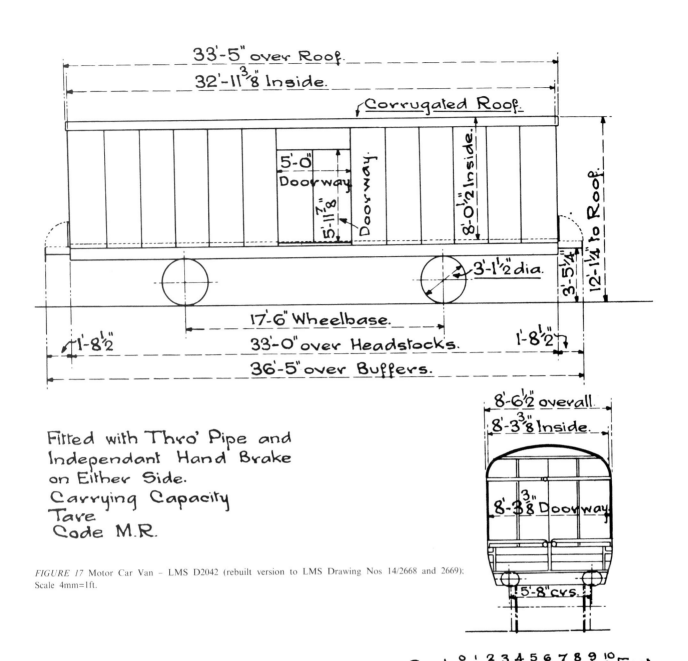

33'-5" over Roof.

32'-11 3/8 Inside.

Corrugated Roof.

5'-0" Doorway

5'-11 7/8"

Doorway

8'-0 1/2 Inside.

12'-1 1/4 to Roof.

3'-5 1/4

3'-1 1/2 dia.

17'-6" Wheelbase.

33'-0" over Headstocks.

36'-5" over Buffers.

1'-8 1/2

1'-8 1/2

Fitted with Thro' Pipe and
Independant Hand Brake
on Either Side.
Carrying Capacity
Tare
Code M.R.

8'-6 1/2 overall.

8'-3 3/8 Inside.

8'-3 3/8 Doorway.

5'-8" crs.

FIGURE 17 Motor Car Van – LMS D2042 (rebuilt version to LMS Drawing Nos 14/2668 and 2669); Scale 4mm=1ft.

Scale 0 1 2 3 4 5 6 7 8 9 10 Feet.

Plate 104 No. 500 in as built condition, 1925. The livery was crimson with a fine yellow line round the extreme outer edges, probably with a narrow black border outside.

Plate 105 This view of No. 500 in its original configuration with all doors open clearly indicates that part of the experiment was related to the matter of side-loading, a common enough practice on the modern railway, but rather rare in those days.

Plate 106 The rebuilt form of the vehicle as No. M34999 is shown in this view at Birmingham New Street in September 1958. (J. E. Cull)

Motor Car Van – D2026

This design was introduced in 1938 when 150 were built by Metro-Cammell, using a similar modern four-wheel chassis to the D1929 CCTs – above. Building resumed after the formation of BR and, as stated in the introduction, the final Swindon-built series received Western Region Lot numbers. When the LMS examples came out, they were given the new freight style insignia (small sans-serif characters in the lower left corner) and we think the vans may have been finished either in the new bauxite colour freight livery or in the varnished undercoat style mentioned in Chapter 5. Confirmation is lacking but they do not seem to have ever been crimson lake.

Summary details are given in Table 7 and, like the long wheelbase D1929 vehicles, they lasted well into the 1970s.

Right: **Plate 107** The pioneer example of the first example of D2026 when built, No. 37000, showing the freight style markings.

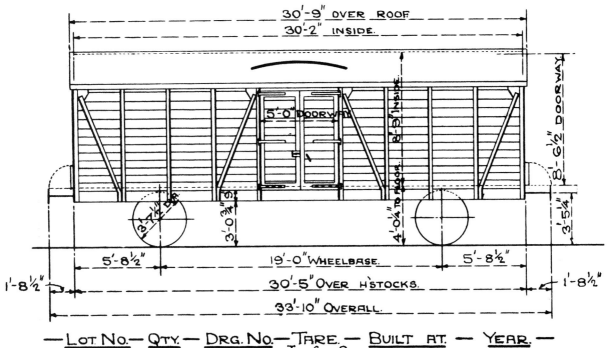

— Lot. No. —	Qty. —	Drg. No. —	Tare. —	Built at. —	Year. —
			T. C. Q.		
1154	150	13/2665	12 - 0 - 0	Metro-Cammell	1938.

FITTED WITH A.V. & HAND BRAKES.

FITTED WITH THRO' STEAM PIPE.

CARRYING CAPACITY:- 8 TONS.

CODE:- M.R.

SCALE. 1 0 1 2 4 6 8 10 feet.

FIGURE 18 Motor Car Van – LMS D2026 (LMS Drawing No. 13/2665); Scale 4mm=1ft.

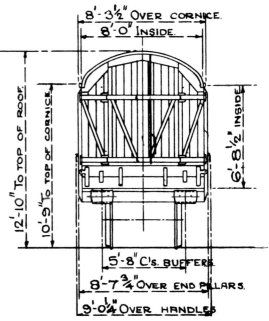

Plate 108 Opposite side view of No. 37037 of the first LMS batch showing the handbrake detail. As with D1929, above, these vans had 'clipped' buffer heads to allow the end flaps to assume proper position for loading and unloading. (A. E. West)

Plate 109 This close-up view of BR-built No. W37238M at Worcester Shrub Hill in 1967 is principally of interest in showing the very comprehensive dimensional branding which BR applied to these vehicles. (J. E. Cull)

Right: **Plate 110** We know of no other views of this type save for this excellent official picture of No. 4853 (later 44302) when new at Wolverton in 1929. The livery was crimson lake with the simplest form of the 'full' pre-1933 NPCS livery: a modest amount of fine yellow lining only round the main panel areas. Again note the 'clipped' tops to the buffer heads to facilitate end-loading.

Aeroplane Van – D1880

These large and impressive vehicles, built to almost the maximum extent of the structure gauge, were rather handsome of aspect and were of patently Midland derivation in design terms – right down to their second-hand underframes, recovered from withdrawn ex-MR Clayton 40ft bogie non-corridor carriages but, it would seem, given LMS wagon-pattern buffer shanks. The five 1929 Wolverton examples survived for almost 40 years, the high roof no doubt proving useful for accommodating large components, though whether these were *always* aeroplane parts is probably doubtful. Summary details are given in Table 7 and the 1933 renumbering details were as follows

Lot 299		Lot 407	
New No.	Old No.	44301	4826
44300	821	44302	4853
		44303	4872
		44304	4881
		44305	4988

FIGURE 19 Aeroplane Van – LMS D1880 (LMS Drawing No. 12/22); Scale 4mm=1ft.

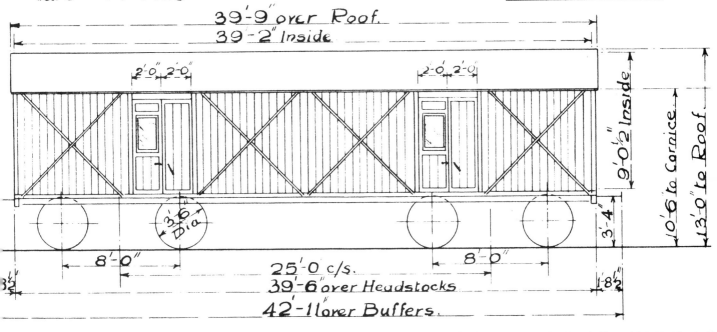

A.V. & Hand Brakes.
Thro' Steam Pipe.
Capacity =
Tare = 17 Tons.

Scale, 0 2 4 6 8 10 feet.

8'10" over Roof.
8'-0" Inside.
8'-7" over Body.
9'-1" over Handles.
5'8½" c/s.

39'-9" over Roof.
39'-2" Inside.
2'-0" 2'-0"
9'-0½" Inside
10'-6" to Cornice
13'-0" to Roof
3'-4"
3'6" Dia
8'-0"
8'-0"
25'-0 c/s.
39'-6" over Headstocks
42'-1" over Buffers.
1'8½"

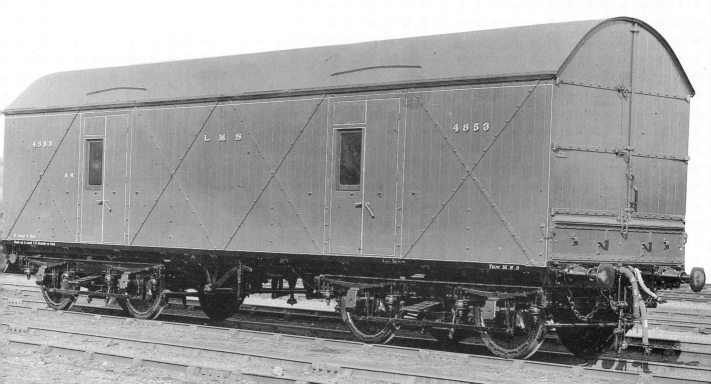

Chapter 8 – Bogie Covered Vans and Open Carriage Trucks

LUGGAGE, PARCELS AND SCENERY VANS

With the exception of the Aeroplane Van mentioned on p.91 this group contains all the end door *bogie* vehicles built to LMS diagrams. In fact, it would be more logical for the LMS to have included its one Aeroplane Van diagram in the Luggage/Parcels Van section of the diagram book since this latter section includes one diagram annotated as 'suitable for aeroplane traffic'. However, this was not the case.

Seven LMS diagrams are covered under the general heading of Luggage, Parcels and Scenery. All were bogie vehicles and in terms of general styling, only two variants were to be seen; semi-flush sided steel panelled types and outside framed wooden bodied designs. Those described as 'Luggage and Parcels' were all of the steel panelled type while the scenery vans were wood bodied. There were three diagrams for each type and the seventh diagram to be considered was another wooden bodied vehicle, this time called simply 'Parcels' Van.

The Luggage and parcels vans all post-dated Stanier's arrival on the LMS scene and, in consequence, shared a great deal in common with the gangwayed full brakes of contemporary age. They had fairly orthodox Period III features but there was no tumblehome and, of course, no gangway connection to the adjacent vehicles.

The standard design was D1870. This was a 42ft vehicle and was extensively multiplied between 1933 and 1937, eventually totalling 240 units. The early examples were given full livery and with their generally coach-like styling, looked very much at home in passenger trains. One of these coaches (37706) was altered in 1937 by fitting steel floor, stronger springs and tethering hooks for the conveyance of elephants! A less light-hearted version of the design was the D2023 version which was built to 13ft 0in height and annotated not to exceed 3ft 6in wheels. Ten of these were built and were rated as suitable for aeroplane traffic.

The final luggage and parcels van was D1933. This was a 45ft version of the standard 42ft vehicle for the simple reason that the coaches were built on the 45ft frames of ex-LNWR open scenery trucks.

The bogie parcels van diagram and the three theatrical scenery diagrams can be considered together since they shared a common exterior styling which resembled the six-wheel CCTs – Chapter 7. All four diagrams also shared another feature, namely an utterly bewildering variety of lengths. Normally, the LMS issued a new diagram for a different length of vehicle but in these cases, several lengths found their way onto one diagram. Some of the vehicles are officially recorded as having second hand underframes and it is the authors' belief that all, in fact were built on older underframes. Further confusing the matter is the fact that the diagrams themselves do not seem to indicate any logical pattern to the segregation into four separate 'designs', except in the matter of overall height where there was some consistency.

The so called 'parcels vans' were four in number to D1869. Three separate lengths were involved (!) and the vehicles do not seem to have differed a great deal from the three 'Theatrical Scenery Truck' diagrams (D1875/1881/1882). The latter three were all much alike but two were annotated as Westinghouse fitted as well as vacuum braked. Seven different lengths appear on D1875 and two each on the other two theatrical diagrams. It is not even possible to generalise very much about the styling of the vehicles since all were a little different. Two coaches from D1875 are illustrated and the diagram of these vehicles infers that both were built to the same drawing – how this could be is anyone's guess!

An attempt has been made in Table 8 to cover all these variations but, as will be apparent, there is little pattern to any of it.

OPEN CARRIAGE TRUCKS

At the grouping, the LMS acquired more than enough open carriage trucks to satisfy its needs for almost 20 years. Most of the time, these vehicles would be standing waiting for traffic anyway. The only LMS diagram of the type was for a four-wheel design (D2027) which was somewhat longer than most pre-group four-wheel types although not as long as some of the six and eight-wheel pre-group examples.

TABLE 8. SUMMARY OF LUGGAGE, PARCELS AND SCENERY VANS

Diag	Lot	Qty	Date	Wt Built		Dimensions (LxWxH)	Running Numbers	Withdrawals First	Last
Luggage and Parcels Vans									
1870	690	50	1933	Wolverton	24T		37700-37749	12/64	
	750	25	1934	Wolverton	24T		37750-37774	12/65	
	751	25	1934	Wolverton	24T		37775-37799	2/65	Many
	848	50	1935	Derby	24T	42'x8'6"x12'4⅝"	37800-37849	11/65	extant
	863	25	1935	Wolverton	24T		37850-37874	3/66	(1969)
	864	25	1935	Wolverton	24T		37875-37899	4/66	
	1050	40	1937	Wolverton	24T		37900-37939	3/64	
2023	1051	10	1938	Wolverton	22T	42'x8'6"x13'0"	44306-44315*	11/65	11/67
1933	793	15	1934	Wolverton	25T	45'x8'6"x12'4⅝"	38253-38267†	4/64	extant (1969)

* Numbered as Aeroplane Vans.
† Converted from ex-LNWR open scenery trucks.

Parcels Van									
1869	250	4	1926	Derby	see below	see below	34500-34503	10/54	7/56

Theatrical Scenery Trucks

1875	134	10	1925	Derby	see below	see below	37500-37506 37530-37532	4/42 2/54	6/55 5/56
	160	20	1925/6	Derby	see below	see below	37507-37512 37538-37540 37543-37553	1/52 5/55 10/53	7/54 10/57 4/62
1882	308	9	1927	Derby	see below	see below	37513-37519 } 37541-37542 }	1/52	4/55 2/54
1881	400	15	1929	Derby	17T	see below	37420-37529 37533-37537	10/53 12/44	7/56 11/58

Diagram differences, etc., for Parcels and Theatrical Vehicles

Running Number	*Diagram*	*Dimensions* (LxWxH)	*Wt*	*Other remarks*
34500-1	1869	42'5"x8'5$\frac{1}{4}$"x12'4$\frac{1}{4}$"	16T	All four rated 8T capacity and vacuum fitted only.
34502	1869	44'5"x8'5$\frac{1}{4}$"x12'4$\frac{1}{4}$"	17T	
34503	1869	53'5"x8'5$\frac{1}{4}$"x12'4$\frac{1}{4}$"	21T	
37500-12	1875	42'5"x8'5$\frac{1}{4}$"x12'4$\frac{1}{4}$"	16T	Vacuum fitted only.
37513-19	1882	42'5"x8'5$\frac{1}{4}$"x12'6$\frac{3}{4}$"	16T	Dual fitted.
37520-9	1881	42'9"x8'5$\frac{1}{4}$"x12'11"	17T	Dual fitted.
37530-2	1875	44'5"x8'5$\frac{1}{2}$"x12'4$\frac{1}{4}$"	NK	Vacuum fitted only.
37533-7	1881	44'5"x8'5$\frac{1}{4}$"x12'1$\frac{1}{4}$"	17T	Dual fitted.
37538-9	1875	47'5"x8'5$\frac{1}{4}$"x12'4$\frac{1}{4}$"	NK	Vacuum fitted only.
37540	1875	49'5"x8'5$\frac{1}{4}$"x12'4$\frac{1}{4}$"	NK	Vacuum fitted only.
37541-2	1882	53'5"x8'5$\frac{1}{4}$"x12'6$\frac{3}{4}$"	21T	Dual fitted.
37543-9	1875	54'0"x8'5$\frac{1}{4}$"x12'4$\frac{1}{4}$"	21T	Vacuum fitted only.
37550-2	1875	57'0"x8'5$\frac{1}{4}$"x12'4$\frac{1}{4}$"	21T	Vacuum fitted only.
37553	1875	57'11"x8'5$\frac{1}{4}$"x12'4$\frac{1}{4}$"	21T	Vacuum fitted only.

N.K. Weight not known. D1875 gives 16T and 21T as the weight for these vehicles but there were several intermediate weights between the two extremes.

Luggage and Parcels Vans – D1870

These extremely versatile vehicles were built over a five year period and the final survivors lasted until the 1970s. They were the first of the purely LMS design NPCS vehicles to display genuine 'passenger carriage' lineaments and their construction first overlapped and then followed on without break from the large numbers of six-wheel CCTs to D1871/1872 which we considered in the previous chapter. For all practical purposes, they were used for much the same sort of work and the later designation 'General Utility Van' (GUV) has always seemed to us a rather more accurate description of their function.

They were very much in the 'Stanier' carriage family and it may well be that it was he who determined that this type of vehicle should move away from the old fashioned outside framed styling hitherto favoured. At all events, their livery always reflected their genuine passenger rated status. The first 100 from Wolverton were all put into service in the fully lined style and the simplified livery came in from Lot 848 onwards. We have located a good selection of ex-works official views and summary details are to be found in Table 8.

Plate 111 This view shows an early Lot 690 example of D1870, No. 37714. The full livery and 'standard' insignia placing should be noted.

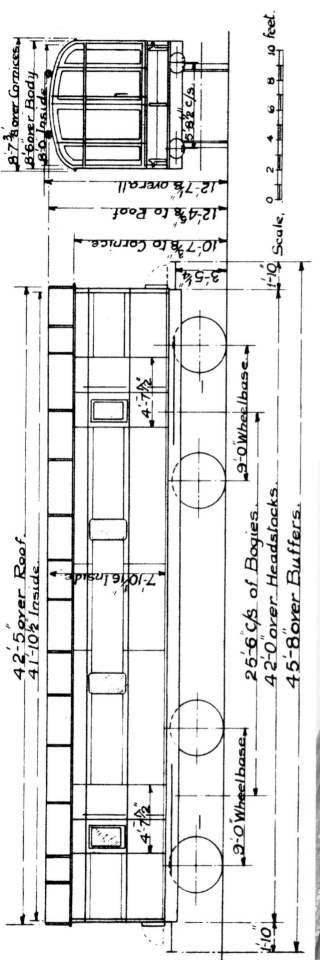

Fitted with A.V.Brakes.
2 tiers of shelves on each side.
Electric Lighting.
Capacity = 8 Tons
Tare = 24-6-2
Code = P.M.R.

8'-7⅜"over Cornices.
8'-6"over Body
8'-0"Inside
5'-8½"c/s.
12'-7⅞"overall
12'-4⅜"to Roof
10'-7⅞"to Cornice.
3'-5¼"
1'-10 Scale.
0 2 4 6 8 10 feet.
Scale,

42'-5"over Roof.
41'-10½"Inside.
7'-10⅝"Inside
25'-6"c/s of Bogies.
42'-0"over Headstacks.
45'-8"over Buffers.
4'-7½"
9'-0"Wheelbase.
4'-7½"
9'-0"Wheelbase.
1'-10

FIGURE 20 Luggage and Parcels Van – LMS D1870 (LMS Drawing Nos. D14/2172A for Lots 690/750/751) and (D14/3471 for the remainder); Scale 4mm=1ft.

Plate 112 We have included this second and almost identical view of the last of the full-liveried examples, No. 37799 of Lot 751, to show the slight changes which had by then taken place in the design. Note particularly the introduction of a hand brake wheel just below the solebar and the very slightly 'clipped' tops to the buffer heads. These changes probably commenced with Lot 750.

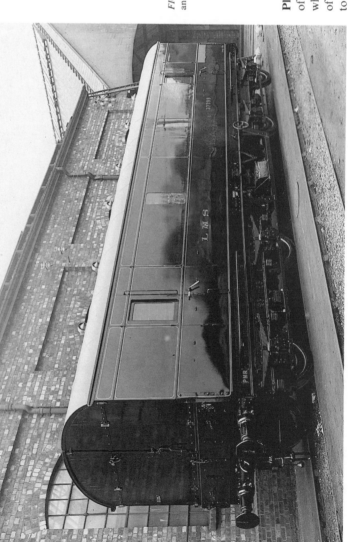

Plate 113 No. 37801 was an early example from Lot 848 with simple livery but otherwise little changed save for shell roof ventilators, a feature obviously introduced with this Lot. This view shows the cell box side; note that the hand brake wheel appeared at one end only of these vehicles but on both sides.

Plate 114 A few further changes had appeared by the time No. 37914 of Lot 1050 appeared in 1937. The buffer heads are much bigger and have a larger 'clipped' portion, the bogies are now of welded construction and shaded numerals have appeared on the side. We presume that these changes came in with this Lot.

Plate 115 The lack of gloss on the rather grimy plain red BR livery of No. M37794M, seen at Birmingham New Street on 28th August 1956, serves to emphasise both the raised beading and general panel construction of these familiar vehicles. (J. E. Cull)

Luggage and Parcels Van – D2023

Described as 'Suitable for Aeroplane Traffic', these ten vehicles, obviously derived from D1870, gave considerably more headroom on the track centreline and the note on the diagram concerning wheel diameter was certainly warranted. Movable padded bars at floor level were provided with tethering straps, no doubt very necessary when large yet somewhat fragile fabric-covered components such as fuselages, tail units and wings were carried. The date of introduction (at the start of the pre-war re-armament period) and their numbering in the 44XXX series after D1880 (Chapter 7), does suggest that aircraft components were their most likely loads in the early days but we have no doubt that they were used for other purposes too whenever bulky loads were to be conveyed.

They were always painted red (LMS and BR respectively), none of them, we think, having lasted long enough to become BR blue. Interestingly, they were slightly outlived by the earlier D1880 series – Chapter 7. Summary details are given in Table 8.

Plate 116 LMS No. 44307 is seen here, as built in 1938. Note the general similarity in shape and proportion to D1880 (Chapter 7).

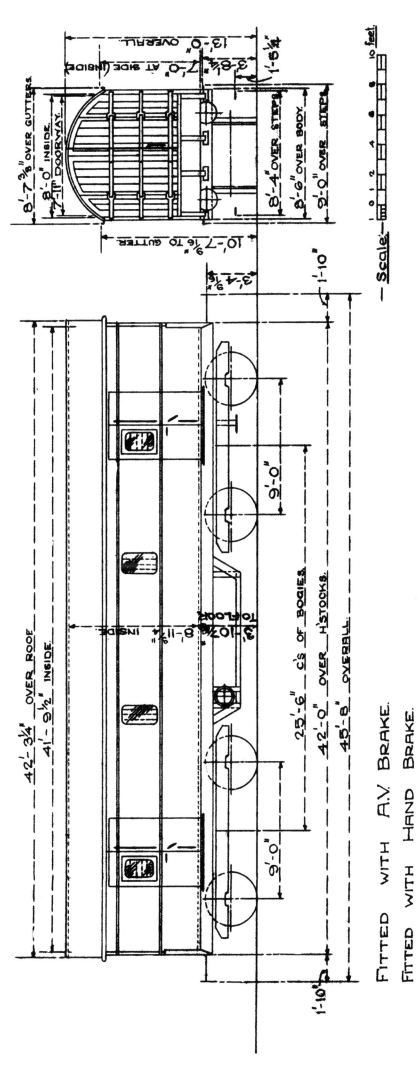

FITTED WITH A.V. BRAKE.

FITTED WITH HAND BRAKE.

FITTED WITH THROUGH STEAM PIPE.

CARRYING CAPACITY. 8 TONS.

TARE: 22 TONS.

CODE: A.R.

WHEELS NOT TO EXCEED 3·6"DIA.ON TREAD.

FIGURE 21 Luggage and Parcels Van – LMS D2023 (LMS Drawing No. 143032);
Scale 4mm=1ft.

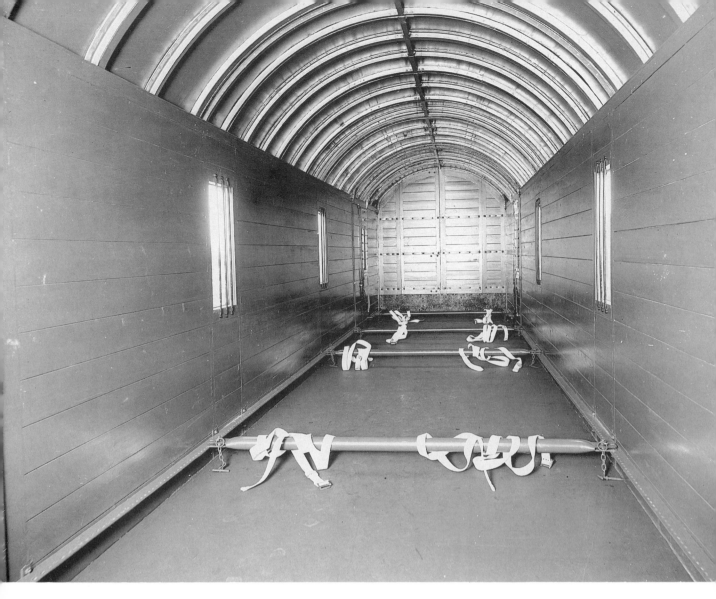

Plate 117 Interior view of No. 44307, showing the padded bars on the floor and the tethering straps.

Plate 118 No. M44315M was photographed in plain red BR livery in 1965, soon before withdrawal but still in remarkably good condition.

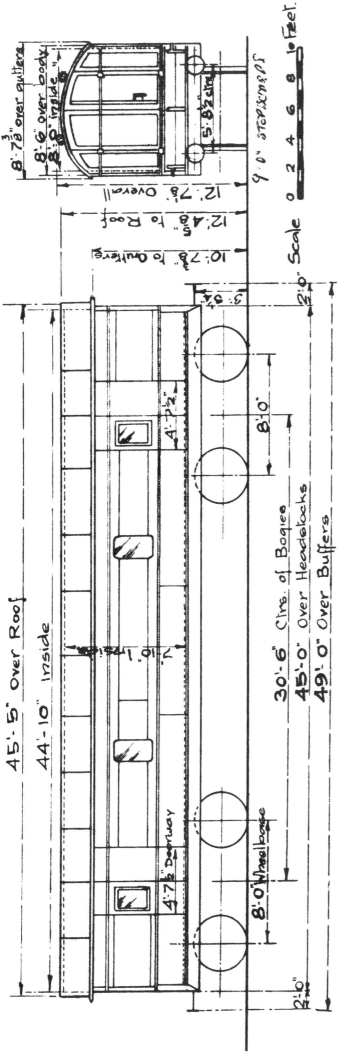

FIGURE 22 Luggage and Parcels Van – LMS D1933 (LMS Drawing No. 13/2053);
Scale 4mm=1ft.

Luggage and Parcels Van – D1933

Pursuing its customary policy of re-using serviceable underframes, the LMS in 1934 put new Stanier style bodies onto fifteen recovered 45ft chassis from open scenery trucks. They were otherwise identical in configuration to D1870 (above). As far as we know, the LMS took no official pictures and they also seem to have escaped the attention of other photographers, unless readers know differently! We cannot therefore offer any views but we have no reason to believe that they were given anything other than the simplified LMS livery, followed by BR styles in turn. Summary details are given in Table 8.

66

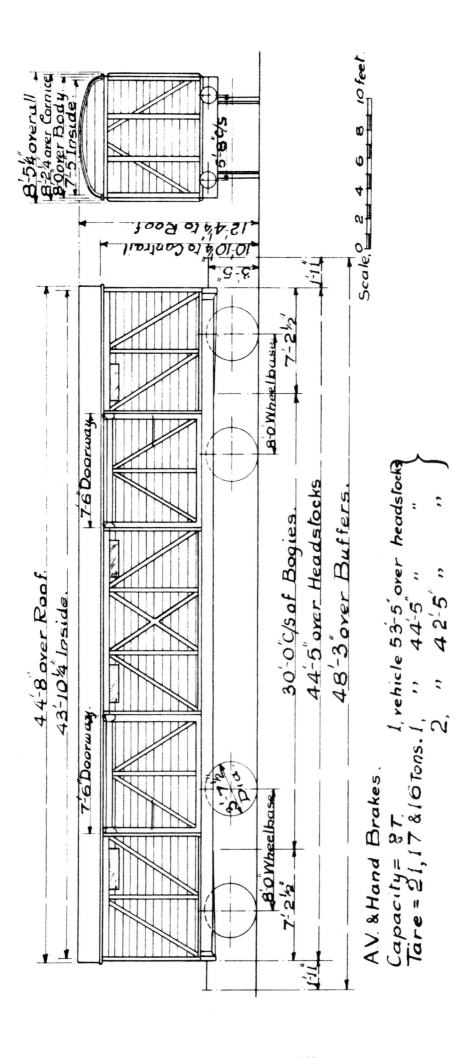

AV. & Hand Brakes.

Capacity = 8T.

Tare = 21, 17 & 16 Tons.

8'-5¼" overall
8'-2¼" over Cornice
8'-0" over Body
7'-5" Inside

5'-8½"

12'-4½" to Roof.

10'-10½" to Contrail

3'-5"

1'-11"

44'-8" over Roof.

43'-10¼" Inside.

7'-6" Doorway.

7'-6" Doorway.

8'-0" Wheelbase

7'-2½"

8'-0" Wheelbase

7'-2½"

3'-7½" Dia.

30'-0" C/s of Bogies.

44'-5" over Headstocks.

48'-3" over Buffers.

1'-11"

Scale, 0 2 4 6 8 10 feet

1, vehicle 53'-5" over headstocks
1, " 44'-5" "
2, " 42'-5" " "

FIGURE 23 Bogie Parcels Van – LMS D1869 (LMS Drawing No. 13/536); Scale 4mm=1ft. The length quoted suggests ex-MR 45ft bogie stock as the origin of the underframes.

Bogie Parcels Vans and Theatrical Scenery Trucks – D1869/D1875/D1882/D1881

We have grouped these interesting diagrams together since, as stated in the introduction to this chapter, they all seem to have been built to a common philosophy – not that we can quite work it out! The parcels van diagram (D1869) was distinguished from the others by virtue of its lack of end loading doors but otherwise, all shared the one common factor of being built to a variety of lengths on recovered second hand underframes and displaying broadly 'Midland' outside framed body styling.

We include all four diagrams and let them mostly speak for themselves. As far as we can judge, the only reason for having three different 'Theatrical' diagrams was to differentiate the various height variations – conceivably a matter of rather more importance than their length when assessing suitability for conveying bulky scenic items; but this is only speculation on our part. We suspect that all four types were used for broadly similar work but have been hampered in our researches by a total lack of photographic coverage other than that offered. Given the various lengths etc., we feel certain that there must have been many detail differences and if readers know more, we will try to include any further information in one of the two future volumes in this series.

Summary details are given in Table 8 and the 1933 renumbering details are listed below. In this context, we cannot give renumbering details for D1869, this being one of the very few pages missing from our copy of the 1933 list. It is also perhaps quite typical of these curious diagrams that even the 1933 numbers are somewhat randomly scattered between the types (see also notes to Table 8).

D1875

Lot 134

New No.	Old No.
37500	6535
37501	6565
37502	6584
37503	6593
37504	6595
37505	6597
37506	6632
37530	6516
37531	6525
37532	6526

Lot 160

37507	50
37508	46
37509	282
37510	310
37511	319
37512	504

37538	274
37539	300
37540	323
37543	232
37544	246
37545	271
37546	250
37547	264
37548	267
37549	294
37550	62
37551	68
37552	269
37553	329

D1882

Lot 308

New No.	Old No.
37513	3917
37514	3967
37515	4611

37516	4668
37517	4692
37518	4700
37519	4714
37541	4832
37542	4941

D1881

Lot 400

New No.	Old No.
37520	1881
37521	1882
37522	1887
37523	4760
37524	4766
37525	4767
37526	4768
37527	4769
37528	4770
37529	4771

Plate 119 Theatrical Scenery Truck No. 6516, later 37530, to D1875, a 44ft 5in vehicle on an ex-MR underframe. This vehicle conforms very closely with the diagram details.

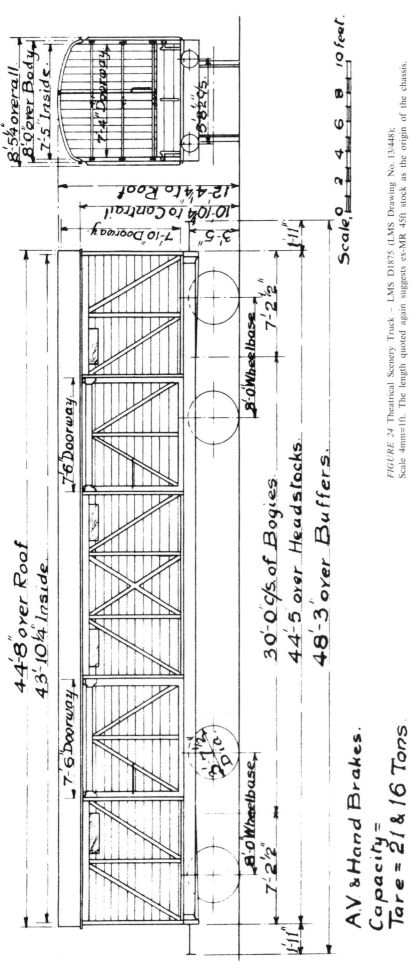

44'-8" over Roof
43'-10¼" Inside

7'-6" Doorway

7'-6" Doorway

8'-0" Wheelbase
7'-2½"

D 3'-1½"

8'-0" Wheelbase
7'-2½"

30'-0" c/s of Bogies.
44'-5" over Headstocks.
48'-3" over Buffers.

A.V. & Hand Brakes.
Capacity =
Tare = 21 & 16 Tons.

8'-5¼" overall
8'-0" over Body
7'-5" Inside

7'-4" Doorway

3'-8¼" c/s.

12'-4¼" to Roof
10'-10½" to Cantrail.
7'-10" Doorway
3'-5"
7'-2½"
1'-11"

Scale. 0 2 4 6 8 10 feet.

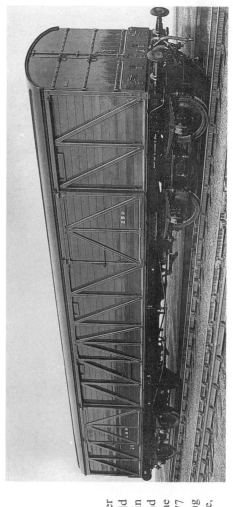

FIGURE 24 Theatrical Scenery Truck – LMS D1875 (LMS Drawing No. 13/448): Scale 4mm=1ft. The length quoted again suggests ex-MR 45ft stock as the origin of the chassis.

Plate 120 This example does not conform with anything on the diagram! Its running number (250, later 37546) puts it onto D1875 – but how it could be built to the same drawing as the previous example is difficult to explain. This is in fact a much longer vehicle than is included on any of the three theatrical diagrams and was one of quite a number of 'long' examples whose dimensions do not appear on the diagram but which we list at Table 8. However, contrary to our comment in the 1977 book, it displays an ex-LNWR underframe, not MR as stated, and is recorded as being of 54ft length. Ex-MR chassis of similar dimensions were 53ft 5in long and in any case, the buffer shanks are quite late LNWR pattern.

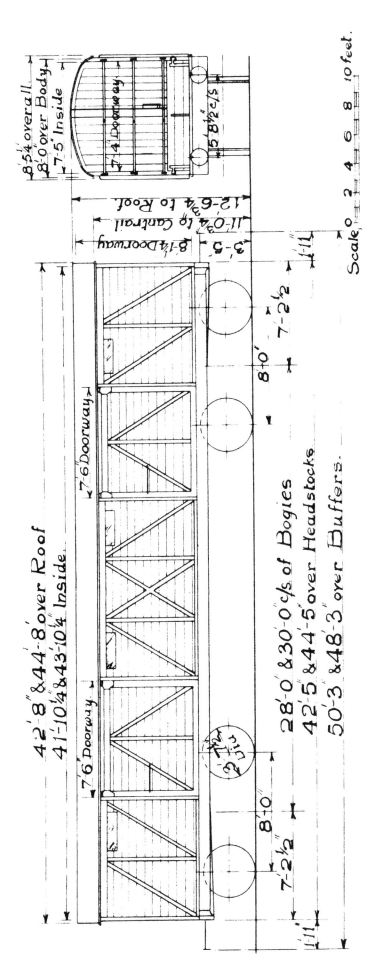

A.V. & Hand Brakes
Steam & West'house Thro' Pipes.
Capacity =
Tare = 21 & 16 Tons.

FIGURE 25 Theatrical Scenery Truck – LMS D1882 (LMS Drawing No. 13/706);
Scale 4mm=1ft. The quoted lengths indicate ex-MR 43ft and 45ft bogie stock underframes and we do *not* believe
the 50ft 3in over buffer dimension – we think it should be 46ft 3in!

Plate 121 The small centre panel of this vehicle tempts us to believe it is a 43ft example
from D1882 but we cannot be sure. There are faint signs of a running number at the
LH end. The indistinct two figure number at the top of the centre panel which could
be 62, cannot be a running number, for No. 62, later 37550, was a 57ft vehicle on an
ex-LNWR chassis! (Authors' Collection)

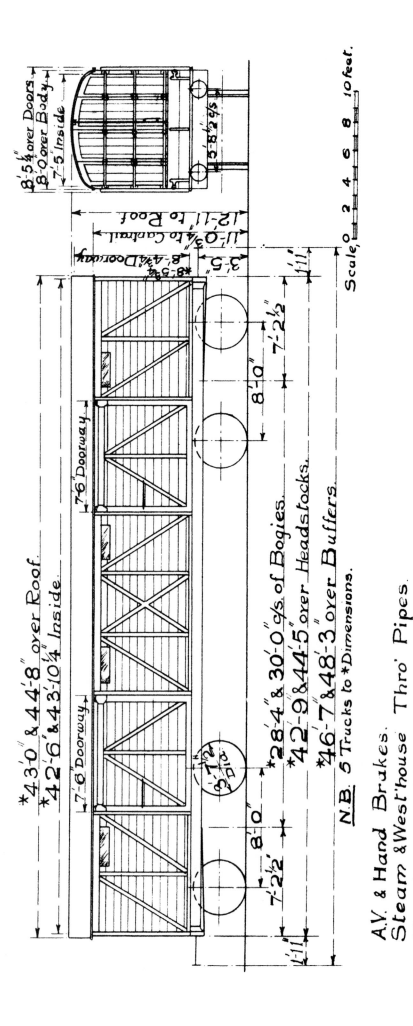

*43'0" & 44'8" over Roof.
*42'6" & 43'10¼" Inside.
7'6" Doorway.
7'6" Doorway.
3'1½" DIA.
8'0"
7'2½"
1'11"
8'5¾"*
8'4¾"Doorway.
11'0¾"to Cantrail.
12'11"to Roof.
3'5"
1'11"
*28'4" & 30'0" c/s. of Bogies.
*42'9"&44'5" over Headstocks.
*46'7"&48'3" over Buffers.
8'0"
7'2½"
1'11"

N.B. 5 Trucks to *Dimensions.

A.V. & Hand Brakes.
Steam & West'house Thro' Pipes.
To carry 8 Tons.
Tare = 17 Tons.

8'5¼" over Doors.
8'0" over Body.
7'5" Inside.
5'8"⅝s.

Scale, 0 2 4 6 8 10 feet.

FIGURE 26 Theatrical Scenery Truck – LMS D1881 (LMS Drawing No. 12/102);
Scale 4mm=1ft. Ex-MR 43ft and 45ft chassis origin again.

104

Open Carriage Truck – D2027

The need for more open carriage trucks did not arise until 1939 when the first of an eventual 40 vehicles to this diagram entered service. They are thought to have been built in connection with an increase in wartime traffic of army vehicles. They were given the bauxite coloured 'wagon' livery and we offer the only views we have of this type. We have a note that the height was increased by ¾in soon after building, presumably because of thicker tyres or conceivably heavier springs to carry greater loads.

They were very different from the customary pre-group OCTs and they made use of a modern long wheelbase four-wheel arrangement similar to some of the modern LMS CCTs covered in the previous chapter. A summary is given below but, regrettably, we have no withdrawal dates:

Lot 1185, 25 built Derby 1939, Nos 41200-24
Lot 1263, 15 built Derby 1940, Nos 41225-39

FIGURE 27 Open Carriage Truck – LMS D2027;
Scale 4mm=1ft.

FITTED WITH A.V. & HAND BRAKE.

FITTED WITH THRO' STEAM PIPE.

CARRYING CAPACITY :- 10 TONS. (DISTRIBUTED.)

CODE:-

8'-6" OVER SOLEBARS.
8'-0" WELL.
4'-4½" TOTAL HEIGHT
3'-11½"
9⅛" DEPTH OF WELL
5'-8" C's. BUFFERS.

— SECTION THROUGH WELL —

SCALE.

15'-0" WELL.
⅜" 8 PLATE.
3'-2" RAIL TO TOP OF FLOOR
13'-½" DIA
3'-11½" 10
3'-5¼"
4'-0"
20'-0" WHEELBASE
4'-0"
1'-8½"
28'-0" OVER H'STOCKS.
1'-8½"
31'-5" OVERALL.

LOT No.	QTY.	DRG. No.	TARE T. C. Q.	BUILT AT.	YEAR
1185	25	11/385A	9. 0. 0.	DERBY.	1939
1263	15	" C	8. 0. 0.	"	1940

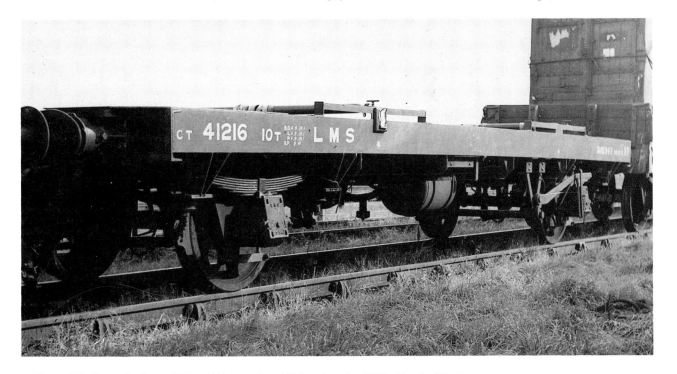

Plate 122 General view of No. 41216 to Lot 1185, taken in 1939. (A. E. West)

105

Plates 123 and 124 Detail views of Nos 41211 (brake end) and 41212, taken in 1939 and 1940 respectively. (A. E. West)

Chapter 9 – Fruit and Milk Vehicles

FRUIT AND MILK VANS

The three diagrams covered under this classification were all of six-wheel type and all but two of the vehicles concerned bore a close family resemblance to the six-wheel CCTs considered above.

The earliest design to D1873 was a developed version of a Midland design. They were slatted sided vehicles and 145 were built between 1923 and 1933. They shared the same profile as the six-wheel CCTs but, of course, did not have the end opening doors. In later years, many were classified 'Fish' and some of them had the slatted sides boarded up. The diagram refers to them as 'Fruit and Milk' whereas the next design to appear was subtly re-titled 'Covered Milk'. It shared the same size and profile as D1873 but the sides were solid from the outset with louvre vents in the upper portions (D1874). At the 1932/3 renumbering, the two lots to this diagram were renumbered separately, one into the fish van series (401XX) and the other into the milk series (385XX). This reflected a pre-1933 distinction between the two lots since only the later versions were actually lettered 'Milk' on the outside.

The final vehicles were two experimental 'Insulated Milk Vans' built to D1936 in 1935. These were austere looking vehicles with very plain exterior styling and the design was not repeated.

TABLE 9a. SUMMARY OF FRUIT AND MILK VANS

Diag	Lot	Qty	Date	Built	Wt	Dimensions (LxWxH)	Running Numbers	Withdrawals First	Last
1873*	112	15	1924	Derby	12T		38300-38314†	11/46	6/61
	223	100	1926	Wolverton	12T	30′5″ x 8′5¼″ x 12′4¼″	40000-40099‡	5/57	12/63
	364	25	1928	Derby	12T		38500-38524	8/56	12/61
	663	5	1933	Derby	12T		38545-38549	10/58	7/63
1874	304	25	1927	Derby	11T	30′5″ x 8′5¼″ x 12′4¼″	40100-40124‡	6/57	11/61
	442	20	1929	Wolverton	11T		38525-38544	7/53	extant (1969)
1936	887	2	1935	Derby	16T	31′ x 8′8″ x 11′10⅛″	38550-38441	2/58	7/66

* Fitted with Westinghouse through pipe as well as vacuum brake.
† Originally 38000-14.
‡ These numbers are in the 'Fish Van' series.
All types were six-wheeled with 21′0″ wheelbase.

Fruit and Milk Van – D1873

These once familiar vehicles were of clear Midland parentage and there is little doubt that a fair number ran on recovered second hand underframes whose buffer bodies, wood centred Mansell wheels and other details only too quickly revealed their MR origins. There was a considerable overlap of use and categorisation between this and the next diagram and examples of both types were in later years also used for fish traffic – a fact which the 1933 renumbering attempted to sort out to some extent.

Part of the reason for the confusion in usage for this type of vehicle is that liquid milk was very much a one-way traffic, for obvious reasons. This meant that at least twice as many empty churns could be returned to the areas of milk production in one vehicle than it could carry loaded to the cities. By long tradition, the railways had always sought 'return' revenue traffic for this 'spare' vehicle capacity, preferably also of a one-way nature which justified passenger train speed of haulage, thus commanding higher carriage rates! The most usual candidates were such things as fruit and parcels which tended to be distributed outwards from the cities to the country districts. One thus had dual purpose 'Fruit and Milk' and 'Milk and Parcels' vans to name but two. But meat and fish also came into the reckoning as well and the LMS, like all railways, could see no reason for having two sorts of vehicles if one type would do.

D1873 was very much the traditional milk van design, whose slatted sides ensured at least some element of 'in transit' cooling of the milk churns which it conveyed. This body structure also had similar relevance to fruit transit as well. As years went by and milk began to be hauled in bulk using tank wagons – below – there developed a gradual excess of traditional milk van capacity and opportunity was therefore taken to get rid of elderly pre-group fish vehicles by converting a considerable number of the more modern surplus milk vans to this alternative function. This was usually done by boarding up the sides and fitting side-louvre ventilation. Lot 233 was the chosen series and in this new form the vans were hardly distinguishable from the D1874 version – built from the outset to this style. In rebuilt form they were simply classified 'Fish' and renumbered in a separate series in 1933.

The diagram is summarised at Table 9A and the 1933 renumbering details were as follows:

Lot 112

New No.	Old No.
38000	192
38001	758
38002	773
38003	781
38004	785
38005	787
38006	895
38007	913
38008	917
38009	1616
38010	1619
38011	1621
38012	1627
38013	1633
38014	1656
Later to 38300-38314	

Lot 233

40000	28	40017	286	40034	572
40001	76	40018	289	40035	628
40002	79	40019	293	40036	725
40003	123	40020	318	40037	739
40004	163	40021	321	40038	763
40005	168	40022	322	40039	779
40006	209	40023	344	40040	784
40007	218	40024	394	40041	793
40008	229	40025	447	40042	796
40009	230	40026	505	40043	817
40010	243	40027	535	40044	824
40011	244	40028	536	40045	833
40012	249	40029	537	40046	898
40013	253	40030	538	40047	902
40014	268	40031	554	40048	912
40015	278	40032	562	40049	925
40016	281	40033	567	40050	1036

40051	1289		40072	3889		40093	6296		38512	7603
40052	1488		40073	3984		40094	6297		38513	7608
40053	1490		40074	4677		40095	6298		38514	7626
40054	1491		40075	4696		40096	6299		38515	7746
40055	1492		40076	4697		40097	7899		38516	7968
40056	1494		40077	4698		40098	7900		38517	8014
40057	1495		40078	4705		40099	7893		38518	8015
40058	1496		40079	4716					38519	8016
40059	1498		40080	6201		**Lot 364**			38520	8018
40060	1913		40081	6203		38500	6596		38521	8019
40061	1919		40082	6204		38501	6620		38522	8020
40062	1952		40083	6229		38502	6621		38523	8022
40063	3472		40084	6232		38503	7168		38524	8023
40064	3693		40085	6233		38504	7200			
40065	3700		40086	6256		38505	7225		**Lot 663**	
40066	3711		40087	6259		38506	7231		38545	6394
40067	3740		40088	6287		38507	7258		38546	6567
40068	3761		40089	6288		38508	7485		38547	6568
40069	3822		40090	6290		38509	7572		38548	6571
40070	3826		40091	6294		38510	7586		38549	6604
40071	3858		40092	6295		38511	7593			

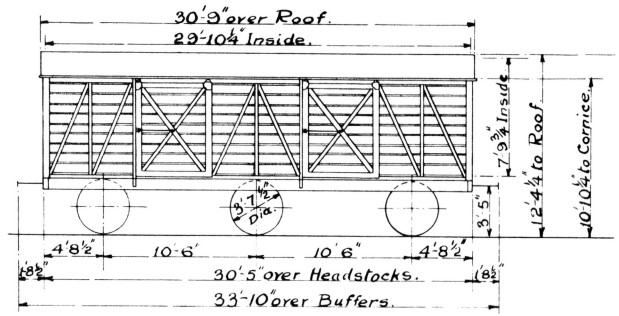

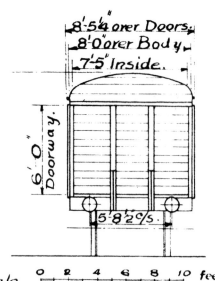

Fitted with A.V. & Hand Brakes.
Steam & West'house Thro' Pipes.
Capacity = 8 Tons.
Tare = 12 Tons

FIGURE 28 Fruit and Milk Van – LMS D1873 (LMS Drawing 13/974);
Scale 4mm = 1ft. The diagram shows the original form of bodywork but when Lot 233 was rebuilt this was to Drawing No. 5141.

Plate 125 LMS No. 8016 was part of Lot 364, later becoming No. 38519, still in the milk van series. It is seen here as built in typical lined out NPCS livery and clearly making use of an ex-MR chassis. It is interesting to note that the side inscription confines it to use in passenger trains only.

Plate 126 This example No. M38509 still displays slatted sides and remains in the milk van number series, but the sides have been filled in at the rear and the vehicle has received the BR classification PMV. Steel wheels have replaced the older Mansell type but the MR chassis remains very much unchanged. (Authors' Collection)

Left: **Plates 127 and 128** These views show the 'Fish Van' version of Lot 233, No. 40004, before and after re-railing following an accident during the 1930s. They reveal the very strong similarity with D1874 – indeed one wonders why they were not put on that diagram. If this vehicle is typical, this particular series was built with new steel underframes – note also the LMS wagon-pattern buffer bodies. The livery appears to be unlined crimson lake as would be expected by this time.

Plate 129 Close-up detail of the framing and louvres of No. M40086 of Lot 233 towards the end of its service. (T. W. Bourne)

Covered Milk Van – D1874

This diagram was introduced in the middle of the construction of D1873 and we have wondered whether the conversion of Lot 233 (above) may have had something to do with the change of style. We also feel that the relatively fewer numbers on this diagram may also have been connected with the wholesale conversion to Fish Vans of no fewer than 100 out of the original 145 D1873 examples. When both series were in service, 125 were categorised as 'Fish' and only 65 as 'Milk' – a vivid reflection of the change to bulk tank milk haulage already mentioned. Thus, though designated 'Milk' on the diagram, we have little doubt that the first Lot of D1874 to be built was designated from the outset for fish traffic. The two official views appended clearly show that the Wolverton batch (Lot 442) had open slatted sides below the upper ventilation louvres, thus revealing the 'Milk' function, whereas Lot 304 had the same close-boarded lower sides as the converted Lot 233 vans to D1873. Both series were built on second hand ex-MR underframes from former 31ft six-wheel passenger coaches.

The series is summarised at Table 9A and the 1933 renumbering (below) put them into the correct categories which their structure had always revealed:

Lot 304

New No.	Old No.
38525	1563
38526	1649
38527	1650
38528	5900
38529	5989
38530	5991
38531	7273
38532	7285
38533	7287
38534	7292
38535	7293
38536	7294
38537	7296
38538	7298
38539	7299
38540	7302
38541	7314
38542	7316
38543	7319
38544	7320

Lot 442

New No.	Old No.
40100	7370
40101	7382
40102	7383
40103	7385
40104	7392
40105	7394
40106	7395
40107	7396
40108	7400
40109	7401
40110	7402
40111	7407
40112	7408
40113	7409
40114	7412
40115	7413
40116	7414
40117	7419
40118	7426
40119	7472
40120	7504
40121	7514
40122	7563
40123	7610
40124	7410

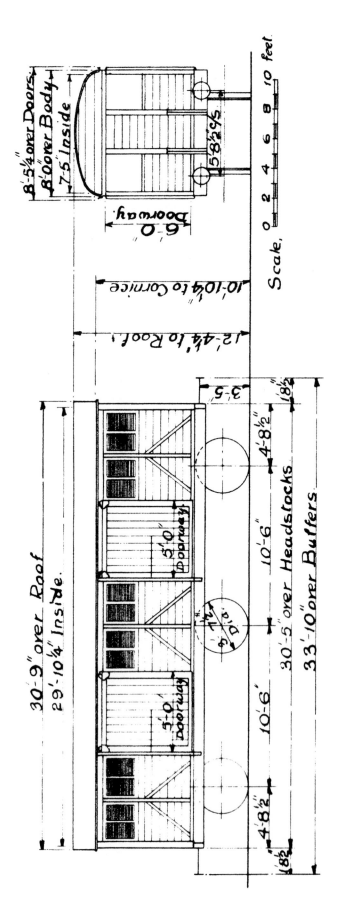

FIGURE 29 Covered Milk Van – LMS D1874 (LMS Drawing No. 13/1020, later No. 6629);
Scale 4mm =1ft.

112

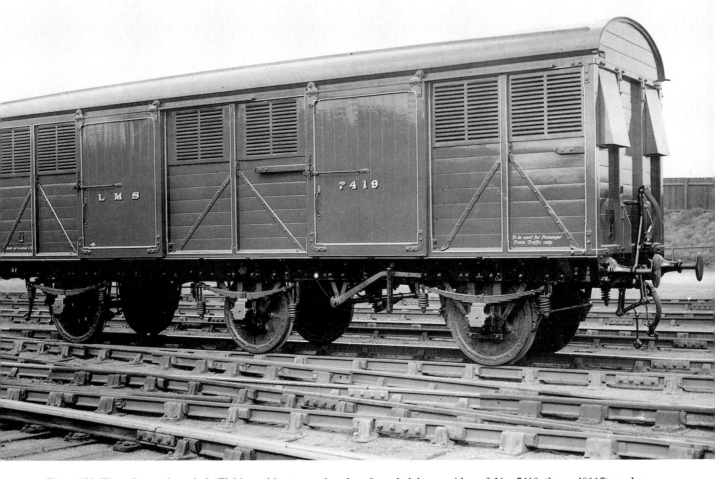

Plate 130 Though not branded 'Fish' at this stage, the close-boarded lower sides of No. 7419 (later 40117) to Lot 304 clearly reveal that this version of D1874 was not really intended for milk. Note the MR pattern chassis and full NPCS livery.

Plate 131 LMS No. 7316 (later 38542) of D1874, Lot 442 was branded 'Milk Van' from the outset, but even without this wording, the lower slatted sides would have revealed its purpose. The underframe and livery are all but identical to the previous example.

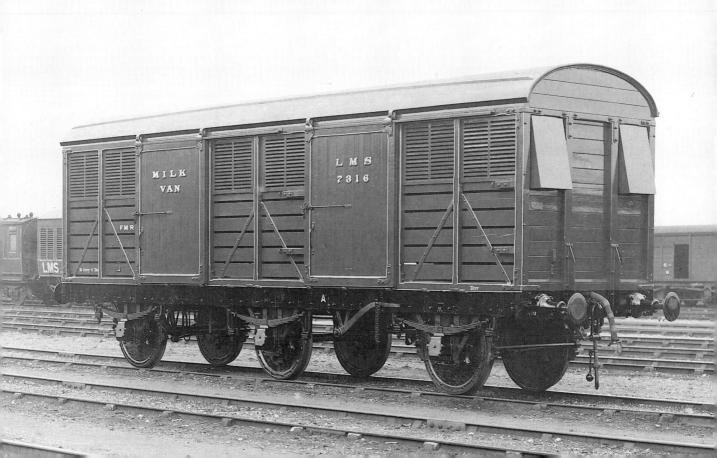

Insulated Milk Van – D1936

These experimental vans appear to have been an attempt to produce a new design of vehicle for the remaining orthodox churn traffic but were never repeated. They were put on heavier duty LMS steel underframes (note the carriage pattern buffer bodies for example) yet were only plated for 6 Tons carrying capacity rather than the 8 Tons of most of the earlier two series. We have no knowledge of any specific use for which they may have been designed.

Plates 132 and 133 These two opposite side official views of the D1936 milk vans are the only ones known to us. They reveal the plain crimson livery and large side-lettering adopted on this type. Note too that the 'LMS' and running numbers are transposed in position compared with normal carriage stock. The use of the elongated 4in 'LMS' was also somewhat less usual for NPCS, though it did come into greater use with several of the more modern smooth-sided vehicles.

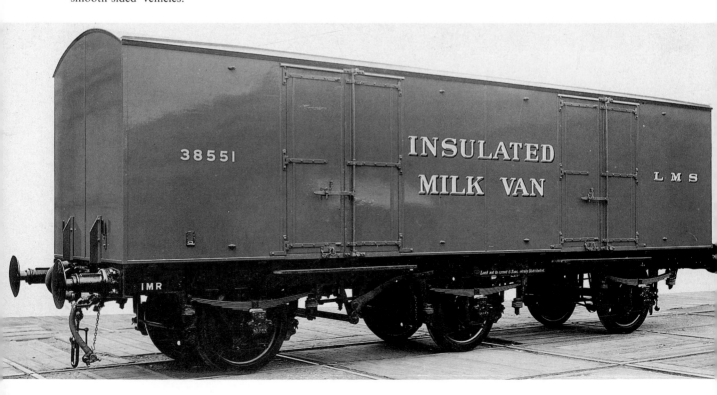

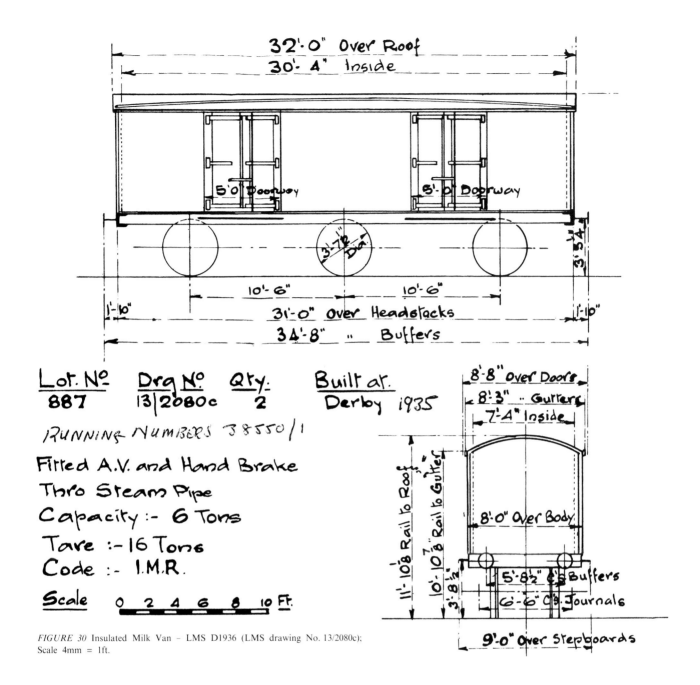

FIGURE 30 Insulated Milk Van – LMS D1936 (LMS drawing No. 13/2080c);
Scale 4mm = 1ft.

MILK TANKS

The rail-carried milk tanks listed in the LMS non-passenger coaching stock are something of a mystery since in some cases the identical lot numbers are also listed in the freight stock book but with different diagram numbers! This section will deal with those examples which were officially classified as passenger rated.

Eight diagrams were involved, six being genuine milk tanks and the other two being underframes for carrying road milk tank trailers. All the six milk tank diagrams differ in slight detail although sharing a common six-wheel chassis, 20ft 6in over headstocks with a 13ft 0in wheelbase. Some of the six-wheel diagrams were issued to cover the conversion of the pioneer milk tanks from four-wheel chassis. The earliest examples were built in this way but in 1937 it was decided to convert all tanks to a six-wheel chassis and the old diagrams were removed from the book. Hence, only the six-wheel diagrams can be quoted in this work. The only logical way to deal with them is diagram by diagram. Running numbers were mixed up amongst the diagrams and are therefore given in Table 9b. Most other details are given in the narrative.

D1992 This diagram was issued in 1937 to cover the conversion to six-wheel chassis of the original 2000 gallon four-wheel tanks. Fourteen vehicles were involved from various pre-1937 lots but the rebuilding was given a fresh Lot number, being classed as part of Lot 1077. All were liveried for 'United Dairies'. This was the only 2000 gallon milk tank diagram. The tanks on these vehicles were quite small being 15ft 9in x 5ft 3in diam.

D1991 This was an early 3000 gallon diagram being issued in 1931. It contained three vehicles only to Lot 613, all of which were built for Nestlés. Tank size was 17ft 2¼in x 6ft 3¼ in.

D1993 These were virtually identical to D1991 except that the tank size was 16ft 9in x 6ft 3in. They were, like D1992 (above) ex-four-wheel tanks to various pre-1937 lots and the batch of 25 concerned in the rebuilding was also classed as part of Lot 1077. Some were 'United Dairies' and some were 'Nestlés'. The conversion took place in 1937.

D1994 This was the earliest 3000 gallon diagram and dated from 1931. It contained an impressive number of different lots but none totalled very many vehicles. All are listed in Table 9b. This diagram was again similar to D1991 but had a tank dimension of 18ft 0½in x 6ft 1in. Both new vehicles and converted ex-four-wheel tanks were included on the diagram which was, in a sense, the LMS 'standard' milk tank.

D2173 D1994 continued to be current until 1946 and was superseded by D2173 which was introduced in 1950. Again a 3000 gallon diagram, these tanks differed from all their forerunners in having the tank hatch and access ladder offset to one end of the tank. Tank dimensions were almost identical to D1994 (actually half an inch longer!).

D2170 This was another 1950 diagram and the last to be listed in the LMS book. It had a centre hatchway type tank but only six vehicles were built. The style was virtually identical to D1994 but this time with a half inch shorter tank and some changes to the tank supporting structure.

The two road milk tank diagrams (D1989/D1990) seem to have been very similar. In D1989 the chassis was a fairly conventional six-wheel structure, identically dimensioned to that of the milk tanks proper. Both types were designed to carry 2000 gallon road trailers but D1990 was designed to carry a six-wheel as opposed to a four-wheel road trailer and, in consequence, was built to a greater length (24ft 6in) over headstocks and had a longer wheelbase (16ft 0in).

As stated above, the milk tanks were numbered indiscriminately although all were in the 44XXX series. It is believed that the railway owned the underframe only, the tank belonging to the dairy concerned. As far as can be deduced, the 1932/3 renumbering system for milk tanks took account of the owning dairy and number blocks were allocated to each company. New tanks were placed in the appropriate series by ownership rather than by taking the lowest available number in a continuous series. The allocations as listed in the diagram book were as follows:

44000–74:	United Dairies
44075–139:	Nestlés
44140–69:	Co-operative Wholesale Society
44170–249:	Express Dairy
44250–2:	Cow & Gate
44295–8:	H. Edwards & Son
44253–94/9 } 44500 upwards }	Not listed as allocated to a particular owner – many were railway owned.

TABLE 9b: SUMMARY OF MILK TANKS

Diag	Lot		Qty	Date	Built	Running Numbers	Withdrawals First	Last	Remarks
1992*	part	1077	14	1937-8	Derby	44006-11; 44016-9; 44032-5	7/41		
1991		613	3	1931	Derby	44091-2; 44096			
1993	part	1077	25	1937-8	Derby	44000-5; 44012-5; 44020-31; 44075-7	1/65		
1994		596	3	1931	Derby	44087-9	6/64		
		599	5	1931	Derby	44090; 44171-2; 44174-5	4/61		
		615	6	1931	Derby	44093-5; 44097-8 plus one scrapped before renumbering?			
		631	2	1931	Derby	44180-1	6/61	2/66	
		632	2	1931	Derby	44170; 44173			
		633	6	1932	Derby	44036-41			
		640	6	1932	Derby	44099-104	9/58	1/68	
		651	3	1932	Derby	44105-7	6/65		
		656	4	1932	Derby	44176-9	9/62		
		668	3	1932	Derby	44250-2			
		705	12	1933	Derby	44182-93	1/64		
		727	2	1933	Derby	44042-3			
		781	3	1934	Derby	44194-6			
		782	1	1934	Derby	44197			
		791	3	1934	Derby	44253-5	2/67		
		812	6	1934	Derby	44044-9	4/61		
		874	5	1935	Derby	44276-80	6/56		Withdrawal details are not entirely complete but many examples ran on into the 1970s.
		875	4	1935	Derby	44281-4	3/61		
		881	3	1935	Derby	44198-200			
		882	1	1935	Derby	44201			
		893	3	1935	Derby	44050-2			
		936	1	1935	Derby	44285		3/61	A number of the railway owned vehicles have been renumbered into the 'dairy' series to replace withdrawals during the 1960s.
			12	1937	Derby	44078-86; 44150-2—these 12 were rebuilt ex-four wheel	12/56		
		1067	5	1937	Derby	44053-7	2/66		
		1068	1	1937	Derby	44058			
		1129	2	1937	Derby	44059-60			
		1172	3	1938	Derby	44061-3			
		1232	2	1939	Derby	44256-7			
		1306	6	1941	Derby	44064-9			
		1328	4	1942	Derby	44258-61			
		1378	4	1944	Derby	44562-5†			
		1434	6	1946	Derby	44230-5	5/67		
2173‡		1580	10	1950 }	Derby &	44500-9			
		1614	2	1950 }	Earlestown	44510-1			
		1640	50	1950-1	Derby	44512-61	2/61		
2174		1641	6	1950	Derby	44263-8	7/67		
1989*		878	3	1935	Derby	44297-9			
		931	1	1935	Derby	44296			
		932	1	1935	Derby	44295			
1990*		1008	5	1936	Derby	44140-4	6/56		
		1240	2	1939	Derby	44153-4	7/61	6/64	
		1491	1	1947	Derby	44155			

*2000 gallon types, the remainder being 3000 gallon.

†These four vehicles were built in 1943/4 on behalf of the Ministry of War Transport for Messrs Libby, McNeil and Libby Ltd. When built they were never given LMS series numbers nor taken into LMS stock. The numbers quoted are those which were allocated when the vehicles were finally taken into stock in 1951.

‡ United Dairies owned some, at least, of these 445xx series vehicles and probably most of them.

A considerable number of milk tanks were in service before the renumbering and as far as we can deduce, Lot 705 of D1994 was the first batch to come into traffic from new with its 1933 series running numbers. The renumbering details of the earlier examples are as follows, followed by a type by type survey of the fleet, generally in diagram page number order but with some changes to aid interpretation of the general development of design:

United Dairies						Co-operative Wholesale Society	
New No.	Old No.	44025	6000	44082	1693	New No.	Old No.
44000	638	44026	1630	44083	1702	44150	1618
44001	639	44027	1689	44084	1735	44151	1644
44002	640	44028	1744	44085	7315	44152	1749
44003	641	44029	5818	44086	7324		
44004	642	44030	7289	44087	1620	Express Dairy	
44005	643	44031	7307	44088	1641	New No.	Old No.
44006	644	44032	7275	44089	1668	44170	1614
44007	645	44033	7277	44090	1741	44171	1639
44008	646	44034	7282	44091	1745	44172	1648
44009	647	44035	575	44092	1746	44173	1674
44010	648	44036	1652	44093	6058	44174	1699
44011	649	44037	1676	44094	6060	44175	1733
44012	5251	44038	1711	44095	7276	44176	1996
44013	5291	44039	1751	44096	7290	44177	1997
44014	5297	44040	1840	44097	7305	44178	1998
44015	5363	44041	2903	44098	7323	44179	1999
44016	5188			44099	25	44180	6093
44017	5220	Nestlés		44100	39	44181	6096
44018	5289	New No.	Old No.	44101	185		
44019	5364	44075	1635	44102	346	Cow & Gate	
44020	1565	44076	8128	44103	356	New No.	Old No.
44021	1637	44077	8168	44104	467	44250	7801
44022	1651	44078	1625	44105	603	44251	7802
44023	1667	44079	1634	44106	1028	44252	7803
44024	1842	44080	1640	44107	1047		
		44081	1646				

3000 Gallon Milk tank – D1991

This diagram, the earliest of the six-wheelers, only contained three vehicles, all originally in the Nestlés fleet and which were, in four-wheel form, allocated to D1835 in the freight wagon diagram book. Regrettably, we have been unable to find any pictures and can only offer the diagram itself.

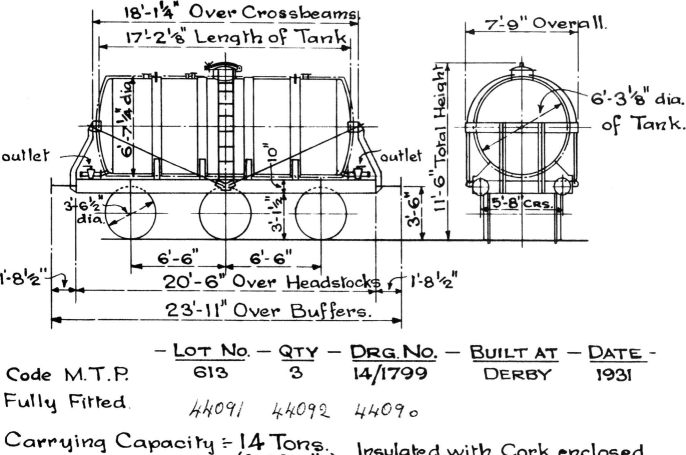

Code M.T.P.	– LOT No. –	QTY –	DRG. No. –	BUILT AT –	DATE –
	613	3	14/1799	DERBY	1931

Fully Fitted. 44091 44092 44090

Carrying Capacity = 14 Tons. (3,000 galls)   Insulated with Cork enclosed in sheet steel covering.

Tare = 14 Tons.

Type of Brake; "Morton."   Fitted with wheel splash plates.

FIGURE 31 3000 Gallon Milk Tank – LMS D1991 (LMS Drawing No. 14/1799);
Scale 4mm = 1ft.

117

2000 Gallon Milk Tank – D1992

These, the only 2000 gallon six-wheel tanks, were converted in 1937-8 from a number of earlier four-wheel types whose original Lot numbers are listed on the diagram itself. The diagram was introduced during the building of D1994 (below) and may well have been influenced by the success of that type. For running numbers see Table 9b.

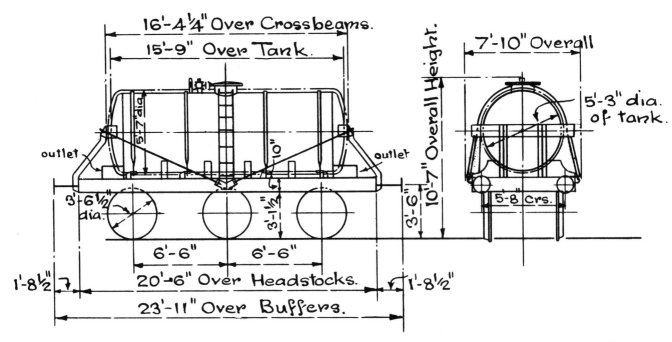

Code M.T.P. Fully Fitted.

```
     – Lot No. – Drg. No. – Qty. – Built at – Year. –
    { Pt 1077    14/2861A    14    Derby      1937
    { Converted from  Lots 358(4), 403(2), 425(4), 317(3), 620(1).
```

Carrying Cap^y, 12 Tons.
(2000 galls.)

Tare ÷ Tons. Cwts.

Insulated with cork & enclosed
in sheet steel covering.

FIGURE 32 2000 Gallon Milk Tank – LMS D1992 (LMS Drawing No.14/2861A);
Scale 4mm = 1ft.

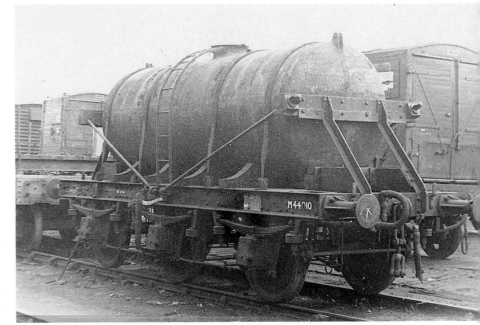

Plate 134 This view at Willesden in July 1961 shows No. M44010, originally United Dairies No. 648. The smaller tank is very noticeable when compared with other six-wheel tanks. (C. M. Strevens)

3000 Gallon Milk Tank – D1993

The second diagram covering the 1937-8 conversions of former four-wheel tanks to six-wheel arrangement dealt with the 3000 gallon variety. The conversions were part of the same Lot as D1992 and again, their original four-wheel Lot numbers are listed on the diagram, running numbers being in Table 9b.

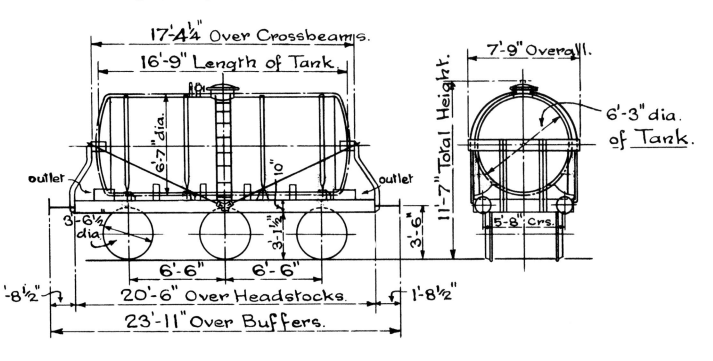

```
— Lot No. — Drg. No. — Qty. — Built At — Year
{ Pt. 1077    14/2862A    25      Derby     1937
{ Converted from  Lots 357(6), 424(4), 458(6), 474(4), 481(5).
```

FIGURE 33 3000 Gallon Milk Tank – LMS D1993 (LMS Drawing No. 14/2862A); Scale 4mm = 1ft.

Code M.T.P.

Fully Fitted.

Carrying Capacity, 14 Tons.
(3000 Galls.)

Tare :- Tons   Cwts.

Type of Brake, "Morton."

Insulated with cork & enclosed in sheet steel covering.

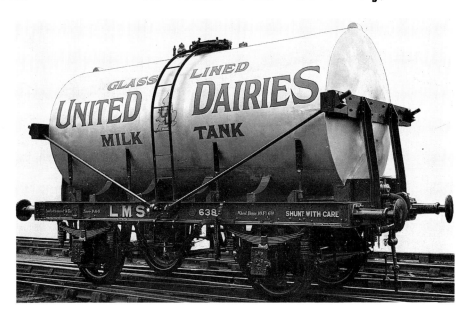

Plate 135 United Dairies four-wheel Milk Tank, LMS No. 638 later No. 44000, seen here in original form, was the first example to be converted to D1993.

Plates 136 and 137 Milk Tank No. 8168 was originally a four-wheel Nestlés vehicle and is seen in the first view as built in full red livery. It became a D1993 six-wheeler and by an astonishing coincidence (second view) was also photographed at Willesden by one of the authors in the summer of 1964 as M44077! (R. J. Essery)

3000 Gallon Milk Tank – D1994

This diagram, the most numerous of the LMS six-wheel milk tank designs, was in effect the 'standard' type and was in continuous use for new vehicles from 1931 to 1946; it probably established some sort of LMS record for longevity in terms of one type in production. The diagram itself states that some of the earlier examples were conversions – presumably from further four-wheelers. There also appear to have been several changes of drawing – see caption to Figure 34 – but we cannot say how significant these were. They may simply have applied to some of the minor detail changes shown in our pictures.

This design was built for a wide number of 'owning' dairies and official bodies – some examples of which are illustrated. In earlier days, some of them had an outer cover, some one inch away from the main tank. This was supposed to help force cooling air round the tank itself while the vehicle was in motion, but does not seem to have been strictly needed and was soon removed. Our picture coverage is quite comprehensive but there were undoubtedly many other liveries to be seen on this one time very colourful series of vehicles.

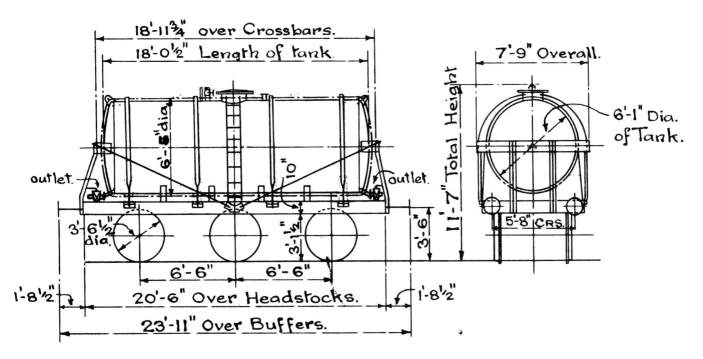

– LOT NO. –	DRG. NO. –	QTY –	BUILT AT –	DATE –
H.O.O. 321	14/2164A	12	DERBY	1937

Converted from Lots 524(2), 565(5), 586(2), 595(3).

Code M.T.P.
Fully Fitted.
Carrying Cap.ʸ, 14 Tons.
(3000 galls.)
Tare :- 14 Tons. 8 Cwts.
Type of Brake, "Morton".
Insulated with Cork & enclosed in sheet steel covering.
Fitted with wheel splash plates.

FIGURE 34 3000 Gallon Milk Tank – LMS D1994 (LMS Drawings: D14/1745 – up to Lot 668; D14/2164 – Lots 705 to 791; D14/2164A – Lots 812 to 1129; D14/3294 – Lot 1172 onwards);
Scale 4mm = 1ft.

Plate 138 This splendid view shows LMS No. 1999 (later 44179) as built to D1994 in 1932. The blue of the Express Dairy livery extended to the solebars; lettering was white. Note the outer cover on the upper half of the tank with its flared air-gathering ends.

Plate 139 Milk Tanks tended to be built in smallish batches. One of the larger series was the twelve built to Lot 705 in 1933 of which Nos 44190-3 (left to right) are seen here.

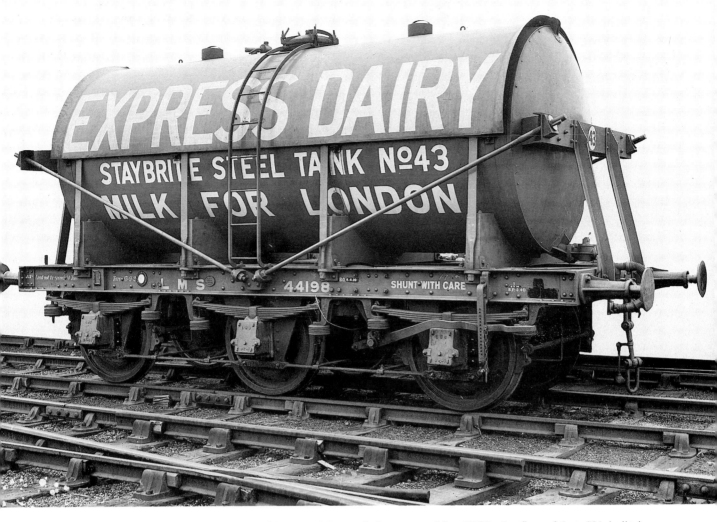

Plate 140 A later form of outer cover, without end 'scoops', is seen on No. 44198, the first of Lot 881 built in 1935. Note that now, the tank number appears as part of the livery on the side tank as well as centrally on the tank-end cross-support and that the lower two lines of lettering have been transposed.

Plate 141 This group of six vehicles from D1994 for Independent Milk Supplies Ltd, were almost certainly Nos. 44276-81, although not arranged in that order. Built at Derby in 1935 to Lots 874 and (part) 875, this series had no outer tank covers which suggests (see No. 44198 in the previous view) that 1935 was the year of changeover.

Plates 142 and 143 Detailed side and end views of No. 44276 of Lot 874. Regrettably, the livery colour is not known.

Plate 144 Milk tanks got just about everywhere and this interesting view shows two unidentified early examples from D1994 being filled at Ecton Creamery in 1932 while standing on the narrow gauge 'transporter' wagons of the former Leek & Manifold Valley Light Railway. They would have been 'United Dairies' examples and probably destined for Finsbury Park. This traffic provided the only stable factor in the revenue of the L&MVLR and the closure of the creamery in the same year as this picture was taken was a key factor in the demise of the line itself only two years later. (Authors' Collection)

Plate 145 No. 44257 was built at Derby in 1939 and discreetly branded for 'Cow and Gate Limited', though we do not know the main colour. By now, some of the elaborate liveries were being superseded by plainer styles.

Plate 146 This second view of No. M44257 at Derby in August 1966 shows that apart from the addition of roof top footboards, little structural change had taken place. (Authors' Collection)

Plate 147 In 1944, a batch of four tanks to D1994 was ordered (Lot 1378) by the Ministry of War Transport for Messrs 'Libby, McNeill and Libby Ltd'. This is the first of them: MWT No. 1. Again we do not know the livery colour. They were taken into BR stock in 1951. MWT No. 1 becoming No. M44562. (Authors' Collection)

Plate 148 In 1946, No.44230 was one of the last examples (Lot 1434) to be built to D1994. By now, the Milk Marketing Board had taken over control of much distribution and this tank carries MMB markings; but again we are unable to offer livery colours. Note the fitting of tank top footboards (see also previous two pictures).

Plate 149 From the war years onwards and until the end of their active life, milk tanks rarely looked as bright and cheerful as was once the case. They were usually painted all-over aluminium (which soon got dirty) and carried only modest sized ownership markings. This is No. M44179 of the 1932 Lot 656 at Appleby in June 1962 carrying a small 'Express Dairy' identification plate. It probably started life rather like No.1999 (Plate 138) but has long since lost its top cover and has now received additional tank supports at the outer ends. (D. Jenkinson)

3000 Gallon Milk Tank – D2173

This 1950 design represented the first basic change for almost 20 years and differed principally in the location of the upper filling hatch, though we know not why. It was of lighter tare weight than D1994 and did have the distinction of seeing the largest ever single lot of LMS/LMR tanks to be built in one batch – Lot 1640 of 1950-51: 50 vehicles. There appear to be no known official views and we can only offer one picture.

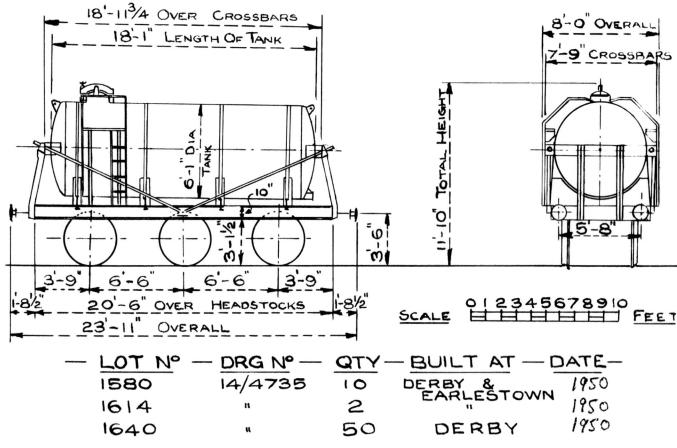

— LOT Nº —	DRG Nº —	QTY —	BUILT AT —	DATE —
1580	14/4735	10	DERBY & EARLESTOWN	1950
1614	"	2	"	1950
1640	"	50	DERBY	1950

TEL CODE :- MTP

FULLY FITTED.

CARRYING CAPACITY. 14 TONS

TARE :- 12 TONS 4 CWT.

TYPE OF BRAKE. MORTON.

INSULATED WITH CORK & ENCLOSED IN SHEET STEEL COVERING

FIGURE 35 3000 Gallon Milk Tank – BR (LMR) D2173 (BR Drawing No. 14/4735); Scale 1mm=1ft

Plate 150 No. M44501, seen at Willesden in July 1964, was branded 'United Dairies' and clearly shows the changed position of the tank filling hatch. (R. J. Essery).

3000 Gallon Milk Tank – D2174

This design – the last of the Milk Tank diagrams to be issued – retained the centre hatch but only six were built. It seems to have been a slightly lighter weight version of D1994 and the tank top footboards, added later to D1994, are now marked on the diagram itself. We have no pictures of this type.

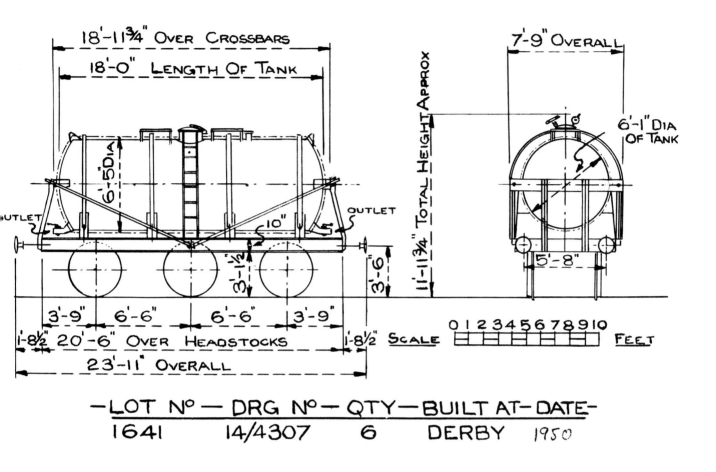

TEL CODE   MTP
FULLY FITTED
CARRYING CAPACITY   14 TONS
TARE   13 TONS 3 CWT.
TYPE OF BRAKE   MORTON
INSULATED   WITH CORK & ENCLOSED
IN   SHEET STEEL COVERING

FIGURE 36 3000 Gallon Milk Tank – BR (LMR) D2174 (BR Drawing No. 14/4307);
Scale 4mm = 1ft.

Underframes for 2000 Gallon Road-Rail Milk Tanks – D1989/D1990

We conclude our survey with two broadly identical types designed for the onward rail haulage of road milk tanks. This reflected an early move towards a practice which has now removed all bulk milk haulage from the railway system. Not all the early concentration depots of the 1930s were rail connected and milk was sometimes loaded into road tanks rather than directly into rail vehicles; the LMS therefore came up with this sensible solution to the problem. The two types differed mainly in terms of length, that for the six-wheel road option being surprisingly little heavier in tare weight.

Relatively few were built – see Table 9b – but given the present day road congestion one cannot help but think that the railways might have done more to develop this type of 'inter-modal' approach, to use the currently fashionable term – perhaps it will return one day.

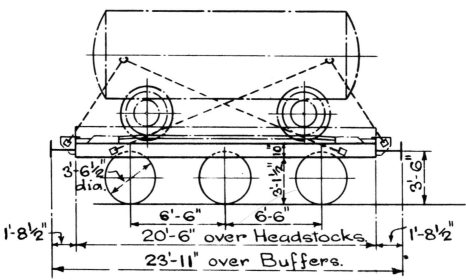

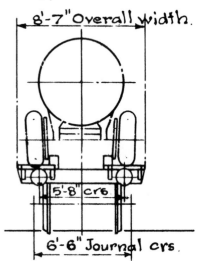

Fully Fitted.

Carrying Capacity, 2000 Galls.

Tare ÷ Without Tank, 12 T. 6 c.

    With empty Tank, appx. 16 T. 12 c.

    " Full " " 25 T. 16 c.

Type of Brake, "Morton"

Code, T.U.P.

FIGURE 37 Underframe for 2000 Gallon four-wheel Road-Rail Milk Tank – LMS D1989 (LMS Drawing No.14/2539): Scale 4m = 1ft.

Plate 151 Ex-works view of the D1990 underframe No.44140 for six-wheel road tanks. We believe the 'upperworks' to have been either red or bauxite in colour but cannot be 100% positive. Note the small hinged flaps to bridge the gap over the buffers between the loading bay and the vehicle floor.

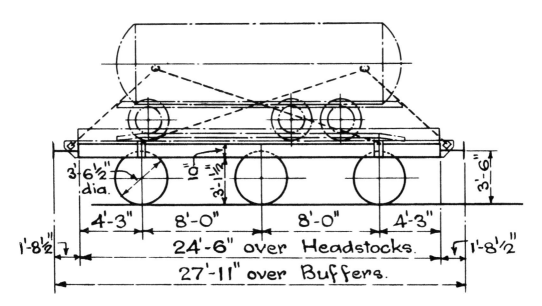

A.V., Hand Brake & Steam pipes.

Carrying Capacity, 2000 Galls.

Tare. :- Without Tank, 12 Tons 14 Cwt.

With empty Tank, 18 Tons 4 Cwt.

With full Tank, 27 Tons 14 Cwt.

Code. T.U.P.

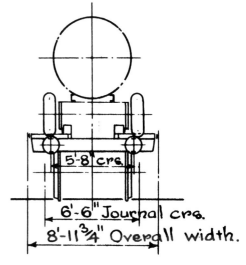

FIGURE 38 Underframe for 2000 Gallon six-wheel Road-Rail Milk Tank – LMS D1990 (LMS Drawing No.14/2796); Scale 4mm = 1ft.

Chapter 10 Other Vehicles for Perishable Traffic

The next vehicles to be considered were for perishable traffic of various kinds and fall into two natural groups. The first of these groups contains exclusively four-wheel vehicles which would be more at home, stylistically at all events, in the freight stock book. However, they were given the passenger livery and listed in the passenger book. They were used for the carriage of meat or fish. The second group was more variable and contained four, six and eight-wheeled vehicles, mostly for the sausage traffic but also including two coaches rejoicing in the name of 'Cream Vans'.

Dealing first with the meat/fish van group, nine diagrams were involved, all concerning standard 17ft 6in long four-wheel goods van type vehicles. Two diagrams concerned meat vans, the remainder were variations of design in vehicles for fish traffic.

The meat vans were all initially built to D1883 as ventilated refrigerator vans. They were orthodox tidy looking vehicles and, other than their passenger rating, they differed little from contemporary freight vehicles. At a later stage (believed c.1950), all were altered to D1883A which was a modification involving the removal of the refrigeration equipment which gave a larger interior load space. They were then reclassified ventilated insulated vans and although retained in the passenger book, it is thought they were given the BR fitted freight bauxite livery. They had 9ft 0in wheelbase.

The fish vans exhibited quite a number of detail changes as time went by and are best considered in diagram order. The first vans were to D1884 which was a slatted type van. Some were fully fitted, others merely carried a through pipe and, in addition, the diagram only involved part of one lot (105). The remainder of the vans to Lot 105 were built to D1885 (below). The D1884 vans were transferred to the wagon stock as Banana Vans in 1937 and finally to Ale Wagons in 1944.

The next fish van diagram (D1885) introduced solid sides which remained standard for all future construction to LMS design. The style is illustrated and needs little further description save to remark that as with D1884, some were fully fitted and others had a through pipe only. These vans evolved into the D1886 version which dispensed with the side louvre vents and diagonal side strapping but had louvre vents at both sides of both ends. Again there were fully fitted and 'piped only' examples and this diagram saw an increase in wheelbase from 9ft 0in to 10ft 0in. With D1887, the side vents re-appear, this time at the expense of the end louvres. All of this batch were fully fitted and retained the 10ft 0in wheelbase.

During the evolution of these designs, which took place during the period 1924-31, there was introduced a rather different fish van design to D1982 which first appeared in 1929. These were, outwardly, orthodox ventilated vans with side strapping, vertical planking, roof-top torpedo ventilators and no louvre vents at all. They are recorded as having been built with 9ft 0in wheelbase, later converted to 10ft 0in – date of conversion not known.

The final LMS four-wheel fish van diagrams were D2059 and D2107. They appeared in 1941 and 1945 respectively and were identical save for the wheelbase (10ft 0in and 10ft 6in respectively). The exterior of these vehicles was completely devoid of strapping apart from strengthening plates at the corners and doors. They were given neither louvres nor roof vents which, in view of the traffic carried, must be considered a little unusual.

The final group of perishable vehicles to be considered were of more orthodox non-passenger coaching stock design. The first to be considered is the six-wheel 'Express Fish' van (D2115) introduced in 1947. Although taken out of date sequence, this design forms a logical conclusion to the above description of LMS four-wheel fish vans since its body style was all but identical to that of the final four-wheel diagrams. Moreover it was rated at the same carrying capacity (6T) as the four-wheel designs.

The remaining vehicles were the colourful vans built mainly for the sausage trade during the later 1930s. Four types were involved and all carried the highly distinctive Palethorpes livery. In diagram order, the first design was a six-wheel vehicle (D1955) bearing a marked similarity to the contemporary insulated milk vans. The main difference was the presence on the sausage vans of end ladders and roof hatches. A bogie equivalent was built at about the same time to D1957. It was 50ft long but shared the same style of body with roof hatches and end ladders.

A second bogie design to D2001 was introduced in 1938. These vehicles were unusual for non-passenger coaching stock in that they were given gangway connections. The interior space was arranged in side-corridor fashion. The corridor side elevation contained three standard Period III 4ft 0in windows between the two pairs of double doors and another 4ft 0in window between each double door and the extreme end of the vehicle. Double doors opposite those on the corridor side led into the van from the side corridor while the van side itself presented the same austere aspect as the non-corridor equivalent with but two pairs of double doors to relieve the completely flat sided exterior. Like the non-gangwayed version, the D2001 coaches had completely flat sides.

Two all but identical 50ft gangwayed vans were built to D2002 at the same time as D2001. These were annotated 'Insulated Cream Vans' and rated at 10½T capacity rather than the 6T of the gangwayed sausage vans.

The four-wheel sausage van was to D1958 and was contemporary with the six and eight-wheel designs. It had but one pair of double doors and was rated at 3T capacity. During 1956, the two examples of the type were converted to 'Passenger Vans'.

TABLE 10: SUMMARY OF PERISHABLE STOCK

Diag	Lot	Qty	Date	Built	Wt	Dimensions*(LxWxH)	Running Numbers	Withdrawals First	Last
Ventilated Refrigerator Van (Meat)									
1883†	133	30	1927/8	Derby	10½T	17′6″x8′0″x12′2¼″	38700-38729	5/56	5/64
Fish Vans									
1884	part 105	53	1924/5	Derby	8T	17′6″x7′8″x11′10½″	39021-39073	to wagon stock 1937	
1885	66	20	1926	Wolverton	8T		39000-39019	11/52	6/61
	part 105	47	1925	Derby	8T	17′6″x7′8″x11′10½″	39020 39074-39119	5/56	7/61
	336	50	1928	Ntn Heath	8T		39120-39169	3/48	4/61
	399	50	1929	Ntn Heath			39170-39219	2/55	9/63
1982	456	60	1929	Ntn Heath	8T	17′6″x7′8″x11′10¼″	39220-39279	2/53	‡
1886	589	66	1931	Wolverton	9½T	17′6″x7′8″x11′10¼″	39280-39345	9/58	‡
	592	34	1932	Wolverton	9½T		39346-39379	4/59	5/64

1887	660	20	1932	Wolverton 9¼T ⎫	17'6"x8'0" x11'10¼"	39380-39399	5/59	‡
	691	40	1933	Wolverton 9¼T ⎬		39400-39439	9/59	‡ 9/64
2059	1299	75	1941	Earlestown 9T (bodies built at Derby)	17'6"x8'0"x11'10¼"	39440-39514	2/59	‡
2107	1390	35	1945	Wolverton 9T	17'6"x8'0"x11'10¼"	39515-39559	11/58	‡
2115	1428	50	1946/7	Wolverton 17T ⎫		40200-40249	4/64	‡
	1445	50	1949	Wolverton 17T ⎬ 31'0"x8'0"x12'1"		40250-40299	7/66	‡
	1509	40	1949	Wolverton 17T ⎭ (six-wheel)		40300-40339	10/65	‡
Insulated Sausage Vans/Cream Vans								
1955	986	4	1936	Wolverton 17T	31'0"x8'0"x12'2⅜"	38732-38735	6/66	10/66
1957	984	2	1936	Wolverton 28T	50'0"x8'0"x12'2⅜"	38877-38878	6/67	6/67
2001	1125	3	1938	Wolverton 29T ⎫	50'0"x8'0"x12'2⅜"	38874-38876	5/67	6/67
	1157	1	1938	Wolverton 29T ⎬		38873	—	3/65
1958	985	2	1936	Wolverton 11T	21'0"x8'0"x12'3"	38730-38731	10/67	—
2002	1156	2	1938	Wolverton 29T	50'0"x8'0"x12'2⅜"	38998-38999§		not known

* Width is given over body.
† Rebuilt to D1883A retaining original numbers but reclassified 'Ventilated Insulated Van (Meat)'.
‡ Survivors to wagon stock (c.1965) and some remained in service until the late 1970s (at least).
§ These two vehicles classed as 'Insulated Cream Vans'.

Ventilated Refrigerator Van – D1883

What little we know of this small group (by LMS standards) is mostly given in the introductory summary. However, since the painted inscription on the only known official view calls for the van to 'Return to the Northern Division', we deduce that some if not all were used for high speed transit of prime Scottish beef to England! Until the refrigeration equipment was removed (on conversion to D1883A), they were given plain crimson livery with passenger style insignia and, we believe, the type designation was applied in unshaded yellow lettering. It seems likely that the BR bauxite livery (on conversion) may have been preceded by a period when, if repainted, the LMS used much the same sort of treatment. Like many other types, they vanished during the mass slaughter of specialist cargo vehicles during the depressing period when BR almost 'gave up' on the business of promoting non-passenger carrying activities in the late 1950s and early 1960s.

A general summary is given in Table 10 and the 1933 renumbering details were as follows:

New No.	Old No.	New No.	Old No.	New No.	Old No.
38700	6311	38710	6495	38720	6936
38701	6312	38711	6506	38721	6937
38702	6322	38712	6507	38722	6938
38703	6344	38713	6633	38723	6939
38704	6352	38714	6635	38724	6940
38705	6372	38715	6638	38725	6941
38706	6410	38716	6648	38726	6942
38707	6425	38717	6933	38727	6943
38708	6435	38718	6934	38728	8186
38709	6492	38719	6935	38729	8187

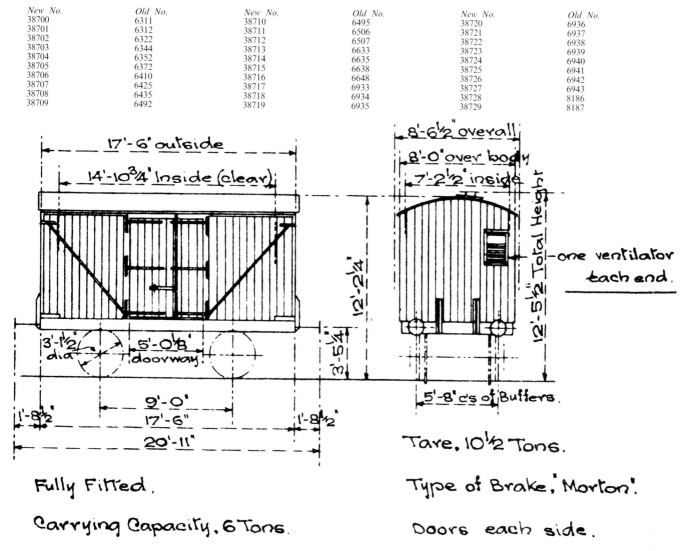

FIGURE 39 Ventilated Refrigerator Van – LMS D1883 (LMS Drawing No. 6429);
Scale 4mm=1ft.

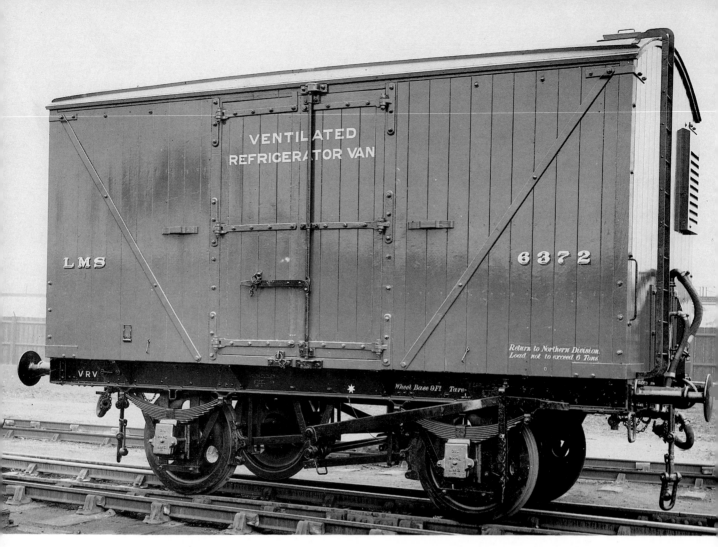

Plate 152 LMS No. 6372, later 38705, when brand new in 1927.

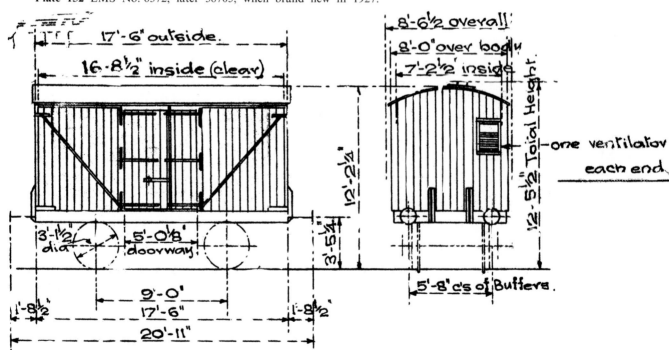

Fully Fitted,

Carrying Capacity, 6 Tons.

Tare, 10½ Tons.

Type of Brake, "Morton".

Doors each side.

FIGURE 40 Ventilated Insulated Van – LMR D1883A;
Scale 4mm=1ft. The same diagram was repeated with but the one change to show the greater internal length created by removal of the refrigeration equipment.

Fish Van – D1884

In the mid-1920s the LMS issued its first two Fish Van diagrams, one each to be built at Derby and Wolverton. D1884 was the 'Derby' version and Lot 105 was allocated to the first Derby batch. In the event, the Lot number was divided between this diagram (with slatted sides) and D1885, the 'boarded' side version (below). We can only conclude that the alternative design was found preferable. Interestingly, D1884, or something very like it, re-emerged in 1929 in the form of a series of new slatted sided vans, this time for Burton beer traffic and put in the freight book. In 1937, D1884 was itself transferred to wagon stock, probably as a result of its 9ft wheelbase combined with its older-fashioned body style. As seen with the converted six-wheel milk vans in the previous chapter, the close-boarded form of the body construction with high level louvres was preferred for fish.

The picture offered is the only known view of D1884, from which it seems to have been attractively finished in full gloss crimson lake with a modest amount of additional lining. We presume all were identical. A summary is given at Table 10 and the full 1933 renumbering was as follows:

New No.	Old No.	New No.	Old No.	New No.	Old No.
39021	1029	39039	1455	39057	6505
39022	1141	39040	1456	39058	6508
39023	1152	39041	1772	39059	6517
39024	1158	39042	1782	39060	6521
39025	1161	39043	1797	39061	6529
39026	1169	39044	1808	39062	6533
39027	1217	39045	6310	39063	6540
39028	1223	39046	6319	39064	6562
39029	1233	39047	6338	39065	6624
39030	1241	39048	6355	39066	6628
39031	1295	39049	6370	39067	6630
39032	1379	39050	6419	39068	6631
39033	1380	39051	6438	39069	6637
39034	1384	39052	6440	39070	6884
39035	1425	39053	6441	39071	6885
39036	1431	39054	6442	39072	6886
39037	1434	39055	6498	39073	6887
39038	1441	39056	6504		

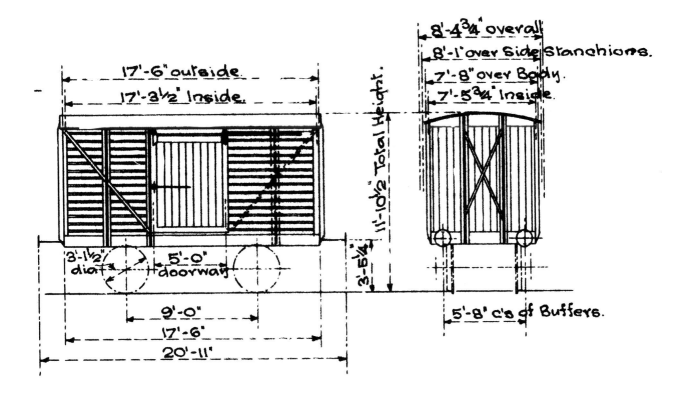

Some Fully Fitted.
Some with thro' pipe.
Carrying Capacity, 6 Tons.
Tare, 8 Tons.

Type of Brake, "Morton".
Sliding door each side.
Asphalt floor.

FIGURE 41 Fish Van – LMS D1884 (LMS Drawing No. 5937);
Scale 4mm=1ft.

Plate 153 No. 1295, later 39031, shows the attractive way by which the full version of the NPCS crimson lake livery could enhance what was nothing much more than a goods van. It is one of those with a 'through pipe only' (see annotation, Figure 41), indicated by the 'one end only' hand brake and lack of vacuum brake cylinder. This expense-saving exercise allowed the addition of a few vans of this type to passenger or fully fitted trains without destroying the vacuum or seriously affecting the braking power. We shall come back to this matter in a later view.

Fish Van – D1885

This, the second of the two original Fish Van diagrams also turned out to be the largest numerical type to appear in the LMS NPCS book: 167 vehicles. Also, judging from the second LMS numbering series and confirmed by its Lot number, Lot 66 seems to have been introduced at Wolverton ahead of the construction of D1884 at Derby (above), although the exact building dates given at Table 10 are not 100% certain. As stated above, the second batch of D1885 to be built was in fact the residual 47 vehicles from Lot 105 at Derby, but just to add confusion to the exact commencement of both series, the lowest 1933 running number of all in the 'split' Lot 105, was a D1885 example from Derby! D1885 was also one of the few passenger-rated types to be constructed at Newton Heath as well as Derby and/or Wolverton.

As with D1884, many examples were 'through piped' only. Lot 66 was, we think, 'piped' only, as was Lot 399, but Lots 105 and 336 had a mixture of full AVB and 'piped' only examples. When new, all were given crimson lake livery and the Derby and Wolverton examples would certainly get 'full' lining as shown on the picture of No. 6893. We cannot give the ex-works livery for the Newton Heath series. The date of build suggests that lining may, by then, have been left off – eg the broadly contemporary 1927-8 meat vans to D1883 (above).

The outline summary is given in Table 10 and the full 1933 renumbering was as follows:

Lot 66

New No.	Old No.						
39000	4665	39015	5195	39080	6894	39095	6928
39001	4667	39016	5284	39081	6895	39096	6929
39002	4670	39017	5310	39082	6896	39097	6930
39003	4673	39018	5317	39083	6897	39098	6931
39004	4676	39019	5345	39084	6898	39099	6932
39005	4678			39085	6899	39100	7633
39006	4679	**Part Lot 105**		39086	6900	39101	7661
39007	4680	*New No.*	*Old No.*	39087	6920	39102	7662
39008	4681	39020	910	39088	6921	39103	7663
39009	4684	39074	6888	39089	6922	39104	7664
39010	4686	39075	6889	39090	6923	39105	7665
39011	4688	39076	6890	39091	6924	39106	7666
39012	4690	39077	6891	39092	6925	39107	7667
39013	5070	39078	6892	39093	6926	39108	7668
39014	5179	39079	6893	39094	6927	39109	7669

New No.	Old No.	New No.	Old No.	New No.	Old No.	New No.	Old No.
39110	7670	39136	6579	39165	1007	39191	4334
39111	7671	39137	6582	39166	1008	39192	4335
39112	7672	39138	6662	39167	1009	39193	4336
39113	7673	39139	7270	39168	1010	39194	4337
39114	7674	39140	7280	39169	1011	39195	4338
39115	7675	39141	7313			39196	4339
39116	7676	39142	7321	**Lot 399**		39197	4340
39117	7677	39143	7573	*New No.*	*Old No.*	39198	4341
39118	7678	39144	7582	39170	1800	39199	4342
39119	7679	39145	7911	39171	1801	39200	4343
		39146	7912	39172	1802	39201	4345
Lot 336		39147	7926	39173	1803	39202	4346
New No.	*Old No.*	39148	8121	39174	1804	39203	4348
39120	886	39149	8153	39175	1875	39204	4349
39121	889	39150	8172	39176	1876	39205	4350
39122	926	39151	8183	39177	1877	39206	4351
39123	1807	39152	894	39178	4320	39207	4657
39124	4458	39153	1815	39179	4321	39208	4661
39125	4466	39154	4455	39180	4322	39209	4662
39126	4618	39155	4619	39181	4323	39210	4664
39127	5069	39156	5201	39182	4324	39211	6573
39128	5207	39157	5216	39183	4325	39212	6577
39129	5337	39158	5340	39184	4327	39213	6581
39130	5585	39159	5352	39185	4328	39214	6641
39131	5639	39160	6572	39186	3229	39215	6642
39132	5646	39161	7301	39187	4330	39216	7204
39133	5666	39162	1004	39188	4331	39217	7206
39134	5980	39163	1005	39189	4332	39218	7207
39135	6257	39164	1006	39190	4333	39219	7208

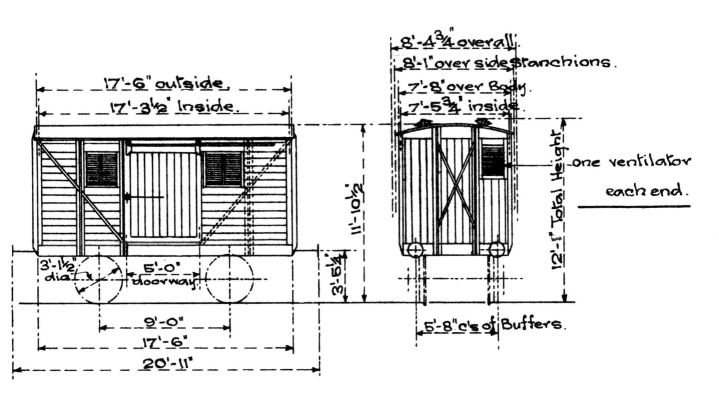

Some Fully Fitted.

Some with thro' pipe.

Carrying Capacity, 6 Tons.

Tare, 8 Tons.

Type of Brake, "Morton".

Sliding door each side.

Asphalt floor.

FIGURE 42 Fish Van – LMS D1885 (LMS Drawing No. 6220);
Scale 4mm=1ft.

Plate 154 No. 6893, later 39079, splendidly turned out in 'full' NPCS red livery when brand new at Derby. This was a fully fitted example from Lot 105, shared with D1884 – note the brake cylinder. Some 60 of this lot were fully fitted but we do not know the exact numerical 'split' between the two diagrams.

Plate 155 No. 39019, the last example from Lot 66, is seen here at Gourock on 12th April 1947. It now has plain red livery and is clearly 'through pipe' only. We believe that all this lot were similar in this respect. Note that the side planks are all of equal width compared with the Lot 105 example illustrated in the previous view. (A. G. Ellis)

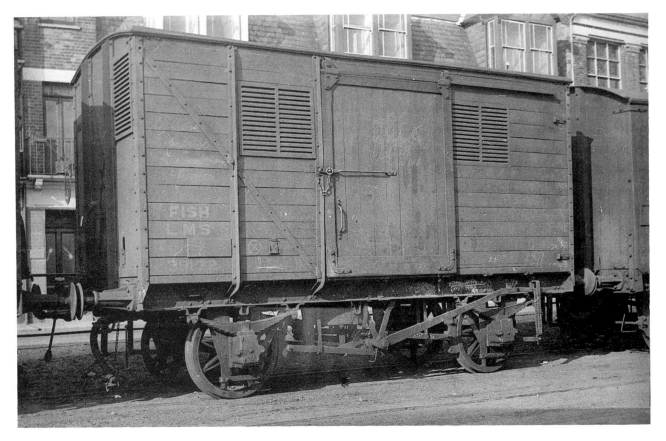

Plate 156 This view of a rather scruffy example of Lot 399, No. 39172, was probably taken after the war and shows a fully braked Newton Heath vehicle from 1929. This too has equal width side planks, thus inferring that Lot 105 may have been different from the rest. The insignia layout suggests that the body livery could well be either freight stock bauxite or (varnished?) undercoat – see Chapter 5. Note the end lamp bracket; these were not fitted to 'piped' only vehicles since these were not allowed to run at the rear of a train. Finally, the open spoked wheels are worthy of some comment: they are obviously replacement wheel sets and by no means unique, but were not usually expected in association with a passenger rated type.

(Authors' Collection)

Fish Van – D1982

This diagram was the slightly 'maverick' design alluded to in our introductory remarks and emerged from Newton Heath in 1929. It seems clear that they were part of the series originally placed on page 7 of the freight wagon book and they had no specific distinguishing external features, except for their lettering, and 'passenger' series numbers and livery, to identify them as being for fish traffic. We do not know their original livery but imagine it to have been plain crimson, probably with sans-serif yellow lettering on the doors – rather in the manner of the meat van seen at Plate 152.

Summary details are given in Table 10 and the 1933 renumbering details were as follows:

New No.	Old No.						
39220	5181	39235	5281	39250	5974	39265	7257
39221	5182	39236	5288	39251	5975	39266	7260
39222	5213	39237	5304	39252	5977	39267	7261
39223	5219	39238	5311	39253	5979	39268	7555
39224	5223	39239	5341	39254	5984	39269	7602
39225	5224	39240	5356	39255	6272	39270	7609
39226	5227	39241	5357	39256	6277	39271	7617
39227	5236	39242	5360	39257	7236	39272	7620
39228	5247	39243	5361	39258	7238	39273	7628
39229	5248	39244	5812	39259	7240	39274	7834
39230	5253	39245	5968	39260	7244	39275	7845
39231	5264	39246	5970	39261	7245	39276	7993
39232	5268	39247	5971	39262	7249	39277	8034
39233	5269	39248	5972	39263	7250	39278	8048
39234	5273	39249	5973	39264	7256	39279	8050

FIGURE 43 Fish Van – LMS D1982 (LMS Drawing No. 5669A);
Scale 4mm=1ft.

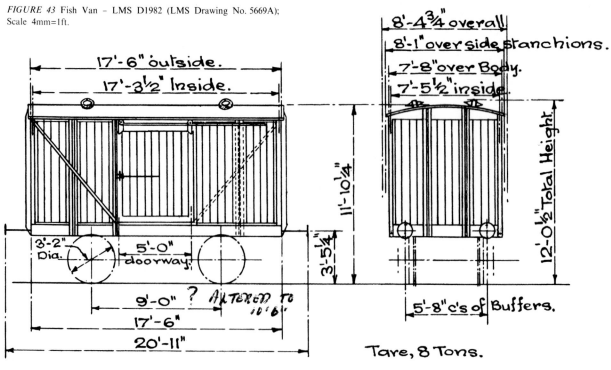

17'-6" outside.
17'-3½" Inside.

8'-4¾" overall.
8'-1" over side stanchions.
7'-8" over Body.
7'-5½" inside.

12'-0½" Total Height

11'-10¼"

3'-5¼"

3'-2" Dia.

5'-0" doorway.

9'-0" ? ALTERED TO 10'6"

17'-6"

20'-11"

5'-8" c's of Buffers.

Tare, 8 Tons.

Some Fully Fitted.   STEAM PIPED

Some with thro' pipe.

Carrying capacity, 6 Tons.

Type of Brake, "Morton".

Sliding door each side.

Decolite floor.

Left: **Plate 157** This design does not seem to have been officially photographed in LMS days, conceivably a reason why this official BR ex-works view was taken of No. M39249 on or about 7th January 1949, its marked date of overhaul. The livery is plain red with plain yellow lettering and LMS pattern shaded transfers for both 'M' and numerals – the latter, interestingly, being the now long obsolete pre-war shaded sans-serif style. Note too the through steam pipe to allow for use in passenger trains.

Fish Van – D1886

This 1931 design marked the resumption of the mainstream evolution of the LMS four-wheel fish van from D1885 with some simplification and alteration to the bodywork but, more importantly, an increase to 10ft wheelbase to give greater running stability. Once again, there was a mixture of 'piped' only (Lot 592) and fully AVB-equipped examples (Lot 589). Double clasp brakes also appeared on this design and all were equipped with a through steam heating pipe to allow for marshalling in passenger trains. The steam heat was not, of course, diverted through the van itself!

The usual summary is in Table 10 and the 1933 renumbering details are given below:

Lot 589

New No.	Old No.								
39280	4319	39305	8483	39331	8583	39354	6590
39281	4658	39306	8485	39332	8588	39355	6598
39282	6566	39307	8488	39333	8591	39356	6619
39283	6602	39308	8489	39334	8592	39357	7218
39284	7214	39309	8497	39335	8593	39358	7221
39285	7223	39310	8506	39336	8594	39359	7226
39286	7908	39311	8510	39337	8595	39360	8404
39287	8333	39312	8511	39338	8596	39361	8486
39288	8334	39313	8516	39339	8597	39362	8490
39289	8335	39314	8522	39340	8598	39363	8494
39290	8336	39315	8526	39341	8599	39364	8498
39291	8337	39316	8529	39342	8600	39365	8499
39292	8347	39317	8530	39343	8601	39366	8509
39293	8357	39318	8535	39344	8602	39367	8521
39294	8358	39319	8541	39345	8603	39368	8527
39295	8370	39320	8543			39369	8532
39296	8374	39321	8548	**Lot 592**		39370	8536
39297	8416	39322	8554	*New No.*	*Old No.*	39371	8546
39298	8463	39323	8562	39346	1774	39372	8557
39299	8466	39324	8565	39347	1806	39373	8563
39300	8470	39325	8567	39348	1818	39374	8568
39301	8471	39326	8570	39349	1822	39375	8576
39302	8474	39327	8573	39350	4258	39376	8604
39303	8481	39328	8577	39351	4274	39377	8614
39304	8482	39329	8581	39352	4659	39378	8619
		39330	8582	39353	6560	39379	8634

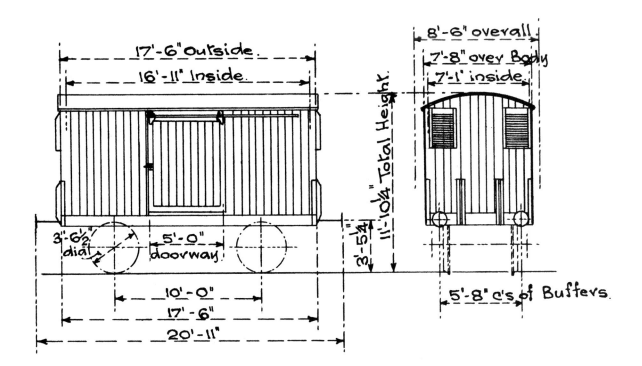

Some Fully Fitted.

Some with thro' pipe.

Carrying Capacity, 6 Tons.

Tare, 9 Tons 9 cwts.

Type of Brake, 'Morton'.

Sliding door each side.

Asphalt floor.

FIGURE 44 Fish Van – LMS D1886 (LMS Drawing No. D/12/64); Scale 4mm=1ft

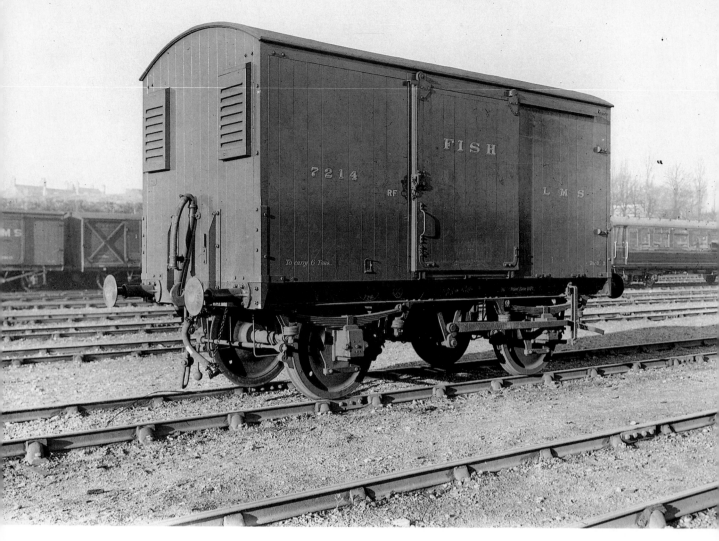

Plate 158 We only know of one view of this type – the appended official picture of No. 7214, later 39284, at Wolverton, taken when it was fairly new. The livery is now plain crimson with a slight rearrangement of insignia compared with D1885.

Fish Van – D1887

With this design, the side louvres returned at the expense of the end variety on the preceding D1886, but with little other change and a retention of the new 10ft wheelbase. This design concluded the series of four consecutively numbered Fish Van types from D1884 to D1887, an unlikely state of affairs other than that it reflected a simultaneous transfer of Fish Van diagrams to the NPCS diagram book from the freight book, where they had occupied pages 7A to 7D.

We summarise them in Table 10, but only 20 (Lot 660) had appeared before the great renumbering, so the pre-1933 list is shorter than usual:

New No.	Old No.	New No.	Old No.	New No.	Old No.
39380	6960	39387	7008	39394	7373
39381	6961	39388	7037	39395	7451
39382	6971	39389	7046	39396	7471
39383	6976	39390	7075	39397	7476
39384	6980	39391	7286	39398	7487
39385	6993	39392	7300	39399	7499
39386	7001	39393	7328		

Right: **Plate 159** Once again we only have one view of this type – ex-works No. 7476, later 39397 at Wolverton in 1932. The livery is plain crimson with yet further subtle changes to insignia layout. This time the word 'Fish' no longer appears and the only indication is the LMS 'RF' code on the solebar – not to be confused with the BR classification 'RF' – Restaurant First!

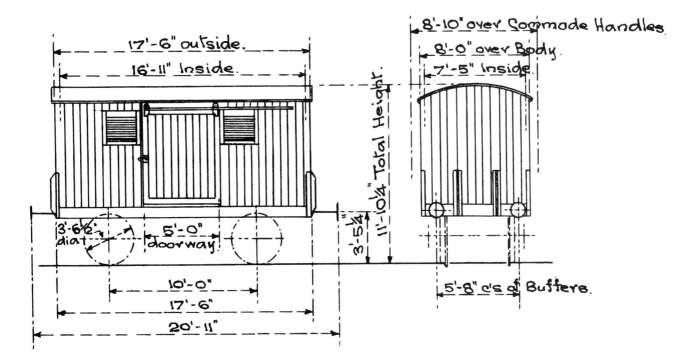

17'-6" outside.

16'-11" Inside.

8'-10" over Soapmode Handles.

8'-0" over Body.

7'-5" Inside.

11'-10¼" Total Height.

3'-6½" diat

5'-0" doorway

3'-5¼"

10'-0"

17'-6"

20'-11"

5'-8" c's of Buffers.

Fully Fitted.   *STEAM PIPED.*   Type of Brake, "Morton".

Carrying Capacity, 6 Tons.   Sliding door each side.

Tare, 9 Tons 10cwts.   Asphalt floor.

FIGURE 45 Fish Van – LMS D1887 (LMS Drawing Nos. 12/212A,12/212B); Scale 4mm=1ft.

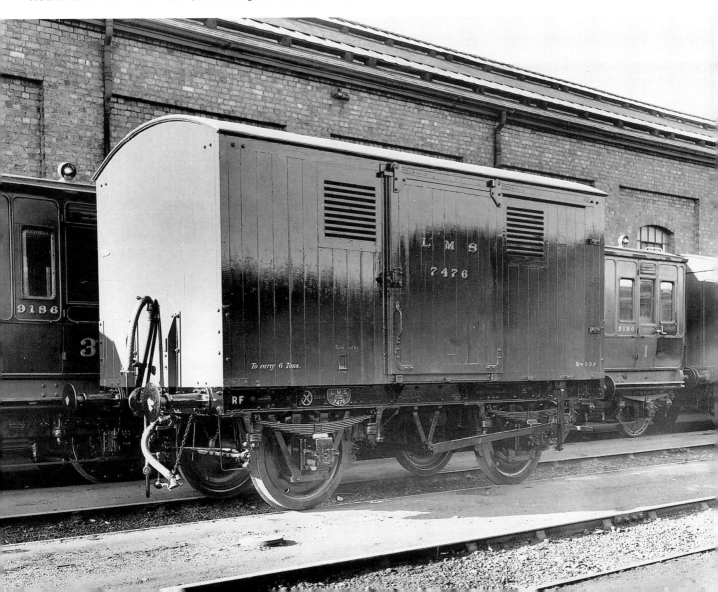

Fish Van – D2059

Austerity came in with a vengeance with these vans of 1941. The bodies came from Derby but were fitted to underframes built at Earlestown where the final assembly took place. No doubt this was related to the early wartime use of the main railway works for military as well as railway construction, but we cannot give further details. We have little other information on these vans but we guess they came into traffic either in bauxite or undercoat livery with freight style markings much as D2107 (below); summary details are given in Table 10.

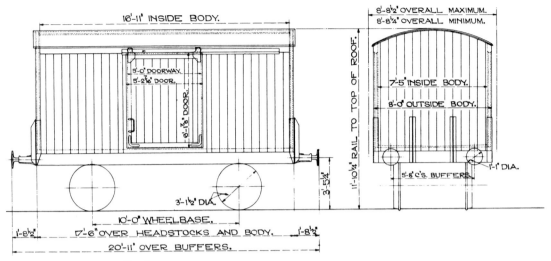

CODE R.F. TARE 8^{T}15^C TO 8^{T}19^C. CARRYING CAPACITY 6 TONS. FULLY FITTED WITH HAND BRAKE. SLIDING DOOR EACH SIDE. ASPHALT FLOOR.

FIGURE 46 Fish Van – LMS D2059 (LMS Drawing No. 12/611B – body; No. 13/3339 – underframe). Scale 4mm=1ft.

Plate 160 Being built in 1941, D2059 was not officially photographed but one of us came across No. M39512 at Wolverton in 1965. As well as the vacuum brake recorded on the diagram, we were able to confirm through steam pipes on this series of vans. A shorter hand brake lever also came in with this type. (R. J. Essery)

Fish Van – D2107

The only significant difference between this and the previous type was an extra six inches on the wheelbase. They came out with freight style insignia and our views on the livery are given in the caption to Plate 161; though we are quite open to correction by readers who may have further details.

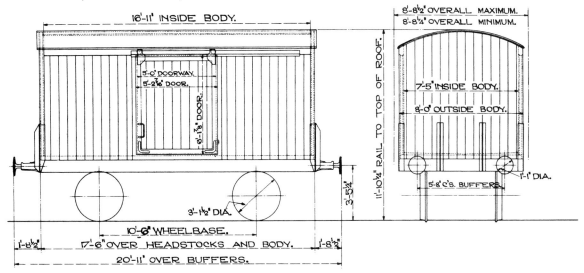

CODE R.F. TARE 8^T 15^C TO 8^T 19^C. CARRYING CAPACITY 6 TONS. FULLY FITTED WITH HAND BRAKE. SLIDING DOOR EACH SIDE. ASPHALT FLOOR. STEAM THRO' PIPE

FIGURE 47 Fish Van – LMS D2107 (LMS Drawing No. 12/699 – body; No. 13/1618 – underframe);
Scale 4mm=1ft.

Plate 161 We base our argument for the livery layout of D2059 (above) on this official picture of No. 39529 to D2107. The use of freight style markings is clear but the livery colour is less certain. The gloss finish suggests red, in which case the lettering would be plain yellow but given the 1945 building date, the body could equally well be finished in varnished undercoat which would look a bit like bauxite – see also livery remarks on D2115, below.

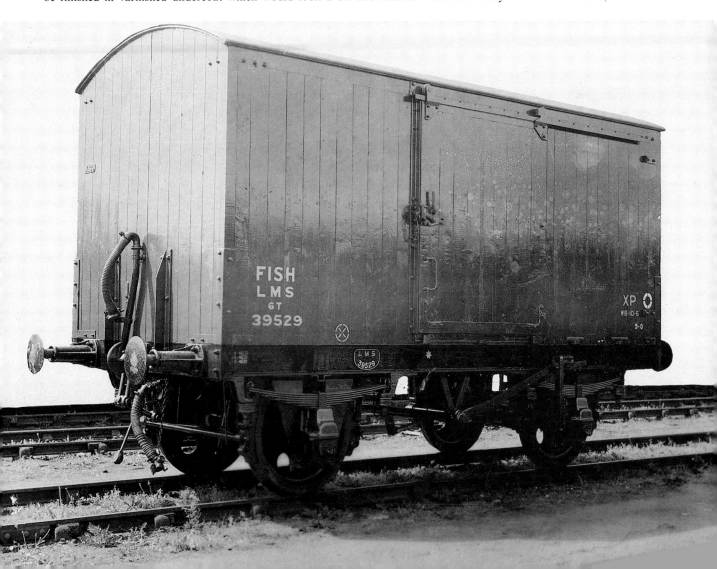

Fish Van – D2115

The post-war construction by the LMS marked a change from the traditional four-wheel Fish Van to a more robust vehicle running on a very substantial six-wheel chassis. Experience with the converted Milk Vans – see Chapter 9 – may have had some influence but the payload remained at the same 6 Tons as the four-wheel predecessors, but with an almost doubled tare weight!

In spite of their traditional appearance, these vans made some concession to modern thinking in that the hardwood frame was mounted directly onto the chassis rather in the manner of much of the later-built Stanier passenger stock. The body frames were wood-sheathed inside and out thus providing an air cavity which offered a measure of thermal insulation. The sliding doors were similarly built and the roof was reinforced with steel carlines below the conventional board and canvas covering. The asphalt floor was arranged to 'fall' towards drains along the centreline to facilitate swilling out and interior walls were protected by varnish. No ventilation was provided. The underframes were clearly built to full passenger standards but they did retain hand brake levers. Through steam pipes were also provided. The livery was plain crimson lake but proper LMS passenger style insignia did re-appear and this does just make us wonder whether use of freight style markings on the earlier four-wheelers reflected a lower standard of finish. The six-wheelers continued building after Nationalisation but all seem to have been put into service with LMS style markings and livery.

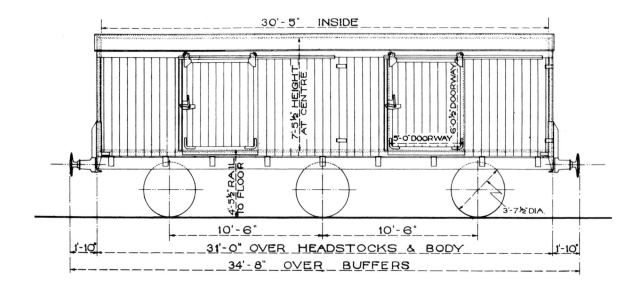

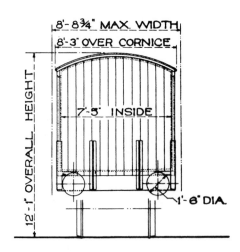

FIGURE 48 Fish Van – LMS D2115 (LMS Drawing No. 13/3708);
Scale 4mm=1ft.

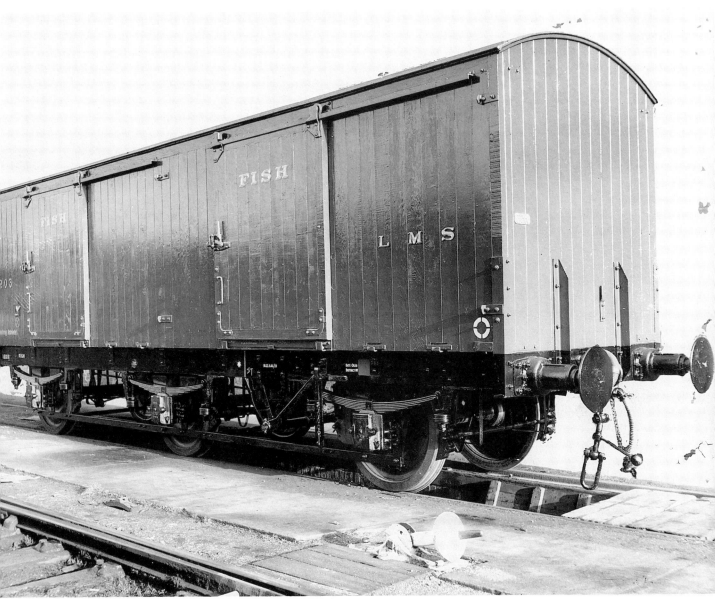

Plate 162 The official view of No. 40203 when built. Note the return of 'Fish' branding as well as passenger style company markings.

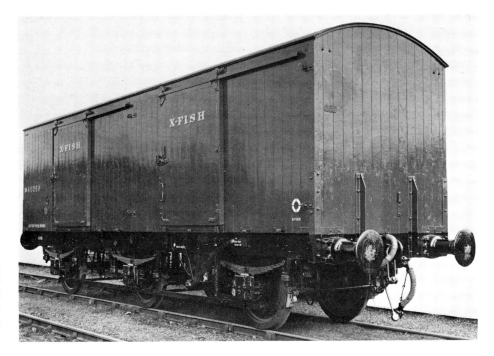

Plate 163 This second official view shows the first BR-built example No. M40250. LMS pattern transfers are still in use but the type designation is now 'X-Fish', denoting higher traffic status.

Plate 164 BR-built No. M40265M at Normanton on 9th September 1964, is seen displaying the final BR form of branding. (Authors' Collection)

Plate 165 The solid construction of these vehicles combined with the rapid erosion of rail-borne fish traffic made them admirable choices for further use in departmental service, thus following on a very long tradition of using serviceable six-wheel ex-fish vans on LMS/LMR lines. This example shows M&E Stores Van No. DM40259 at Springs Branch in February 1968, branded 'Return to Crewe Locomotive Stores'. The retention of the former capital stock number was interesting and rather uncommon. We have a strong feeling that some of these robust vans probably survived in departmental use into the 1990s. (Robert Fysh)

Insulated Sausage Van – D1955

Along with the GWR, the LMS introduced some specialised vehicles for the sole use of the Palethorpes Company and as is often the way of these things, the relatively few vehicles involved were well recorded and a few words regarding their use will not be out of place. The factory was rail connected and during the course of the day, production was loaded onto the vehicles which were then worked away to be attached to scheduled passenger trains, thus ensuring speedy delivery to customers.

Eight were introduced in 1936 to three lengths, though broadly alike in most essentials; four more followed in 1938 to a modified design and we presume that the variety of sizes, combined with the small quantities built of each version, reflected the likely sizes of the separate consignments. It is worth noting that all varieties of van were eventually available in multiples of two and we presume that this was to allow them to work in pairs (one each way) on a daily basis.

The four vans to D1955 were six-wheelers whose livery after Nationalisation was similar, but not identical to the LMS version – see pictures. During the late 1950s and early 1960s, the pictorial sausage emblem ceased to be present on some (all?) of this series though we have no precise dates or details. The vans were equipped with interior lighting and air circulation in the form of an axial flow streamline fan, both systems being driven by a typical 'Wolverton' lighting set. Air circulation could be adjusted by shutter controlled vents located in ceiling air ducts, while the van doors were arranged to stop the fans and switch on the lights when opened – and vice-versa.

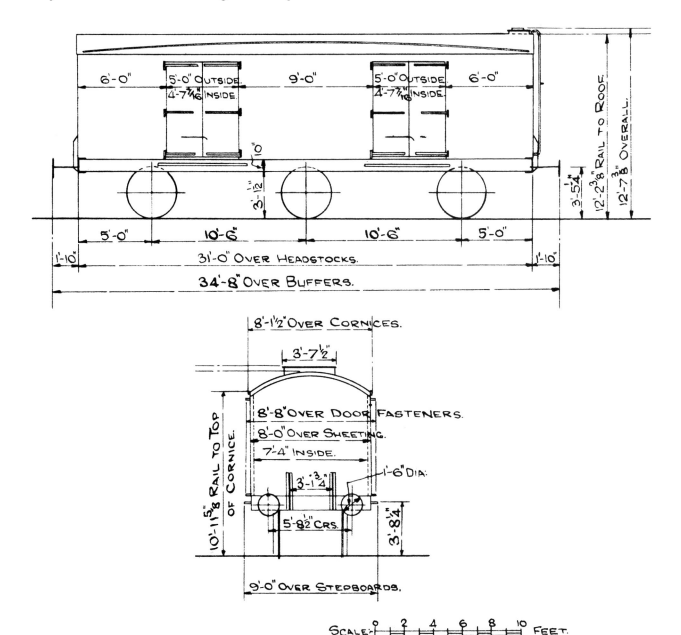

FITTED WITH A.V. BRAKE
& THROUGH STEAM PIPE.

TARE :- 17T. 7C. 3Q.

CARRYING CAPACITY :- 6 TONS.

DYNAMO, ELECTRIC LIGHT & 1 FAN.

FIGURE 49 31ft 0in Insulated Sausage Van – LMS D1955 (LMS Drawing No. 13/2422);
Scale 4mm=1ft.

Plate 166 LMS No. 38733 of D1955 when built. The advertising potential of a plain van side was well and truly exploited. As M38733M, this van retained the 'sausage' emblems until at least 1956, during which year it was seen thus finished at Stourbridge Junction.

Left and top Right: **Plates 167 and 168** End and roof detail views of LMS No. 38733 when new.

Plate 169 This undated BR official view of No. M38732M at Stafford shows the slight change in lettering: 'Royal Cambridge' has given way to 'Pork Sausages'. The picture cannot be earlier than 1956 in view of the all-maroon BR MkI carriage on the right.

Insulated Sausage Van – D1957

This design, the largest of the three similar 1936 diagrams, consisted of two bogie vans equipped much as for the six-wheelers save that two internal axial flow fans were provided. The general changes described for the six-wheelers also applied to this group, except that we have pictorial evidence (appended) which shows the full livery to have lasted until at least 1966 on one of them.

Plate 170 Ex-works view of LMS No. 38877 when new in 1936, showing how the extra length allowed the display of two sausage motifs per side.

Plate 171 This rather poor picture of one of these two vans at Dudley in 1966 confirms the retention of the full livery almost until the date of withdrawal in 1967. The wording has been changed as per D1955 (above) and the note on the print states that the van was annotated 'In use for parcels traffic'. As the van is marshalled with examples of D2001 (below), also marked for Palethorpes, we wonder if sausages were classed as parcels traffic! (Authors' Collection)

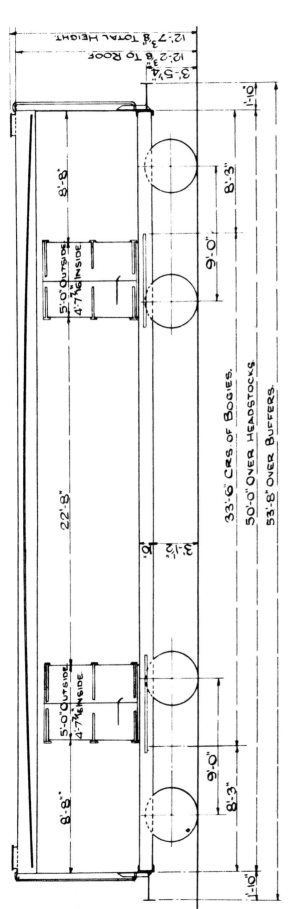

FITTED WITH A.V. BRAKE
& THROUGH STEAM PIPE.

TARE:- 28T. 3C. 2Q.
CAPACITY:- 7TONS.
DYNAMO, ELECTRIC LIGHT & 2 FANS.

SCALE.

FIGURE 50 50ft Insulated Sausage Van – LMS D1957 (LMS Drawing No. 13/2354); Scale 4mm=1ft.

153

Insulated Sausage Van – D1958

The third diagram of the 1936 series was for a very neat pair of four-wheelers. Again they were very similar to the larger versions other than that ice bunkers were used for cooling in transit and portable electric fans were used for cooling prior to despatch. Arguably the neatest of the lot, they seem to have eluded photographers and we only have one picture apart from the official view. In 1956, they were taken off Palethorpes traffic, possibly because they were four-wheel types, and converted to 'Passenger Vans'.

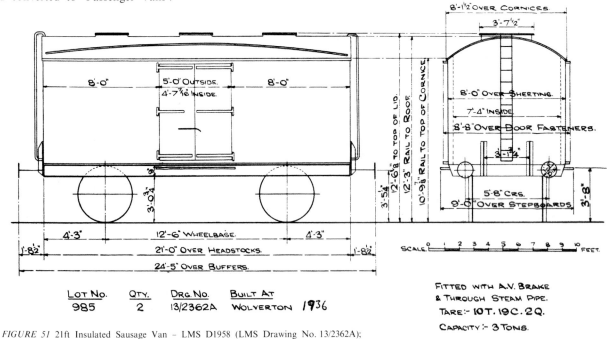

LOT No.	QTY.	DRG. No.	BUILT AT	
985	2	13/2362A	WOLVERTON	1936

FITTED WITH A.V. BRAKE
& THROUGH STEAM PIPE.
TARE :- 10 T. 19 C. 2 Q.
CAPACITY :- 3 TONS.

FIGURE 51 21ft Insulated Sausage Van – LMS D1958 (LMS Drawing No. 13/2362A); Scale 4mm=1ft.

Plate 172 This official view of LMS No. 38731 to D1958 shows how similar were all the original Palethorpes vans.

Plate 173 This undated view shows one of the four-wheelers plus the end of another Palethorpes van on the right (a six-wheel example). The 'M' prefix on the solebar of the six-wheeler denotes the BR period but obviously 'Royal Cambridge' has not yet been changed to 'Pork Sausages' on the four-wheeler so it may be an early BR view. We do not know if the four-wheel type was re-lettered before being taken off Palethorpes traffic. (Authors' Collection)

Insulated Sausage Van – D2001

Two years after the first Palethorpes vans were built, there was clearly a need to have some vehicles which permitted gangway access from adjacent vehicles and which incorporated a side corridor. Three vehicles were supplied at first, thus suggesting that 'paired' operation was not essential; but these three were soon followed by a fourth example whose Lot number (1157) suggests that it was built alongside the D2002 Cream Vans (below).

We do not know the precise reason for the design, nor have we discovered much about them, but we suspect that their purpose may have been similar to the previous type but for smaller consignments for various destinations which could be packed in one vehicle. This could then be sent on a train which made several intermediate stops and be progressively off-loaded en-route, hence the value of the gangway plus corridor arrangement. This is pure speculation on our part but if we are even half right, it suggests that this type would be the most appropriate for modellers to choose!

On the plain side they were painted in very similar manner to D1957 but on the corridor side, because of the windows, a different but still striking arrangement was adopted – see pictures. We do not know if 'Royal Cambridge' gave way to 'Pork Sausages' on this design but perusal of Plate 171 wherein parts of two of them can be seen, does suggest that some livery changes were made.

Plate 174 The non-window side of LMS No. 38874 to D2001 reveals a general similarity to D1957.

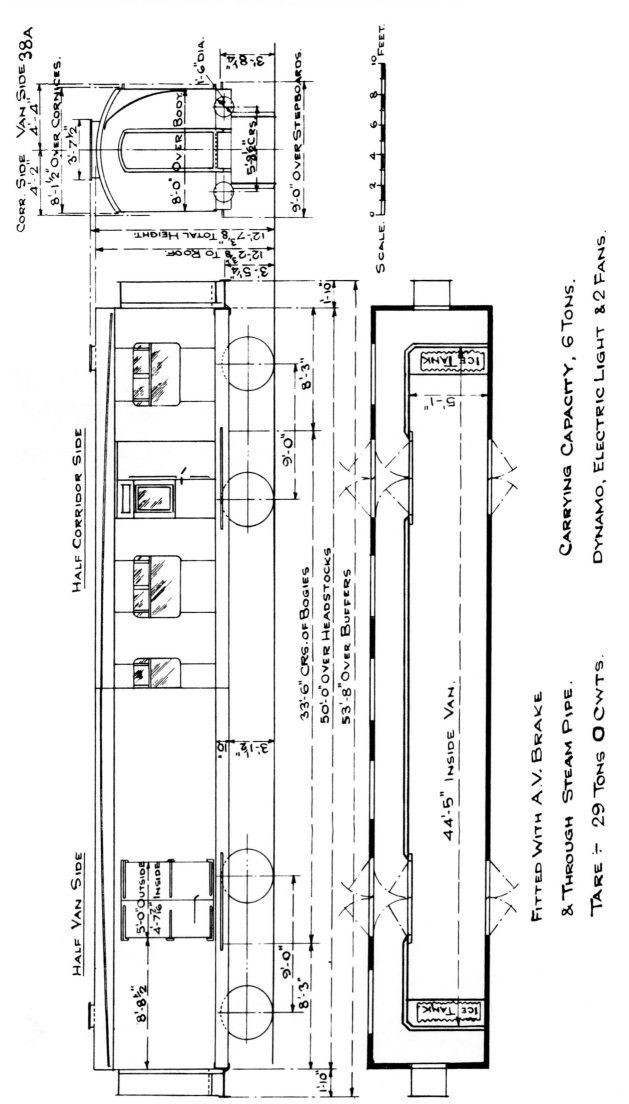

FIGURE 52 50ft Insulated Sausage Van – LMS D2001 (LMS Drawing No. 11/299);
Scale 4mm=1ft.

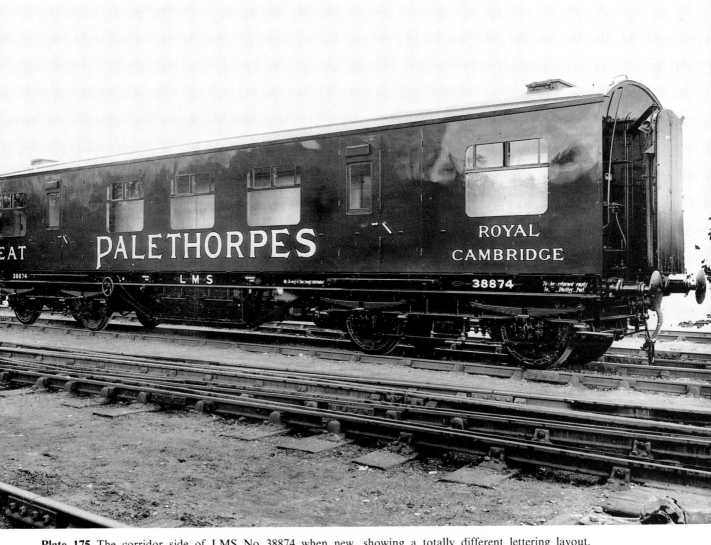

Plate 175 The corridor side of LMS No. 38874 when new, showing a totally different lettering layout.

Plate 176 An undated view of No. 38876 at Birmingham New Street. The faint solebar numbers still seem to be of LMS style and there is no obvious livery change, but it could be early BR in date. Note the hand brake wheel.

(Authors' Collection)

Insulated Cream Van – D2002

We conclude our NPCS survey with one of the most mysterious LMS NPCS designs we have met. The Diagram and Lot numbers plus the configuration of the vehicles themselves clearly indicate that they were identical to the D2001 Sausage Vans – and they were certainly built to the same drawings – but we have no idea how they looked when new, what their livery was or how they were used.

No official views seem to have ever been taken of these vans and in these circumstances, it is lucky that we have pictures of both of them, and from both sides too! We guess that they too were probably used for part loads of high value perishable traffic of a 'Dairy' nature and we feel that they must have been associated with one specific service, possibly even one manufacturer. They were clearly long-lived, lasting until the 1970s (exact withdrawal date not known), and if readers can help, we will try to include further details in one of the future volumes.

Plate 177 Corridor side view of M38998M in plain maroon livery at Willesden in August 1964. (R. J. Essery)

Plate 178 Van side view of M38999 in what looks like plain BR blue livery on 5th April 1969. (D. P. Rowland)

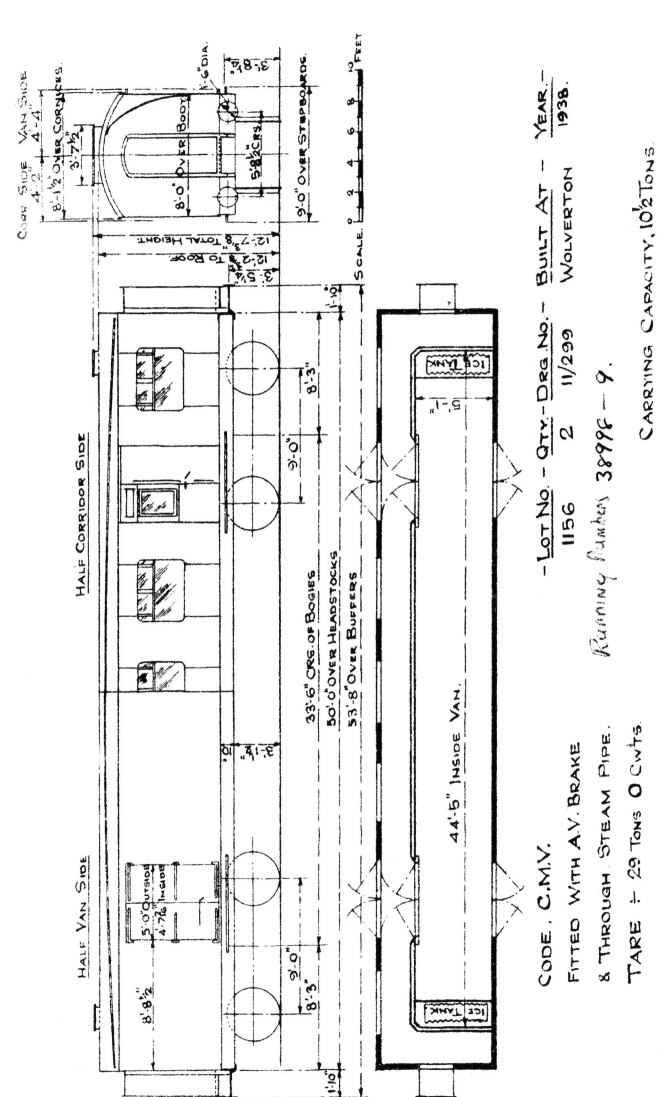

COOK SIDE. VAN SIDE
4·2" — 4·4"

8-1½" OVER CORRIDORS
3·7½"
3·7½"

1·6" DIA.

8·0" OVER BODY
5·8½" CRS.

3·8½"
3·8½"
9·0" OVER STEPBOARDS

12·7⅜" TOTAL HEIGHT
12·3⅞" TO ROOF
3·5¼"

HALF CORRIDOR SIDE

8·3"
9·0"

33·6" CRG. OF BOGIES
50·0" OVER HEADSTOCKS
53·8" OVER BUFFERS

HALF VAN SIDE

5·0" OUTSIDE
4·7½" INSIDE

8·8½"

9·0"
8·3"

1·10"
3·1½"

ICE TANK
ICE TANK
5·1"
44·5" INSIDE VAN.
ICE TANK

SCALE.
0   2   4   6   8   10   FEET

CODE, C.M.V.

FITTED WITH A.V. BRAKE

& THROUGH STEAM PIPE.

TARE ÷ 29 TONS 0 CWTS.

— LOT No. — QTY. — DRG. No. — BUILT AT — YEAR. —
1156 — 2 — 11/299 — WOLVERTON — 1938.

Running Numbers 38996 — 9.

CARRYING CAPACITY, 10½ TONS.

DYNAMO, ELECTRIC LIGHT & 2 FANS.

FIGURE 53 50ft Insulated Cream Van – LMS D2002 (LMS Drawing No. 11/299);
Scale 4mm=1ft.

Appendix I Standard Codes for Coaching Stock

The BR system of coding coach types is based on the old LNER system and following parts of it are relevant to LMS standard coaches discussed in this book, the LMS codes being given for comparison:

Dining and Kitchen Vehicles	BR Code	LMS Code
First Class Kitchen/Dining car	RF	1st RKC
Composite ,, ,,	RC	Compo RKC
Third Class ,, ,,	RT	3rd RKC
Unclassified ,, ,,	RU	Common RKC
Kitchen/Buffet car	RB or RKB	BRC
Kitchen only car	RK	KC
First Class vestibule dining coach	RFO	QL (Dining)
Composite ,, ,, ,,	RCO	VC (Dining)
Third Class ,, ,,	RTO	QF (Dining)
Unclassified ,, ,,	RUO	—

Sleeping Cars		
First Class	SLF	SC
Composite	SLC	CSC
Third Class	SLT	SCT
,, ,, (twin berth)	SLT (T)	—

Vestibule Stock		
Vestibule First Class	FO	QL
,, Composite	CO	VC
,, Third Class	TO	QF
,, Third Class Brake	BTO	VH
Semi-open First Class (Corridor/Vestibule)	Semi-Fo or Semi-RFO	CQL
Semi-open Third Class (Corridor/Vestibule)	Semi-TO or Semi-RTO	—

Corridor Stock	3R Code	LMS Code
First Class	FK	CL
,, ,, Brake	BFK	E
Composite	CK	CBC
,, Brake	BCK	CBB
Third Class	TK	CF
,, ,, Brake	BTK	CH

Non-corridor Stock		
First Class	F	L
,, ,, (with lavatory)	FL	LM
Composite	C	BC
,, (with lavatory)	CL	L&C
Third Class	T	F
,, ,, Brake	BT	H
,, ,, ,, (with lavatory)	BTL	LH

Other Coaching Stock		
Passenger full brake with gangway	BG	CBR
6 wheel passenger full brake with gangway	BGZ	CR
,, ,, ,, ,, without gangway	BZ	R
Post Office Sorting Van	POS	POR
Post Office Tender (Stowage Van)	POT	PPR

Note: 1. Articulated stock is prefaced by the word 'Twin' or 'Triple' in the BR system.
2. Codes exist for multiple unit stock but have not been employed in this book.

Appendix II   A Note on the 1923 LMS Coaching Stock Numbers

When the LMS was formed in 1923, the ex-Midland carriages mostly kept their old numbers and the former M&GSWR/M&NB Joint stock was eventually assimilated into this series in 1923 and 1928 respectively. The other pre-group companies were then allocated blocks of new numbers following on in sequence, each company being kept together before going on to another company. Thus, for example, the LNWR/WCJS carriages were allocated the 4301-10700 block, followed by the LYR etc. Non-passenger coaching stock was numbered in a separate series with the ex-MR vehicles again at the head of the list (retaining their numbers) followed by the other pre-group fleets.

For the most part, new LMS carriage numbers for pre-group carriages were allocated in ascending diagram page order and the coaches on any particular diagram were usually numbered in pre-group number order. Although this system was not particularly refined it did, in most cases, collect all coaches of any particular type and diagram into one consecutive number series – often for the first time, given the somewhat random numbering principles followed by most LMS constituents. The basic fault was that inadequate provision was made for the numbering of newly built LMS standard coaches.

The general principle was to use appropriate gaps in the pre-group lists but this was not wholly successful. Where a complete series of old pre-group carriages had been scrapped, this would normally, of course, vacate a fully consecutive LMS number series (given the 1923 renumbering principles) but even when this was added to the existing gaps in the sequence, the blocks of numbers selected in 1923 were frequently too small to absorb the sheer numbers of new carriages. In consequence, the pre-1933 numbers of new coaches could either be found in short consecutive batches (existing gaps or replacing withdrawn pre-group stock) or randomly scattered anywhere in the whole LMS series where any gap (even one only!) was to be found. Even this did not suffice and the LMS itself eventually had to resort to an old LNWR principle of 'cyphering' the running numbers of still existing pre-group carriages. This was done by adding a 'O' prefix to many 1923 LMS numbers, thus freeing the originals for re-use.

By 1932/3, the situation had become so confusing that the LMS felt obliged to introduce a completely new and systematic numbering scheme whose principles are outlined in Appendix III. It is felt that this may have been the main reason for introducing sans-serif carriage number insignia – mainly to allow easy differentiation of new from old numbers during the changeover.

Appendix III   The 1932/3 LMS Coach Renumbering Scheme

The 1932/3 renumbering scheme grouped all coaching stock (pre- and post-grouping) into systematic number blocks according to coach type. Within the pre-group allocations, the numbering order was generally as follows: LNWR (which carried the lowest numbers); MR; LYR; FR; CR; GSWR; HR (which carried the highest numbers). Generally speaking the LMS standard coaches were numbered consecutively upwards from the start of the block and the pre-group coaches were numbered backwards from the end of the block. The pre-group numbers were allocated in such a way that the complete pre-group block of coaches generally occupied the last and highest numbers in any series. This usually left a gap between the end of the LMS standard block and the start of the pre-group block which was available for new construction. In some cases the 1932 planners underestimated the size of the number blocks they would need and certain coaches overflowed into the other blocks – these are annotated below.

1-99 First Class Kitchen/Dining Cars
    1-44   LMS Standard types
    45-58   Vacant
    59-99   Pre-group types

100-199 Third Class Kitchen/Dining Cars and Buffet Cars
    100-148   LMS Standard types
    147-199   Pre-group types (including first 147/8)

200-299   Composite Kitchen/Dining Cars
200-221   Ex-Pullman cars (mostly Scottish)
222-252   LMS Standard types
253-270   Sundry post-1947 cafeteria conversions of LMS coaches
241-299   Original pre-group allocation

300-499   First Class Sleeping Cars
300-402   LMS Standard types
403-437   Vacant
438-496   LNWR (with a few gaps)
497-499   Vacant

500-699   Third Class Sleeping Cars
500-599   LMS Standard SLT
600-624   LMS type SLT(T)
625-699   Vacant

700-799   Composite Sleeping Cars
700-724   LMS Standard types
725-789   Vacant
790-799   LNWR—note second 798 later given to HM The King's and HM The Queen's Saloons

800-999   Special Saloons—mainly pre-group varieties

1000-1199   Corridor Firsts and Semi Open Firsts
1000-1128   LMS Standard types
1128-1199   Pre-group types (including first 1128)

1200-3399   Corridor Thirds
1200-2516   LMS diagrams
2235-3399   Pre-group types (including first 2235-2516)

3400-3499   Push pull conversions of older gangwayed stock—both pre-group and LMS Standard types (some of the pre-group examples were built new as push pull vehicles)

3500-4999   Corridor Composites
3500-4514   LMS Standard types
4357-4999   Pre-group types (including first 4357-4514)
2nd 4800-4899   LMS Standard types

5000-5199   Corridor First Brakes and Open First Brakes
5000-5004   LMS Standard Lounge (open) brakes
5005-5077   LMS Standard BFKs
5078-5144   Vacant
5145-5199   Pre-group types

5200-6599   Corridor Third Brakes
5200-6038   LMS diagrams
5990-6599   Pre-group types (including first 5990-6038)

6600-7399   Corridor Composite Brakes
6600-6876   LMS Standard types
6877-6956   Vacant
6957-7399   Pre-group types

7400-7599   Vestibule Firsts (both FO and RFO)
7400-7575   LMS Standard types (Note: First 7465-89 were later downgraded and the numbers in part used again for later standard coaches)
7556-7599   Pre-group types (including first 7556-7575)

7600-9699   Vestibule Thirds (both TO and RTO)
7600-9518   LMS Standard types
9519-9561   Vacant
9562-9699   Pre-group types

9700-9799   Vestibule Composites (both CO and RCO)
9700-9758   LMS Standard types
9759-9791   Vacant
9792-9799   Ex-LYR

9800-9999   Vestibule Brake Thirds
9800-9999   LMS Standard types
9971-9999   Pre-group types—first coaches with these numbers.

Note: This concluded the initial allocation of numbers for passenger carrying non-articulated gangwayed stock. Extra batches built after the number series filled up were as follows:
Corridor Thirds: 12750-13184
Corridor Composites: 24500-24739
Corridor Brake Thirds: 26100-27095 }
Vestibule Thirds: 27100-27449
Vestibule Third Brakes: 27900-27956 } Some of these also orginally used to re-number pre-group gangwayed stock to clear the original series for standard construction.

10000-10699   Non-corridor Firsts
10000-10131   LMS Standard types
10132-10308   Vacant
10309-10699   Pre-group types

10700-15799   Non-corridor Thirds
10000-12267   LMS Standard types
12268-12277   Downgraded composites from 160xx series
12278-12283   Ex-MSJA trailers (converted 1954)
12284-13610   Vacant (12750-13184 used for overflow numbering of TKs and 13610 downwards used for various downgraded vehicles)
13611-15799   Pre-group types

15800-15999   Non-corridor Thirds—Motor Fitted
15800-15857   Pre-group types
15858-15906   LMS Standard types
15907-15996   Vacant
15997-15999   LMS Standard types (converted)

16000-17899   Non-corridor Composites
16000-16325   LMS Standard types (16000-16006 originally compo. seconds)
16326-16330   Vacant—allocated initially to 17900-4 (Push-Pull version)
16331-16796   LMS Standard types
16797-16876   GWR designs built post-1947 and given LMS series numbers
16850-16937   Originally part of the vacant series but later used in part (post-1947) for ex-CLC stock and marked down pre-group firsts
16938-17899   Pre-group types

17900-17999   Non-corridor Composites—Motor Fitted
17900-17942   LMS Standard types
17943-17957   Vacant but some later used for conversions
17958-17999   Pre-group types

18000-18199   Non-corridor Lavatory Firsts
18000-18029   LMS Standard types
18030-18161   Vacant
18162-18199   Pre-group types

18200-18999   Non-corridor Lavatory Thirds
No LMS Standard designs built but 18614-18999 were pre-group coaches.

19000-19999   Non-corridor Lavatory Composites
19000-19199   LMS Standard types
19200-19386   Originally Vacant but 19377-86 were given to non-lavatory Cs to Lot 1450 (Motor fitted coaches—D1921A)
19387-19999   Pre-group types, also first 19385/6

20000-24399   Non-corridor Third Brakes
20000-21251   LMS Standard types
21252-22214   Vacant (22196-202 later used for ex-North London area LMS Standard brake seconds and 22203-14 for other down graded coaches)
22215-24399   Pre-group types (24317-31 later used again for Push-Pull driving trailers—1950)

24400-24499   Non-corridor Driving Trailer Thirds
24400-24459   LMS Standard types
24460-24499   Pre-group types and LMS standard conversions

24500-24799   Non-corridor Composite Brakes
24500-24717   Vacant (no LMS designs) but later used for overflow numbering of Period III CKs 24500-24739
24718-24799   Pre-group types (including first 24718-24739)

24800-24899   Non-corridor Driving Trailer Composites
24800-24895   Vacant (No LMS Standard types)
24896-24899   Ex-MR and Ex-LYR

24900-24999   Non-corridor Second Brakes
24900-24906   LMS Standard designs for North London sets—later downgraded and renumbered 22196-202
24907-24999   Vacant but 24989-99 later used for marked up BTs (pre-group) which were later marked down again

25000-25699   Non-corridor Lavatory Third Brakes
25000-25272   LMS Standard types
25273-25507   Vacant
25508-25699   Pre-group types

25700-25999   Non-corridor Lavatory Composite Brakes
25700-25777   Vacant (No LMS Standard designs)
25778-25999   Pre-group types

26000-27999   Pre-group four/six wheel passenger carrying coaches—all types
Note: Survivors of this block again renumbered 26000-99 when the 'overflow' numbering began

28000-29899   Electric Multiple Unit Stock
The number allocation in these blocks was a little complex and is best appreciated by studying Volume III.

29900-29999   Miscellaneous Railcars, etc.

30000-30199   Kitchen Cars
30000-30106   LMS Standard types
30107-30196   Vacant
30197-30199   Ex-LNWR

30200-30399   Post Office Vehicles
The numbers in this group were completely haphazard

30400-32899   Bogie Corridor Full Brakes
30400-32019   LMS Standard types and LMS built conversions from other coaches. There were vacant numbers.
32020-32899   Pre-group types built as full brakes

32900-33499   Six Wheel Corridor Full Brakes
32900-33019   LMS Standard types
33020-33441   Vacant
33442-33499   Pre-group types

33500-44999   Non-passenger carrying coaching stock

45xxx numbers   Chairman's and Engineer's Saloons (total of 16 to LMS design)

50000 Upwards   Articulated coaches

Appendix IV Selected Extracts from the LMS Instructions Regarding the Working of Trains

There is much confusion regarding the way in which rolling stock, particularly the passenger rated vehicles, was operated in the traditional steam days. We have therefore felt it would be helpful to readers if we offered extracts from the relevant LMS working documents. In this volume we concentrate on the rules and regulations covering non-passenger coaching stock and in future volumes we hope to include similar details for the passenger carrying fleet.

WORKING OF PASSENGER TRAINS ON GOODS LINES AND GOODS LOOP LINES.

Passenger trains must not be worked on goods lines except in cases where printed instructions have been issued authorising this to be done, or, in case of accident or obstruction, authority is given by the Station Master or by the District Control Office.

In such cases, passenger trains must, except where otherwise provided, be worked on the Absolute Block System on goods lines not normally worked in accordance with the Regulations for Train Signalling by Absolute Block System.

Where printed instructions have been issued authorising passenger trains to be worked on a goods line, the first passenger train required to enter upon the line following a train which has been signalled in accordance with the Permissive Block system or the Regulations for Train Signalling by Telegraph Bells must be stopped and the driver cautioned.

In case of accident or obstruction, before a passenger train is allowed to enter upon a goods line it must be stopped at the home signal and the driver informed of the circumstances.

Passenger trains must not be worked on goods loop lines where the entrance and exit is controlled from the same signal box, except in cases where printed instructions have been issued authorising this to be done, or, in the case of accident or obstruction, authority is given by the Station Master or by the District Control Office, and the loop line is clear throughout.

Before a passenger train is allowed to enter a goods loop line, it must be brought to a stand at the home signal and the driver informed of the circumstances unless printed instructions have been issued authorising passenger trains to be worked on the goods loop line.

CONVEYANCE OF ADDITIONAL VEHICLES BY PASSENGER TRAINS.

Extra vehicles must not be attached to passenger trains for the conveyance of passengers, unless authorised in the programmes or other special train notices, or by the Divisional Passenger Train Control Office, or the District Goods and Passenger Manager.

In exceptional circumstances, when there is insufficient time to telephone the Divisional Passenger Train Control, or District Goods and Passenger Manager, Swansea, as the case may be, the Station Master may attach additional vehicles for the accommodation of passengers, provided the maximum tonnage for the class of engine working the train is not exceeded, and the working of it is not likely to be otherwise upset en route.

An advice must at once be given by telephone to the Divisional Passenger Train Controller, District Goods and Passenger Manager, Swansea, or the District Controller (in cases where he is responsible for the supervision of the working of the train) stating precisely what has been done.

The Divisional Passenger Train Control or District Goods and Passenger Manager, Swansea, must be advised immediately it is known horse boxes, wagons of cattle, fish traffic, etc., for conveyance by passenger train are likely to pass.

CALCULATING NUMBER OF VEHICLES ON PASSENGER, ETC., TRAINS.

The equivalent number of vehicles on passenger, etc., trains must be calculated in accordance with the following table:-

Bogie carriage (12 wheels)	2 vehicles.
Bogie carriage (8 wheels)	$1\frac{1}{2}$,,
Compos, etc. (6 wheels)	1 vehicle.
Horse box	1 ,,
Carriage truck	1 ,,
Fish van	1 ,,

(*This table does not apply when reckoning the amount of brake power on trains—See instructions on page 24 headed "Extract from the Regulations of Railways Act 1889."*)

MAXIMUM NUMBER OF VEHICLES ON, AND WEIGHT OF, PASSENGER, PERISHABLE AND EMPTY CARRIAGE TRAINS COMPOSED OF COACHING STOCK.

The weight of all trains composed of coaching stock is to be calculated on the tonnage system, and the maximum load for the various classes of engines over the different sections of the line is shown in the loading of passenger and freight trains circulars.

L.M.S. coaching stock vehicles are marked at each end, showing the weight in tons, so that the total weight of the train can be readily arrived at.

The tonnage for other Companies' vehicles not marked with the weight is to be counted at 10 tons for horse boxes and carriage trucks, 20 tons for brake vans, 30 tons for passenger carrying vehicles, and 40 tons for a dining car or sleeping saloon.

The maximum weight for a loaded passenger train over L.M.S. main lines, except where otherwise shown in the loading circulars, is 600 tons, and not more than 17 bogie vehicles, or where a train is composed principally of bogie stock, 15 actual vehicles (each vehicle including dining cars, bogie or other coaches being counted as one vehicle) may be run on any train unless definitely laid down in the marshalling circular or specially authorised by the Divisional Superintendent of Operation, or, in the case of the Northern Division, by the Operating Manager.

Where small, other than bogie, vehicles are used to make up a loaded passenger train, a maximum of 22 vehicles must not be exceeded.

(*Refer to Sectional Appendices for sections of the line on which special limitations exist with regard to the number of vehicles to be conveyed by passenger trains.*)

Guards must show on their journals the actual number of vehicles and the total tonnage of the trains and must fill in the required particulars on the driver's slip.

MAXIMUM WEIGHT OF NON-PASSENGER CARRYING COACHING STOCK TRAINS.

The load for the following description of trains must not exceed the maximum number of vehicles shown hereunder except in cases specially authorised:-

Maximum No. of
vehicles including
brake van or vans.

Milk..25
Parcels...25
Horse box and passenger carriages.....................................25
Horse boxes..30
Fish...30

(The 1.55 p.m. fish train Aberdeen to Broad Street is specially authorised to convey up to 40 vehicles north of Carlisle, and up to 35 vehicles inclusive of brake van or vans south of Carlisle.)

Empty coaching stock trains (8 or 12 wheeled vehicles)....................20
     ,,   ,,   ,,   ,,   (4 or 6 wheeled vehicles)....................30

(2 eight-wheeled vehicles to count as 3 six-wheeled or 4 four-wheeled vehicles.)

CONVEYANCE OF FOUR-WHEELED, ETC., VEHICLES BY PASSENGER TRAINS.

Four-wheeled vehicles such as horse boxes, carriage trucks, refrigerator vans, meat vans, etc., with a wheel base of not less than 10ft., may be worked on express passenger trains (except those trains specially prohibited), but they must be marshalled in the following positions only:—

1.— In the rear of all bogie vehicles provided for the conveyance of passengers, but where this is impracticable in traffic working, may be marshalled next the engine.

NOTE.—*When marshalled in front of a train four and six-wheeled vehicles may be intermixed provided they are all attached in front of bogie vehicles.*

2.— On special trains conveying theatrical parties, four-wheeled vehicles with a wheel base of not less than 9 ft. may be marshalled according to destination.

Every effort must be made to maintain the steam heating apparatus through to all loaded passenger-carrying vehicles.

Vehicles with a wheel base of 15 ft. or over, provided they are fitted with oil axle-boxes, automatic brakes or through pipes, screw couplings and long buffers, and with a minimum tare of 6 tons, may be marshalled in any position on the train.

Open fish and open carriage trucks of less than 21 ft. body length, also four-wheeled vehicles with a wheel base of less than 10 ft., are prohibited from working on express passenger trains.

Bogie freight vehicles, and empty one-plank freight wagons fitted with vacuum automatic pipe, are prohibited from being attached to passenger trains.

The restrictions in the first paragraph do not refer to glass-lined milk tanks, which must be dealt with in accordance with the instructions on page 19.

Certain express passenger trains are prohibited from conveying 4-wheeled vehicles. Details of the trains concerned will be shown in the Passenger Train Marshalling circulars as issued by the Divisional Superintendents of Operation from time to time.

CONVEYANCE OF MILK TANKS BY PASSENGER OR MILK TRAINS.

These milk tanks, which are registered for capacities of 2,000 and 3,000 gallons respectively, may be accepted for conveyance irrespective of the amount of milk which they may contain.

Six-wheeled milk tanks, loaded or empty, may be worked on any passenger or milk train without special restriction.

Four-wheeled milk tanks may be run loaded or empty, on passenger or milk trains, but the service by which they are laid down to be conveyed must not exceed a speed of SIXTY MILES PER HOUR at any point on the journey, and, in all cases, whether loaded or empty, they must, except as shown below, be marshalled with a six or eight-wheeled vehicle immediately behind them.

Should it be necessary in cases of emergency to despatch a four-wheeled milk tank by a train which is not laid down for this traffic, the Station Master attaching the milk tank must give an order in writing to the driver and guard of the train to the effect that the speed of such train must not exceed that laid down above.

The arrangements for an alternative service must in these cases be made in conjunction with the Divisional Passenger Control.

Guards when giving drivers particulars of the tonnage of their trains must advise them in every case when they are conveying four-wheeled milk tanks, in order that a speed of SIXTY MILES PER HOUR may not be exceeded at any point.

Between the following points four-wheeled tanks may be run loaded or empty on any passenger train, either in front or extreme rear of train, without necessarily having a six or eight-wheeled vehicle in front or rear of them:—

Market Harborough and Rugby.
Cricklewood and Acton.
Kensington and Mitre Bridge.
Willesden and Kilburn.
Willesden and South Acton.
Willesden and Tredegar Road, Bow.
Uttoxeter and Egginton.

Over S. & D. Joint line (except on express passenger trains).

On the branches named a horse box or other 4-wheeled vehicle may, if required for convenience, be attached in rear of a milk tank for conveyance from one station to another.

The couplings must be screwed up tight so as to hold the tanks together when running at speed.

Not more than 10 tanks must be attached to any passenger train or 20 tanks running together to any milk or non-passenger carrying coaching stock train without special authority.

When one of the loaded tanks is stopped owing to hot axle, or from other causes, making it impossible for the tank to go forward, sender's instructions must be obtained, with the least possible delay, as to the disposal of the milk.

ROAD RAIL MILK TANK WAGONS.

The following instructions in connection with the loading and unloading of these vehicles must be strictly adhered to by all concerned:—

DESCRIPTION OF OPERATIONS.

Loading.

No. 1.—Rail clips fixed.
No. 2.—Bearing spring stop screwed down to stop.
No. 3.—Landing plates across.
No. 4.—Front wheelbar fixed across runway.
TRAILER RUN ON WAGON either by pulling on with the ropes and pulleys provided, or backed on by lorry.
No. 5.—Trailer drawbar fixed up on catch.
No. 6.—Trailer brakes put on.
No. 7.—Back wheelbar fixed across runway.
No. 8.—Trailer bearing spring stop screwed down.
No. 9.—Binding chains fixed.
No. 10.—Wagon bearing spring stop screwed back to solebar.
No. 11.—Rail clips off rails and hung up.
No. 12.—Landing plates back (loose plate on wagon).

Unloading.

No. 1.—Rail clips fixed.
No. 2.—Landing plates across.
No. 3.—Trailer brakes taken off.
No. 4.—Binding chains off.
No. 5.—Trailer bearing spring stop up.
No. 6.—Back wheelbar away.

TRAILER COUPLED TO LORRY
AND PULLED OFF WAGON.

EXTRACT FROM THE REGULATION OF RAILWAYS ACT, 1889.

INSTRUCTIONS WITH RESPECT TO CONTINUOUS BRAKES.

A.—PASSENGER TRAINS.

1.—All passenger trains must be worked with the continuous brake in use by the Company.
To facilitate working, however, the following exceptional arrangements are allowed:—
In passenger trains a proportion of unbraked vehicles may be run on the following conditions:—

(a) That all such vehicles shall have continuous pipes of the pattern in use upon the trains with which they are running.

(b) That the proportion of such vehicles shall not exceed one in four in every passenger train running a distance not exceeding 10 miles without a stop.

(c) That the proportion of such vehicles shall not exceed one in six in every passenger train running a distance exceeding 10 miles without a stop.

Provided that for the purpose of conditions (b) and (c) the number of vehicles forming a train be counted as follows:-

Tender engine, 6 or 8 coupled...as 4 vehicles.
Tender engine, 4 coupled...as 3 ,,
Tank engine, 4 or 6 wheeled coupled...as 2 ,,
Coaching vehicles, 8 or 12 wheeled...as 2 ,,
Coaching vehicles, 4 or 6 wheeled...as 1 vehicle.
Horse box, carriage truck, fish van or other 4-wheeled vehicle not carrying passengers...as $\frac{1}{2}$,,

Table showing what proportion of unbraked vehicles (which must be fitted with continuous pipes) may be attached to a passenger train RUNNING **NOT MORE THAN 10 MILES** WITHOUT A STOP.			Table showing what proportion of unbraked vehicles (which must be fitted with continuous pipes) may be attached to a passenger train RUNNING **MORE THAN 10 MILES** WITHOUT A STOP.		
To a train (including engine) consisting of braked vehicles equal to—		Unbraked vehicles equal to—	To a train (including engine) consisting of braked vehicles equal to—		Unbraked vehicles equal to—
3	may be added	1	3	may be added	$\frac{1}{2}$
$3\frac{1}{2}$	,, ,,	1	$3\frac{1}{2}$	,, ,,	$\frac{1}{2}$
4	,, ,,	1	4	,, ,,	$\frac{1}{2}$
$4\frac{1}{2}$	,, ,,	$1\frac{1}{2}$	$4\frac{1}{2}$	,, ,,	$\frac{1}{2}$
5	,, ,,	$1\frac{1}{2}$	5	,, ,,	1
$5\frac{1}{2}$	,, ,,	$1\frac{1}{2}$	$5\frac{1}{2}$	,, ,,	1
6	,, ,,	2	6	,, ,,	1
$6\frac{1}{2}$	,, ,,	2	$6\frac{1}{2}$	,, ,,	1
7	,, ,,	2	7	,, ,,	1
$7\frac{1}{2}$	,, ,,	$2\frac{1}{2}$	$7\frac{1}{2}$	,, ,,	$1\frac{1}{2}$

8	,,	,,	2½		8	,,	,,	1½
8½	,,	,,	2½		8½	,,	,,	1½
9	,,	,,	3		9	,,	,,	1½
9½	,,	,,	3		9½	,,	,,	1½
10	,,	,,	3		10	,,	,,	2
10½	,,	,,	3½		10½	,,	,,	2
11	,,	,,	3½		11	,,	,,	2
11½	,,	,,	3½		11½	,,	,,	2
12	,,	,,	4		12	,,	,,	2
12½	,,	,,	4		12½	,,	,,	2½
13	,,	,,	4		13	,,	,,	2½
13½	,,	,,	4½		13½	,,	,,	2½
14	,,	,,	4½		14	,,	,,	2½
14½	,,	,,	4½		14½	,,	,,	2½
15	,,	,,	5		15	,,	,,	3

2.—Except as hereinafter provided the last vehicle of every passenger train must be fitted with the continuous brake of the pattern in use upon the train.

Where necessary to avoid delay in working, one vehicle only, not being a passenger carrying vehicle, may be placed in the rear of any such train without being fitted with the continuous brake or with the continuous pipe, except on those sections of the line where the vehicles behind the rear brake van must be provided with the continuous brake or where the practice of running vehicles behind the rear brake van is prohibited. (*See respective Sectional Appendices for sections of line affected.*)

NOTE.—Grooms or attendants travelling in horse boxes, etc., are not counted as passengers.

B.—MIXED TRAINS.

1.—"Mixed" trains for the conveyance of freight and passengers, in which the freight wagons are not required to have continuous brakes, may be run, subject to the following conditions, namely:—

(a) That the engine, tender and passenger vehicles of such "mixed" trains shall be provided with continuous brakes worked from the engine.

(b) That the freight wagons shall be conveyed behind the passenger vehicles with brake van, or brake vans, in the proportion of one brake van with a tare of 10 tons for every 10 wagons, or one brake van with a tare of 13 or more tons for every 15 wagons, or one brake van with a tare of 16 or more tons for every 20 wagons, or fractional parts of 10, 15 or 20 wagons respectively.

(c) That the total number of vehicles of all descriptions of any such "mixed" train shall not exceed 30, except in the case of a circus train when the number shall not exceed 35.

(d) That all such trains shall stop at stations, so as to avoid a longer run than 10 miles without stopping, but nothing in these regulations shall require a stop to be made between two stations should the distance between them exceed 10 miles.

The distance over which a circus train may run without a stop may be increased to a maximum of 50 miles

2.—Upon lines where the maximum speed of trains is limited to 25 miles per hour, all trains may be "mixed".

Upon lines where no trains are booked to travel between stations at an average speed of more than 35 miles per hour, half of the total number of passenger trains may be "mixed". Authority to work a larger proportion of "mixed" trains must be obtained from the Minister of Transport.

Upon lines where trains are booked to travel between stations at an average speed exceeding 35 miles per hour, the like authority must be obtained before any "mixed" trains are run.

Circus trains may be run without such authority during the period from March 31st to November 30th in any year whether the maximum average speed of trains run on the section of line concerned is limited or not.

In no case must the speed of a circus train exceed 30 miles per hour.

3.—Trains for the conveyance of horses, cattle or other stock, when vehicles are added for the conveyance of passengers, shall be subject to the same regulations and conditions as apply to "mixed" trains, but drovers, grooms or other persons travelling in charge of such stock shall not be deemed to be passengers.

A passenger vehicle provided for the special accommodation of persons travelling in charge of stock must, however, be marshalled next the engine, and be provided with the continuous brake worked from the engine.

4.—When, in addition to one goods brake van at the rear of a "mixed" train, a passenger brake vehicle is included as part of the continuously braked stock, it will not be necessary for a guard to ride in the passenger brake vehicle. If the composition of the train necessitates a second (or third) goods brake van, a second (or third) guard will be necessary, unless communication between the vans is such as to enable one guard to operate efficiently the hand brakes on the vans.

All trains booked to be run as "mixed" will be so shown in the Working Time Tables, and the foregoing regulations will apply to such trains.

The expression circus train means a "mixed" train in which livestock, traction engines, trailers, caravans, tenting and other equipment and circus employees belonging to a touring circus are exclusively being conveyed.

NOTE.—The above regulations do not apply to troop trains.

CLEANSING AND DISINFECTING OF HORSE BOXES, PRIZE CATTLE VANS AND GUARDS' VANS.

The attention of Station Masters, Inspectors and others concerned is particularly drawn to the instructions in the "Livestock Handbook" (E.R.O. 29568) respecting the cleansing and disinfection of horse boxes, cattle vans, etc., which have been used for the conveyance of livestock.

Failure to carry out these regulations involves the Company in risk of prosecution and the imposition of heavy fines, and every care must, therefore, be taken to see that the instructions are strictly complied with.

These instructions must be carried out to the smallest detail immediately every horse box, or other vehicle mentioned in the Orders, is unloaded. It is not sufficient merely to sweep the floor of the vehicle; the manger (whether it has been used or not), and the other parts must be cleansed in the prescribed manner.

In cases where vehicles used for animals are unloaded on the platform and the vehicle goes on by the same train to a junction or depot, arrangements must be made with the station to which the empty vehicle is sent for the necessary cleansing and disinfection to be carried out there. The Station Master at the unloading station must see that such arrangements are made.

Empty horse boxes, etc., received at depots must be examined immediately on arrival and cleaned if they are dirty. Each case in which a horse box, etc., is received in a dirty condition must be reported.

Sponges, brushes, disinfectants, etc., must be obtained from the Stores Department, and stations at which large numbers of horses are dealt with, a *set* of the required articles must be kept on or adjacent to the dock, *exclusively* for cleansing and disinfecting horse boxes, etc.

LOADING OF HORSES.

1.—Before any horse box is loaded it must be thoroughly examined, and unless the fittings are in good order and the head stall and ropes complete it must not be used.

2.—In tying up the horse the length of the rope or ropes must be carefully regulated by the height of the animal, so as to keep its head in a natural position and care must be taken to see that the head stall is adjusted to fit the head of the animal.

3.—To assist those engaged in fastening horses in a horse box the following diagram illustrates the proper method of securing the ropes to the rings.

In tying this knot the end of the rope must be taken in the right hand, then passed through the ring downwards, brought out at the left-hand side of that part of the rope attached to the head collar, carried over this rope towards the right, then passed again through the ring downwards, and brought out between the ring and the rope loop; the end rope then being pulled tight, completes the knot.

4.—When only one horse is to be conveyed in a horse box it must, as a rule, be loaded in the centre stall; when there are two horses they should be placed in each of the side stalls.

5.—Great care must be taken that the head doors are securely bolted, also that the head divisions of the stalls are properly fastened.

6.—If the consignor requires any deviation to be made from the ordinary mode of fastening, it must only be made on the distinct understanding that he (or she) undertakes all responsibility, and the live stock ticket must be endorsed accordingly, and the endorsement signed by the consignor or his or her agent.

7.—In the event of a horse injuring itself while in transit, the Station Master or other person discovering the injury must note and immediately record how the animal is tied, and measure the length of top and bottom ropes from rings to headstall. They must also retain the original headstall and ropes where these have been cut or broken in order to release the animal, and the horse box must not again be used until instructions are received from the Chief Commercial Manager.

HORSE BOXES—STALL PARTITIONS.

When a horse box is received with the partitions displaced, immediately the box is unloaded the partitions must be replaced in their proper positions, unless the vehicle is required for further loose loading. Care must be taken to place partitions in their proper places, according to the numbers upon them, with the corresponding numbers inside the horse box.

HORSE BOXES—LIGHTING.

When horse boxes are ordered from point to point to supply orders, the Traffic Department staff must take note of the condition of the vehicles as regards the supply of gas, and, where possible, arrange with the C. & W. Department to fully charge the vehicles before leaving. At stations where vehicles cannot be gassed, advice must be sent to the nearest station where such gassing can be carried out if the vehicles are working in the direction of such a station.

Horse boxes not fitted with gas should be at all times fitted with a fully trimmed and filled oil lamp.

TICKETS OF PERSONS TRAVELLING IN CHARGE OF MACHINERY, ETC., OR LIVE STOCK.

Guards in charge of trains conveying machinery, etc., or live stock, must see that any person, not being a Company's servant, travelling with this traffic is in possession of a proper passenger ticket for his own conveyance, and, in the case of live stock, that he holds a copy of the cattle ticket, or live stock consignment note and waybill, endorsed to the effect that he has signed the indemnity. On completion of the journey for which the ticket is available, the guard must collect the ticket and attach it to his journal, on which should be recorded the name of the person travelling, the number of his ticket, and any circumstances of an unusual or irregular character in connection with the matter. On those sections of the line where no journal is made out, the guard must hand the ticket in at the place at which he books off duty, together with a note showing the required information. A similar record must be made in the case of persons travelling to places off the Company's system, but they will retain the tickets for the completion of their journey.

Should a case arise where a person is found travelling without a ticket, the attention of the station staff at the station where he alights must be specially called to the fact so that the proper fare may be collected.